THE EMPLOYMENT CONSEQUENCES OF TECHNOLOGICAL CHANGE

This volume reports the proceedings of the European Production Studies Group meeting held at Loughborough University in 1980. It contains a collection of papers on the economic causes and consequences of technological change, focusing in particular on the impact of the new technologies on the prospects for employment. The volume not only includes a number of contributions that look at the theoretical frameworks used as a basis for modelling labour demand, but also contains the results of empirical studies at both the micro and macro levels. The wealth of new research in the area and the results of this research point at least to transitional problems in the labour market, if not to the likelihood of long-term unemployment. The volume therefore also contains a number of papers that focus on possible employer, trade union and government responses to these problems. These papers deal with the question of whether present socio-political and economic mechanisms are adequate to cope with the adjustments that will be necessary, given the scale of the problems anticipated, and, if not, what other options are open to ensure that economies achieve a new and acceptable position. The international nature of the data and contributions indicate clearly that this is a topic of world-wide interest rather than a parochial problem faced by the United Kingdom in isolation. Nevertheless, there remains the question of whether the UK will cope with the employment consequences of technological change as adequately as other economies, which are often competitors, and the implications of its failure to do so.

Also by Derek L. Bosworth

PRODUCTION FUNCTIONS: A Theoretical and Empirical Study
WORK PATTERNS: An Economic Analysis

THE EMPLOYMENT CONSEQUENCES OF TECHNOLOGICAL CHANGE

Edited by

Derek L. Bosworth

MACMILLAN PRESS
LONDON

First published 1983 by
THE MACMILLAN PRESS LTD
London and Basingstoke
Companies and representatives
throughout the world

ISBN 0 333 31939 7

Printed in Hong Kong

To Jonathon and Matthew

Contents

List of Figures

List of Tables

Preface

The papers contained in this volume were presented at the
Conference on the Employment Implications of Technological
Change, organised under the auspices of the European
Production Studies Group and held at Loughborough University
(17-19 September 1980). While both employment and technological change are topics of particular interest to members
of the EPSG, the papers contained in this volume reflect the
diversity of interests and, to a somewhat lesser extent, the
variety of disciplines of the participants.

I should like to extend my thanks to members of the Steering
Committee of the EPSG and, in particular, to David Heathfield,
for the help and advice offered during the organisation of
the Conference. Similar thanks go to various members of the
Department of Economics at Loughborough University, particularly Peter Dawkins, for practical help in ensuring that the
Conference ran smoothly, and to Sue Spencer, for all her
efforts in typing the proceedings of the Conference in a form
ready for publication.

Finally, the European Production Studies Group would like
to proffer a formal note of appreciation to the British
Academy for the funds that it contributed towards the travel
expenses of the foreign participants at the Conference.

D. B.

Notes on the Contributors

Derek L. Bosworth is Senior Lecturer in Economics at Loughborough University of Technology.

Tom Bourner is Principal Lecturer at Brighton Polytechnic, currently seconded to the Information Services Unit of the Council for National Academic Awards.

John Clark is Research Fellow in the Science Policy Research Unit at the University of Sussex.

Howard Davies is Head of the Department of Accounting and Economics at Hull College of Higher Education.

Peter Dawkins is Lecturer in Economics at Loughborough University of Technology.

David Deaton is Research Fellow in the Industrial Relations Research Unit at the University of Warwick.

Richard Harrison is Lecturer in Economics at the Queen's University, Belfast, Northern Ireland.

Linda Hesselman is a research worker in the Economic Division of the National Economic Development Office, London.

Athar Hussain is Senior Lecturer in Economics at the University of Keele.

Alan Ingham is Lecturer in Economics at Southampton University.

Bernard James is Senior Lecturer in Industrial Relations in the Department of Management Studies at Middlesex Polytechnic.

Douglas Jones is Economics Research Assistant at Thames Polytechnic.

A. Kervyn is a Research Fellow in the Department of Economics at the University of Southampton.

Val Lintner is a Lecturer in the Faculty of Economic and Administrative Studies at the Polytechnic of North London.

Peter Nolan is a Research Associate in the Industrial Relations Research Unit at the University of Warwick.

Ruth Spellman is a research worker in the Manpower and Industrial Relations Division of the National Economic Development Office, London.

Paul Stoneman is Senior Lecturer in Economics at the University of Warwick.

Stuart Wabe is Senior Lecturer in Economics at the Centre for European Industrial Studies at the University of Bath.

Daniel Weiserbs is Professor of Economics at the Catholic University of Louvain, Belgium.

Sören Wibe is a lecturer at the Institution för Nationalekonomi, Umeå Universitet, Sweden.

A. Woods is a lecturer in the Department of Economic and Administrative Studies at the Polytechnic of North London.

M. Woods is a lecturer in the Department of Economic and Administrative Studies at the Polytechnic of North London.

Introduction

1 SOME INTRODUCTORY REMARKS

This introduction attempts to set the scene for the rest of
the book, emphasising its strengths and its weaknesses. The
conference proved to be an amalgam of interests, disciplines
and styles. The proceedings naturally reflect this hetero-
geneity. While, in some sense, this might be interpreted as
a weakness by the reader seeking a comprehensive and co-
hesive study of the topic, it is also a strength, in so far
as it reveals alternative ways of looking at a problem and
very often, despite differences in approach, shows substantial common ground in the findings of the various studies.
In this introductory contribution, therefore, no attempt has
been made to précis the findings of each of the papers (these
can be found in the conclusions and summaries to each of the
papers); it tries only to draw out some of the more important
topics and themes that were touched upon during the discussions that ensued at the Conference, as well as pointing to
some of the topics that were perhaps given insufficient
attention.

2 NATURE OF TECHNOLOGICAL CHANGE

Many of the authors attempted to examine whether technological unemployment could be isolated as a distinct category.
The general consensus (see the papers by Hussain, Jones, and
Deaton and Nolan) was that, while the cause of technological
unemployment is, in principle, quite distinct, in practice
the resulting unemployed appear in one of the traditional
categories (i.e. the structural and demand deficient types)
and cannot, *ex post*, be distinguished from the other unemployed who reach that state by some other route (i.e. a
change in product mix or a recession). By implication, the
problems of technological unemployment may be (effectively
if not efficiently) removed by the traditionally accepted
instruments (i.e. training and stimulating the level of
demand in the economy). However, there are clearly other

1

routes to alleviating technological unemployment, for example,
through the management of the rate of diffusion of new technology.

3 THEORETICAL ASSUMPTIONS AND PREDICTIONS

The task of modelling technological change involves a certain
theoretical content. In particular, assumptions have to be
made about the underlying technology and market mechanisms.
Thus, the degree of disruption predicted will almost certainly,
in part, depend on the nature of the technology adopted in the
model and the view taken about the efficiency with which market
mechanisms work. The paper by Stoneman, for example, reports
on a model with a restrictive technology and quasi-fixed
factor prices. This model readily generates unemployment during
the transition from one technological state to another (the
two states are distinguished by the extent to which a new
technology is diffused).

The paper by Jones, in using a Harrod-Domar framework, adopts
a technology of production that promises to be relatively unfavourable toward employment where important economic distur-
bances have to be absorbed. In addition, however, he argues
that a number of compensatory mechanisms exist that help to
ameliorate (although not wholly remove) the problems of
unemployment.

Deaton and Nolan, on the other hand, find it extremely
difficult to generate unemployment outcomes in an economy
characterised by a CES production function. Unemployment does
emerge when the assumption of downward rigidity of the real
wage is introduced, but even then, such unemployment only
arises at fairly extreme values of factor augmenting technological change. Deaton and Nolan report that unemployment is
more readily generated (on the basis of *a priori* more acceptable assumptions) using the macro model proposed by Malinvaud
(1980). Even so, while both models produce unemployment outcomes in the medium term, neither manages to generate long-
term unemployment.

From a comparison of the models reported in this volume,
therefore, it seems clear that the predicted size of the
technological unemployment problem depends crucially on the
researcher's view of the nature of the production process, and,
in particular, the degree of substitution between inputs, and
the efficiency of the normal market mechanisms in the real
world, especially with regard to the role played by movements
in the real wage. These are areas that are of interest not
only to the debate on technological change, where much more
empirical investigation is required. Sophisticated model building can be of only limited use without statistical evidence
supporting the basic assumptions adopted.

4 EMPLOYMENT AND THE RATE OF DIFFUSION

While the positions of the economy before and after the
introduction of a new technology are of interest, given the
amount of time it generally takes to complete the diffusion
process, the transition path is the centre of particular
attention. The diffusion process clearly lies at the heart
of models that focus on the employment consequences of
technological change (see, for example, the papers by
Stoneman and Wibe). Models that give predictions of relatively high rates of unemployment tend to adopt the hypothesis of a relatively rapid rate of diffusion (see the
discussion of the Hines model in the paper by Jones). It is
interesting to note, therefore, Harrison's description of
the slow and haphazard diffusion process that characterised
the important transitions from wood to iron and from sail
to steam in the shipbuilding industry (see Chapter 10).

The model developed by Stoneman focuses on such a transition path. It is a two-sector model, with capital and
consumption goods industries. On the assumption of a logistic
diffusion process, the paper investigates the way in which
the time path of employment varies as the speed of diffusion
changes (the latter is assumed to be given exogenously).
Under absolutely labour-saving change, the resulting time
path indicates an initially rising ratio of labour demand to
labour supply, followed by a later downward movement of the
ratio. The upward movement in earlier years is accentuated
by a more rapid rate of diffusion. As Stoneman recognises,
even this effect will depend crucially on leakages through
international trade, although this latter avenue is not
endogenised in this particular model (see, however, Stoneman,
1981).

The assumptions of a predetermined wage and an exogenously
given rate of diffusion may again lead to an inherent tendency of a model characterised by such assumptions toward
pessimistic forecasts of employment outcomes. If, on the
other hand, real markets respond accordingly (e.g. by lowering real wage rates for workers manning older vintages of
capital and raising real wage rates of workers on capital of
more recent vintages), then the rate of diffusion might well
be slowed, with corresponding implications for the predicted
initial upturn and longer-term downturn in employment
opportunities.

Some consideration should also be given to the assumption
of a closed economy. Widening of the model to allow for the
existence of trade with the rest of the world raises a
number of new dimensions. There is the question of the
extent to which the initial rise in employment might be

dampened by the loss of jobs caused by the importation of
new capital goods, which would otherwise have stimulated
growth and employment in the domestic economy. There is also
the question of to what extent persistently high levels of
employment might be achieved by a country with a more rapid
rate of diffusion at the expense of countries with more
moderate diffusion rates.

The paper by Bourner *et al.* attempts to stress this
particular argument. They see the need for a rapid diffusion
of the new microelectronic technologies in the UK, in order
to prevent foreign competition from having a severe adverse
effect on employment prospects within this country. The
raison d'être for their paper is that the theoretical debate
has occurred largely within an empirical vacuum (see also
the paper by Jones). They report the results of a pilot
survey of diffusion of new microelectronic technologies
amongst manufacturing firms in South-East England. Their
study is particularly interesting because it not only
provides empirical results in a much needed area, but also
broaches the question of how to design an appropriate methodology for obtaining information about diffusion from survey
sources.

This contribution also attempts a preliminary assessment
of the employment consequences of the diffusion by comparing
adopters and non-adopters. Given the relatively early stages
of the diffusion process and the inability of the survey to
control for variations in other relevant factors, it is
perhaps not too surprising that there are no statistically
significant differences in employment changes between the
adopters and non-adopters. Nevertheless, the authors do
interpret their evidence as pointing to a rather more pessimistic outcome amongst adopting firms. There seems to be
something of a contradiction here with the demand growth
arguments put forward elsewhere (see the papers by Jones,
Stoneman and Clark). One interpretation, of course, is that
the relatively less successful firms have been forced into
adoption (perhaps along the leap-frogging lines suggested
by Downie, 1958), and that, without adoption, employment
prospects in such firms would have been even worse. It should
be added that the potentially important growth in the demand
for labour in the capital goods industries, which formed a
focus of attention in the Stoneman analysis, and which might
prove to be a particularly important counterbalance in the
real world, lies outside of the scope of this particular
book.

5 INFLUENCES ON THE RATE OF DIFFUSION

On balance, perhaps, less was said at the Conference than
might have been expected about the factors influencing the
rate of diffusion. This was, in part, a reflection of the
technical difficulty of endogenising the diffusion process
within many of the already rather complex models linking
technology and employment (see, for example, the paper by
Stoneman). There was, for example, little or no discussion
of the supply of inventions or of the transfer of technology
between firms, industries or countries. Nevertheless, a
number of interesting aspects relating to this question did
arise during the course of the Conference.

The paper by Harrison, for example, reviewing the influence of technological changes on the longer-term evolution
of the British shipbuilding industry, emphasised the growth
of organisational inflexibilities. These to some extent
explain the stagnation and decline of the Dutch shipbuilding
industry during the 18th century. A similar problem to some
extent pervaded the British shipbuilding industry, contributing to its decline during the inter-war period, when
firms clung to 'practical experience and tradition'. Taking
this argument a step further, successful technological
innovation requires an appropriate environment and this
often means that it will be complemented by organisational
and managerial improvements.

Another influence on the speed of adoption is quite clearly
the availability of relevant and accurate information.
Harrison points to the haphazard adoption of new technologies
in the transition from wood and sail to metal and steam in
shipbuilding, where entrepreneurs are claimed to have mixed
'virtuosity in one field with appalling ignorance in another'.
The importance of information flows is no less acute today,
indeed, perhaps more so. In the survey by Bourner *et al.*,
they conclude that ignorance about new technologies, their
applications and effects, is a major factor in retarding
the adoption of the new microelectronic technologies.

The Bourner *et al.* study, however, indicates that other
factors are at work. They distinguish scarcity of finance,
lack of necessary skills to introduce and exploit the new
technology, cost-effectiveness of the new technology in
activities undertaken by the firm, the business cycle,
labour relations, and firm size. The important question of
labour relations is left until the following section, where
the potentially disruptive effects of the introduction of
new technology are considered. The survey by Bourner *et al.*
fails to find any appreciable differences between small and
large firms in the expected cost-effectiveness of the new

microelectronic technologies. They argue that non-adopters appear to under-emphasise the difficulty of securing the necessary skills to ensure a successful innovation.

6   DISRUPTION AND ADJUSTMENT

Section 3 above emphasised that some part of the differences in the predicted employment outcomes emerged because of the alternative theoretical frameworks and assumptions adopted in the models. Clearly, the more 'flexible' the technology and the greater the efficiency with which market mechanisms work (i.e. adjustments in prices and quantities), the less disruptive the effects of technological change are likely to be. The contributions of Stoneman and Jones emphasise the possible employment-creating effects that may counter-balance the jobs lost through technological change, in particular those of income generation, the stimulation of demand for new consumer goods, and the growth in demand for new capital equipment. Jones, for example, argues that the essential difference between the 1950s/1960s and 1970s/1980s in the level of technological unemployment can probably be traced, not so much to a change in the rate of diffusion of new technologies, but to a breakdown in these compensatory mechanisms.

   In this section, therefore, an attempt is made to review the fairly flimsy evidence relating to the disruptive nature of technological change. The evidence of Bourner *et al.* that there are no statistically significant differences in the employment prospects of adopting and non-adopting firms, has already been mentioned. Nevertheless, the authors did point to a somewhat more adverse employment outlook amongst the adopting firms.

   Wabe and Bosworth, using rather scattered, plant level observations collected by UNIDO, attempted to ascertain whether the effect of vintage on labour productivity could be detected. A statistically significant, positive corre-lation between labour productivity and vintage would have particularly important implications for employment prospects. Approximating different vintages by different ages of the capital stock, the authors could find no substantive evidence that labour productivity was significantly in-fluenced by the age of capital. There are important problems in an analysis of this type, however (i.e. the choice of the underlying technology of production and the set of ex-planatory variables) that make it difficult to isolate the separate effect of the age of capital on productivity in the plant. There are equally important problems in interpreting the results of the statistical estimates obtained. In particular, while the zero order correlation between capital intensity and age did not appear to be unacceptably high, nevertheless, there was a lingering suspicion that the capital intensity variable might represent the main element of the vintage effect.

There is a further piece of evidence relating to the potentially disruptive effects of technological change. The Verdoorn relationship (i.e. that the rate of change of labour productivity is directly related to the rate of change of output) may be interpreted as indicating the existence of forces counteracting the potentially severe effects of new technology on employment. While the Verdoorn relationship can be treated as an empirical 'law', it cannot be assumed to be unchanging. The argument put forward by Jones, that there may have been a breakdown in the counterbalancing effects, has already been noted. In addition, Jones raises the question of whether output can now rise sufficiently to provide employment for those who do not have jobs because of technological change. The contribution by Clark provides some interesting evidence relating to this question, by focusing on changes in the Verdoorn relationship over time in the UK, estimating it over a series of ten-year rolling periods. His basic conclusion is that the empirical evidence indicates that increasingly large rates of productivity growth have become associated with given rates of change in output. The net result is that increasingly large rates of growth of output are becoming necessary to maintain existing employment levels (see also Hussain's discussion of this point). In order to explain the changing Verdoorn pattern, the author searches for evidence of a change in the nature of investment and, in particular, a swing toward rationalisation investment. The author points to a cyclical variation in the relationship between productivity and output growth, that may be linked with the diffusion of more radical, new technologies.

7 RESPONSES TO TECHNOLOGICAL CHANGE

Technological change is inherently disruptive for one group or another. The extent of the disruption depends, in part, on the flexibility within the economy, both in its market mechanisms and with regard to the institutional framework within which these market mechanisms operate. The paper by Hesselman and Spellman explores the market mechanisms and the institutional framework. The latter is certainly complex. The rate of technological change is variously prompted

and hindered (sometimes both) by a large number of groups: the
National Economic Development Council; the National Economic
Development Office; Economic Development Committees and Sector
Working Parties; the Government (through such bodies as the
Department of Industry, Department of Employment and the
Manpower Services Commission); the Confederation of British
Industry; and the Trade Unions - to name but a few. The authors
argue that the NEDO/SWP/EDC mechanism is an explicit attempt
to determine a socially acceptable solution through socio-
political co-ordination. Despite the obvious goodwill and
effort of those involved, one cannot help but feel that the
morass of parties and policies forms a largely unco-ordinated,
if not, on occasion, contradictory, set of influences on the
introduction of new technologies, aggravated by the lack of
any formal Science and Technology Policy (see Stubbs, 1980,
and Bosworth, 1980).

Outside of the institutional framework which the Government
helps to establish (and, indeed, is itself a part), the
Government plays a much more direct role through its manipulation of the level of economic activity. In so far as technological unemployment corresponds to the demand-deficient
category, we may anticipate that a stimulus to the level of
economic activity might help. Nevertheless, a history of
outward shifts in the Phillips Curve (and the possibility of
a vertical long-run Phillips Curve) point to unacceptably high
levels of stimulus that may be politically or socially unacceptable. This is consistent with the finding we reviewed in
the previous section, that a given rate of employment growth
has required increasingly large rates of output growth over
time.

There is clearly another area of government involvement relating to the need to influence or control jobs lost through
the transference of employment from the UK to other countries.
This, as we have already mentioned, has two quite distinct
aspects. First, that the potential growth in employment in
the capital goods industries should not leak abroad in the
form of UK imports of plant and machinery embodying the new
technologies. Second, that the rate of diffusion in the UK
should be controlled to give this country the greatest possible
competitive advantage *vis-à-vis* its foreign competitors in
order to reduce import penetration and increase export
performance.

The rate of adoption will clearly not be wholly independent
of the potential disruption that the diffusion of new technologies will bring. Of the various interested parties,
workers (and those seeking employment) appear to be likely
to be most affected. It is hardly likely, therefore, that
they will remain entirely passive as the tidal wave of
technology washes over them. History is peppered with

examples of workers who attempted to block the introduction
of new technologies, often by means of physical force (e.g.
the 'Captain Swing' and Luddite riots in England). In more
recent years, the introduction of computers has led to disruption and strikes in a number of industries, for example,
in newspaper production. The early examples were largely
individual groups of workers taking independent, localised
action. The growth in the size and power of the trade unions,
however, raises the question of whether this may now form an
institutional inflexibility that will hinder the introduction
of new technologies. From the evidence presented by Bourner
et al. it would appear that labour relations is not perceived
as a particularly important problem in this respect. Indeed,
labour relations problems were mentioned by fewer firms than
any other impediment listed. We might anticipate that this
result would differ between unionised and non-unionised firms.
No direct evidence is available on this point, but a useful
pointer is given in the fact that smaller firms tended to
rate the labour relations aspect more highly than larger
firms and, yet, smaller firms tend, on balance, to be less
unionised.

There is the additional question as to whether existing
forms of representation and collective bargaining remain
adequate in the face of rapid and radical changes brought
about by the introduction of new technology. It seems unlikely, for example, from the paper by Hussain that an
occupationally-based trade union structure is going to be
conducive to technological change. There is also an important
question mark about the representation of the unemployed, as
opposed to the employed, and the distributional implications
of the current system. It is particularly interesting that
the new technologies pose a potentially important threat to
the trade union movement itself (see the paper by James).
This work also indicates that, if collective bargaining and
the New Technology Agreements prove to be inadequate, further,
perhaps more radical, changes can be expected in worker
representation.

Trade unions traditionally bargain over a whole range of
items that form the conditions of employment. The hours of
work-hours of leisure outcome, in particular, is crucial in
determining the level and distribution of income. For the
individual employee, there is a trade-off between leisure
time and income. Across individuals, there is a trade-off
between the numbers of hours worked and the numbers of
workers in employment. If workers remaining in employment
maintain their hours of work, they can expect to receive
higher levels of real income on the introduction of the new
technologies. These higher levels of real income will, in

turn, result in something of an increase in demand (at
least by those still in jobs, and an amelioration of the adverse employment consequences of the technological change.
If, however, workers opt for a lower number of hours (maintaining their real income levels), this may free some jobs
that can be filled by those who would otherwise have been
unemployed. The first of these two avenues would, on balance,
seem to have been more common in the post-war period. This
may, in part, be a reflection of the nature and consequences
of technological change itself resulting in greater uncertainty of future employment and causing individuals to
build up stocks of personal wealth earlier than otherwise,
creating new and improved products, preventing satiation
amongst consumers. These new and improved products have been
heavily advertised by firms attempting to maintain their
share of the market and the position of the market for their
type of product *vis-à-vis* other products (see Cowling and
Brack, 1980). Large firms and oligopolistic market structures
(which may, in part, be a product of the nature of technological change itself), in so far as they rely heavily on
R & D and advertising, may therefore have produced an inflexible labour market response to new technology. As a
result, fewer new jobs have been created and the only major
compensatory mechanisms are likely to have been the extra
demands arising from the higher income levels of workers who
manage to remain in employment and the extra demand for
capital goods in the transitional phase from one technological state to another.

The contribution of Bosworth and Dawkins stresses that
effective responses to technological change may not lie
wholly (or even mainly) in the realms of managing the rate
of introduction of the new technology. A sharing of the
available work is clearly one possible means of redistri-
buting more evenly across the population the wealth created
by the new technologies. This touches on the potentially
important distributional question of sharing the wealth not
only across the 'work-force', but across the whole of the
population. Action on this broader front may well require
not only some form of work sharing, but some form of
arrangement for profit sharing and possibly also a wider
distribution of the ownership of capital.

8   OTHER ASPECTS IN THE TREATMENT OF THE EMPLOYMENT
    CONSEQUENCES OF TECHNOLOGICAL CHANGE

There are a number of areas, some of which were touched
upon during the presentations of the ensuing discussions,

others being omitted, that probably deserve much greater attention than was allotted to them during the course of the Conference. In particular, questions were raised about the impact of technological change on the supply of labour, regarding the maintenance of hours of work in order to increase family income levels and to buy the new products coming on stream. On the other hand, there is the equally important question of the impact of technological change in determining the range and effectiveness of consumer durable goods that, on balance, have increasingly freed labour from time-consuming domestic chores. Such trends have given house-workers the choice of entering paid employment (see the paper by Bosworth and Dawkins). The majority of these freed workers are women and this has almost certainly had an important effect on the sex distribution of the work-force. At the same time, it is probably fair to say that technological changes have opened up many jobs in the factory to women, partly by reducing the amount of physical strength required and partly by reducing the amount of training necessary for certain tasks. There is, however, still a considerable way to go before complete equality of opportunity will prevail between the sexes.

Outside of the level of employment and the training impli-cations of technological change, Bosworth and Dawkins raise the broader questions of health, worker satisfaction and safety in employment. The new technologies are almost cer-tainly affecting the levels of skill required to undertake the tasks being allotted to the worker. Examples can be found of deskilling, but, equally, other changes may require substantial increases in the skill level. Both changes have their dangers, resulting in either dull, boring, stressful jobs or in demanding substantial levels of training or edu-cational attainment, that may well lie outside the range of achievement of many individuals. At the same time, the indi-viduals are working with new materials and on new processes that may have serious, unforeseen health effects. Finally, technological changes, particularly in so far as they are associated with greater capital intensity and more rapid technological obsolescence, give rise to a greater amount of shift-working and working at unsocial hours of the day or week. Again, many authors have pointed to the potentially very important physiological and psychological effects of such activity.

REFERENCES

Bosworth, D. L. (1980) 'Technology Policy and Industrial

Strategy: Discussion', in T. Puu and S. Wibe (eds). *The Economics of Technological Progress* (London: Macmillan).

Cowling, K. G. and J. A. Brack (1980) 'Advertising and Hours of Work in US Manufacturing, 1919-75', Warwick Economic Research Papers, No. 178, Department of Economics, Warwick University.

Downie, J. (1958) *The Competitive Process* (London: Duckworth).

Hines, C. (1978) *The Chips are Down* (London: Earth Resources Research).

Malinvaud, E. (1980) *Profitability and Unemployment* (Cambridge University Press).

Stoneman, P. (1981) 'Technology and Employment in Open and Closed Economics', paper presented at the AUTE Workshop on the Causes and Consequences of Technological Change, Loughborough University, 2-3 April 1981.

Stubbs, P. C. (1980) 'Technology Policy and Industrial Strategy', in T. Puu and S. Wibe (eds). *The Economics of Technological Progress* (London: Macmillan).

1 Theoretical Approaches to the Effects of Technical Change on Unemployment

ATHAR HUSSAIN

1 INTRODUCTION

As yet there is no comprehensive and coherent analysis of the multifarious effects of technical change on unemployment. This furnishes me with an excuse to put together various bits of familiar economic theory which shed light on the issue. This paper is divided into two parts, of which the first is concerned with conceptions of production and the second, very briefly, with some institutional aspects of employment.

2 CONCEPTIONS OF PRODUCTION

Since they are closely interrelated, the way in which we analyse the effects of technical change crucially depends on our conception of production. Broadly speaking, we may distinguish between the black-box view and the functional view of production. According to the former - the main stream view in economics - production is what takes place in the black-box (work-place); and for the purposes of economic analysis the relevant features of production are adequately described by its inputs and outputs. The second view, in contrast, focuses on the performance of technical functions which together constitute production. For the purposes of discussion the black-box view could be divided into the familiar categories of the simple neo-classical and Leontief and von Neumann models of production.

2.1 *Simple Neo-classical Model*

The underlying conception in this model is the familiar view that production essentially consists in combining together land, labour and capital. The primary emphasis in the model is not on the technique but on the functional distribution of income. For the three factors of production are not technical but distributive categories in that each of them

is the source of a particular type of income. Thus production in this model is essentially a process of generation
of income. Leaving aside rent, technology is then described
by possible combinations of the wage rate and the profit
rate.[1] Under certain conditions - for instance when there
is only one good - one can, as is well known, establish a
monotonic correspondence between the distributive and the
physical descriptions of techniques, in terms of capital to
labour ratio.

In the context of the discussion of technology the simple
neo-classical model for all practical purposes becomes a
single good model. It is widely accepted that the one-good
model is a very inadequate framework for the description of
technology. Inadequate though it may be, none the less the
model can be used to analyse at least some of the effects
of technical change on employment. For that analysis does
not in all cases depend on an adequate description of
techniques.

Technical change in the neo-classical model is what
enables the economy to produce more with the given amounts
of labour and capital. Since here we are concerned with the
effect of technical change on employment and not on techniques described in terms of capital to labour ratio, it is
appropriate to specify technical change purely in terms of
an increase in labour productivity, as done by Marx and
Harrod. Therefore the main effects of technical change, for
the present purposes, are: (a) a reduction in the amount of
labour required to produce a given volume of goods, and
(b) *pari passu* an increase in per-capita income. Broadly
speaking, these two effects, *mutatis mutandis*, remain valid
in the complicated multi-commodity model; and these are,
historically speaking, the two most important effects of
technical change.

Ceteris paribus technical change *qua* an increase in the
productivity of labour always creates a problem of unemployment; because, as a result of it, a given volume of production generates a smaller volume of employment. The
problem of unemployment can be re-stated in the terms
employed in empirical work: technology, in conjunction with
other conditions of production, determines the potential
output, which for advanced industrial economies could be
regarded as equal to the full employment level of income;
while the aggregate demand determines the actual level of
output and hence the level of employment in the economy.
Technical change creates a problem of unemployment in so far
as it widens the gap between the potential and actual
output.

When put in this form it becomes clear that the problem

of unemployment created by technical change is no different
from the Keynesian problem of the deficiency of demand.
Therefore the remedy for technical unemployment need not be
any different than that for Keynesian unemployment.[2] There
is, however, an important difference between the two.
Technical change, because of its effect on per-capita
income and the expected rate of profit, has an expansionary
effect on aggregate demand and thus on employment. Therefore
it is perfectly possible for technical change to more than
offset the contractionary effect that it has on employment
through an increase in labour productivity. Indeed, from the
point of view of the Schumpeterian analysis of trade cycles,
it is unwarranted to associate technical change with the
creation of unemployment. For, according to that analysis,
technical change by creating an investment boom eventually
results in an expansion of employment, some of which may be
temporary.

  Briefly, then, the insights into the relationship between
technical change and aggregate employment which the one-
sector model yields are:

(a) technical change does not create a problem of aggregate
    unemployment which is peculiar to it;
(b) technical change results in aggregate unemployment only
    because the growth in output falls short of the rate of
    increase in labour productivity;
(c) when analysing the effect of technical change on
    aggregate employment, one should not focus exclusively
    on reduction in the requirement of labour per unit of
    output; one should also take into account the increase
    in per-capita income brought about by technical change.

Generally valid though these insights are, they are not
sufficient for a comprehensive analysis of the effect of
technical change on unemployment. For, in the one-sector
model, employment has only one dimension: its volume. For
other dimensions of employment we have to turn to other
models of production.

2.2 *Leontief-von Neumann Model*

Production in this model, as in the previous one, is a
process of combination, with the difference that factors of
production are broken down according to their physical
characteristics. In fact, the model can accommodate itself
to a wide variety of classifications of inputs; and it is
in this that the versatility of the model lies.

Technical change in this model can take three forms, of which the simplest and the least plausible is one where the change implies the production of the same range of goods with smaller quantities of inputs. Technical change in this model is Harrod neutral if it reduces the labour requirement of each activity by the same proportion.[3] In this case, however, the multi-commodity model behaves exactly in the same way as the one-good model and adds no extra dimension to the effect of technical change. The alternative case is one where technical change reduces the requirements of other inputs as well as labour; such a change would normally result in a change in the composition of national output, and thus would have a similar effect as the next case.

Technical change in this model assumes its second form when the same range of consumption goods are produced with different arrays of inputs, some of which will be new inputs embodying the new technology. The embodiment is the most visible effect of technical change. Analytically, what it does is to make it impossible to identify the change in the requirement of labour per unit of consumption good by examining the inputs and labour immediately required to produce that commodity, for the inputs before and after the change do not consist of the same items. However, the change in employment generated by one unit of consumption good can be calculated by comparing the employment multiplier before and after the change: the sum of labour required at each stage of the production of the commodity. In concrete terms, the requirement is that when analysing the effect of, for example, automation on employment, one should take into account not only the labour displaced by the automation but also the labour required to produce the automation, and so on. Leaving aside the case where technical change results in the introduction of new consumer goods, we turn briefly to the question of the calculation of employment multipliers.

When there is no joint production in the economy, employment multipliers can be calculated by solving the input-output equations for what is required to produce a unit of the commodity in question, directly or indirectly. In fact, the requirements can be read off straight from the Leontief inverse. Once these are given, one can easily calculate the employment multiplier, with the help of the labour requirements vector. In fact, as has been shown by Morishima, the employment multiplier of a commodity is the same as its value in the Marxist sense.[4]

However, this method may yield negative employment multipliers in the von Neumann model, in which partially utilised capital goods are regarded as joint products. None the less, one can, as Morishima has shown, calculate

employment multipliers in the von Neumann model by the
linear programming method, but the multipliers obtained in
this way do not have the same properties as those obtained by
solving equations in the non-joint products case. In
particular, one cannot obtain the total employment created
by the production of a group of commodities by simply adding
up the employment created by the production of each unit of
the commodities in the combination. The sum of the latter
may well exceed the former, but never falls short of it.[5] The
intuitive reason for this is that joint production introduces
an element of 'waste', in the sense that all joint products
may not be utilisable. Further, producing commodities in
combination rather than a unit of each at a time may economise
on labour, because it may result in the utilisation of
partially used up capital goods which may otherwise remain
unutilised. Employment in the von Neumann model therefore
depends on the composition as well as on the volume of the
commodities produced, as in the Leontief model.

In both the Leontief and the von Neumann models, the
productivity of labour increases when, *ceteris paribus*, the
employment multiplier for at least one of the consumption
goods decreases. In addition, in the von Neumann model the
change in the composition of inputs brought about by an
embodied technical change may decrease total employment
generated by a group of consumption goods over and above
what is implied by changes in the employment multipliers of
each of the individual commodities. Complicated though the
employment multipliers are, a decrease in them raises
exactly the same type of problem of unemployment generated
by an increase in the productivity of labour in the one-good
model.

After this brief discussion of the calculation of employment multipliers and the relation between changes in them
and in labour productivity, we now turn to the relation
between types of technical change and the direction of
change in employment multipliers.

The simplest case is one of disembodied technical change,
where it takes the form of simply a reduction in the quantity
of an input or labour. Such a change is more likely to be an
effect of learning by doing or a reorganisation of production
than of the introduction of a new technique of production; it
would obviously imply a reduction in the employment multiplier
of the commodity in question. Its importance stems from the
implication that the effect of a technical change on employment may not be once and for all but distributed in time.

We turn now to the case of mechanisation or automation,
which was initially analysed by Ricardo.[6] Assuming that the
machine is non-durable, the pre-condition for its profitable

utilisation is that its price should not exceed the sum of
the wages of the labourers which it displaces. One can
justifiably assume that the production of the machine is
profitable, which is equivalent to saying that the price of
the machine exceeds the undiscounted sum of wages paid out
during the course of its production. In light of this, the
precondition for mechanisation becomes that the total sum
of wages paid out in the course of production of the machine
should be less than the sum of wages of the displaced
labourers. If the wages are the same everywhere in the
economy, then this precondition simply means that the
employment generated by the production of the machine should
be less than employment reduced by mechanisation. However,
if the wage rate in the capital goods sector is less than
elsewhere, then mechanisation may end up increasing the
employment multiplier of the commodity. However, in that
case, mechanisation reduces overall labour productivity.

A similar reasoning can be applied to the durable machine
case. Mechanisation in that case implies that the price of
the machine does not exceed the total sum of wages saved by
the machine over its lifetime. In this case, because of
durability, it is perfectly possible for the labour employed
in the production of the machine to exceed the labour it
immediately displaces on its introduction. Later on during
the course of its life, however, the partially used machine
keeps on displacing labour without requiring any labour for
its production, because a partially used up machine is a
joint product. The production of durable capital goods
therefore gives rise to irregular employment - a phenomenon
which Marx identified by reference to fluctuations in
employment in the textiles machines industry. In a general
sense, technical change, apart from reducing the volume of
employment generated by consumption goods, may well introduce an element of irregularity in employment.

At this stage, it is worth raising the question about the
guidance which the examination of changes in the employment
multipliers of individual commodities can provide in
analysing the overall effect of technical change on total
employment. It is clear that one cannot progress very far
by such an examination. The aggregative effect of technical
change on employment must be deduced from secular trends in
real per-capita income and labour productivity. The continual
increase in per-capita income which has taken place in
industrialised economies over, for example, the last hundred
years, indicates that, generally speaking, technical change
is synonymous with a decrease in employment multipliers and
an increase in labour productivity. Further, that the
maintenance of employment entails a continual growth in

output. One may also note that the multi-commodity model, so
long as it is used only for the calculation of employment
multipliers, does not yield any conclusion different from
those yielded by the one-sector model.

As a side issue, it is worth pointing out that though the
term employment multiplier is widely used in the literature,
there is a slight problem in calling the sum of labour
directly or indirectly required to produce a unit of the
commodity its employment multiplier. For that sum is a one-
dimensional entity, while employment is a rate, and thus has
two dimensions. The point, then, is that the same employment
multiplier can give rise to widely different patterns of
employment in time. This is of some importance, because one
is interested not only in the volume of employment during a
time period, but also in its regularity.

Apart from its temporal distribution, employment in the
multi-commodities model has two dimensions: its total volume,
as in the one-sector model, and its distribution over
different industries. Thus, technical change changes not
only the volume, but also the distribution of employment
generated by the production of a group of commodities. It is
only when we are concerned with the distribution of employment and changes in it that the multi-commodity model adds
to the analysis of the one-sector model. For present purposes, it is the introduction of either new consumer goods
or of inputs embodying the new technology which change the
distribution of employment over different industries.

In order to analyse the effect of embodied technical
change on the distribution of employment, we once again turn
to the case of mechanisation. Mechanisation is, in effect,
the substitution of the labour employed in the production of
machines for the labour displaced by them. Such a substitution would, in general, create a problem of unemployment, even in the unlikely circumstance where the mechanisation leaves the employment multiplier unchanged. For,
because of the organisational specialisation in economic
activities, it would normally be tantamount to the substitution of labour employed in one firm for that in another.

The introduction of new consumer goods changes the
distribution of employment, but with the difference that,
unlike mechanisation, the increase in employment which it
brings about is not coupled with a reduction in employment
in some other industry. That makes it equivalent to an
increase in the volume of the already existing range of
consumer goods. However, the introduction of new consumer
goods has a particular significance of its own from the point
of view of aggregate demand: it points to why an increase in
per-capita income brought about by technical change need not

lead to satiation and thus a decline in the propensity to
consume. Further, it points to the general possibility of
maintaining employment in the face of technical change, by
widening the range of activities. It could be argued that
the range of goods and services which are actually produced
in the economy is only partially determined by the existing
state of technology, which offers far more possibilities
than those actually realised in practice. What this suggests
is that it is always technically possible to generate any
volume of employment by widening the range of activities.
Perhaps one should also add that widening need not assume
the pointless form of getting the unemployed to dig holes in
order to fill them up again.

Before we leave the subject of the distribution of employment, it is as well to specify the reason why a redistribution of the labour force among activities creates a problem
of unemployment. In a completely centralised economy, where
the state is the only employer, the redistribution of the
labour force among different activities would, by itself,
create no unemployment. A redistribution of labour in the
centralised economy, in terms of its effects, is identical
with the redeployment of labour within a capitalist enterprise in a decentralised socialist economy, and thus it
creates no problem of unemployment. Therefore, the redistribution of the labour force among activities creates a problem
of unemployment only when activities are partitioned into
distinct organisations, each of which is a unit of employment.

Changes in the distribution of the employed labour force
are as important effects of technical change as increases in
per-capita income and labour productivity. These changes, in
conjunction with the related changes in the composition and
volume of output, will manifest themselves in variegated
combinations of output and employment in each industry.
Generally speaking, during any period of time, industries
would fall into one of the four categories obtained by combining the pair decreasing/non-decreasing employment with the
pair decreasing/non-decreasing output. Before finishing the
discussion of the multi-good model, it is as well to raise
the question of what should be the point of reference when
one is analysing the effects of changes in the distribution
of the employed labour force? Logically speaking, the
reference ought, whatever happens, to be the unit of employment, a firm, or a plant in the case of multi-divisional
firms. However, it could be justifiably argued that, from the
point of view of the determinants of employment, it is not
the unit of employment, but rather the larger units of industry or sectors which are relevant.

2.3 *The Functional View*

This view, rather than restricting itself to inputs and
outputs, focuses on the performance of technical functions
which together make up production of commodities. Thus the
focus of this view is on the work-place. Adam Smith's discussion of the division of labour and Marx's discussion of
the organisation of production could be regarded as exem-
plifications of this view, which is essentially a technological view of production.

According to this view, production consists of the performance of interrelated tasks. Further, the tasks performed
within a branch of production are not all peculiar to that
branch: there is a considerable overlap of tasks between
branches of production. For instance, Rosenberg has pointed
to the overlap between the functions performed in all those
industries which work with metals.[7] A technique under this
view is then a combination of tasks to be performed to
achieve a particular result, as well as the specification of
how those tasks are to be performed. In particular, a technique would indicate whether tasks are to be performed by men
or machines, and the nature of the tasks to be performed by
the men employed in production.

Briefly, the importance of this view consists in the fact
that it enables one to specify the link between techniques
and occupations. To start with, given that functions performed in different branches of production overlap, one would
expect the classification of occupations to cut across industrial divisions. Further, this view also enables one to
see how and why a large number of technical changes affect a
group, rather than one industry at a time. For instance, this
view comes in handy when one is analysing the possible points
of incidence of micro-electronic devices.

Thus technical change under this view is essentially a
change in the range of functions to be performed and the
method by which they are performed. That change, one may
emphasise, is never total; it may only affect certain functions, leaving others unchanged. It is through these functional changes that technical change may have radical implications for particular occupations. For it may make the
very functions on which they are founded redundant. In
addition, by creating new types of functions, technical
change gives rise to new occupations. Just as technical
change in the multi-commodity model is coupled with a change
in the sectoral distribution of the employed labour force,
in the functional sense technical change becomes synonymous
with changes in the composition and the range of occupations.
Such a change may be a cause of unemployment in much the

same way as a change in the structure of production. There is, however, an important difference between the two: the latter results in unemployment only when there is an organ- isational specialisation in different activities. The problem of unemployment created by occupational adjustment would exist even in a completely centralised economy.

The question one may raise here is, whether or not occu- pational readjustments brought about by technical change exhibit a particular long-term trend. There is a vast literature on how technical change makes skills unnecessary and crafts redundant.[8] Indeed, in a general sense, it does, but one cannot conclude just from that fact that technical change continually shifts the occupational pattern towards less skilled occupations - the process of de-skilling. The first point to be made is that technical change, as well as making skills and crafts redundant, creates new functions and thus skills and occupations. Further, technical change has been historically accompanied with expansion of the service sector which has created new skills and occupations.

The second point is that skill is not merely a technical category but also a social category. It refers to the conditions of entry to occupations. These conditions are as much determined by the actual function performed by the labourer as by the importance attached to the occupation and the position it occupies in the hierarchy of occupations. In short, the point is that the significance attached to occu- pations cannot be deduced simply from the technology which is employed in production. In fact, one can argue that the trend is not towards the increasing preponderance of less- skilled occupations; on the contrary, given the expansion of public services and the trend towards the professionalisation of public service jobs, there is a tendency in the other direction. The general argument is that, if by skill one means individual dexterity, then technical change perhaps leads to de-skilling; but if by skill one means a technical *cum* social category then there is no general evidence in favour of de-skilling.

The importance of the effects of technical change on occupations derives from the fact that trade unions are organised around occupations, especially in Britain. The effect of technical change on employment often appears as a problem which hits particular occupations. Further, it is not so much that technical change makes certain occupations completely redundant, which it does sometimes, but that it changes the relative importance of jobs and thus of occu- pations. It is this change in the relative ranking of occu- pations which is often a source of problems. With this, we now move on to the category of employment.

3 CATEGORY OF EMPLOYMENT

When discussing the effect of technical change on employment, one has to keep in view the fact that employment is not a technical but a socio-legal category. Changes either in the category of employment or what constitutes unemployment can alter the effect which technical change has on employment.

To start with, the labour force available for employment is not simply a demographic datum but a variable entity influenced by socio-economic factors: the age of retirement, provision of education, and obligatory service in the army. Further, work and employment are not synonymous categories: there is a large range of activities which keep individuals occupied without employing them. Education and housework are the most important of these.

We turn now to the relationship between remunerated work and the volume of employment. The conversion of, for example, remunerated number of work-hours into the number of employed is based on the socio-legal category of a normal working week. Logically, the same number of work-hours can create widely different volumes of employment. Historically, technical change and the concomitant increase in per-capita income have been coupled with a reduction in the standard working week. That reduction has, however, also been coupled with what may seem like a contradictory tendency of increase in the rate of participation of adults of working age. Technical change gives an additional significance to a reduction in the working week; it opens up the possibility of such a reduction without a decrease in the per-capita income of the employed. One could look at increase in labour productivity not in terms of the possibility it offers of increasing the wage rate while keeping the rate of profit constant, as is done in the theory of growth, but in terms of the possibility of decreasing the length of the working week while keeping the per-capita income of the employed constant.

4 SOME GENERAL PROPOSITIONS

(a) The problem of unemployment caused by technical change is not necessarily *sui-generis*, thus the remedies required for it need not be any different than those created by other factors.

(b) Technical change provides for the possibility of an increase in per-capita income, and that increase itself may mitigate the effect of technical change on unemployment.

(c) Technology does not set a limit on the volume of employment; that limit is determined by economic as well as social factors.

(d) Technology influences the range of economic activities, only in so far as it indicates whether or not they are possible. In general, the range of technically feasible activities far exceeds the range of actual activities.

(e) The actual problems of unemployment created by technical change crucially depend on institutional factors.

NOTES

1. This view could be said to be embodied in the application of duality theory to production. See, for instance, A. K. Dixit, *The Theory of Equilibrium Growth* (London: Oxford University Press, 1976) Ch. 2.
2. R. M. Solow, 'Technology and Unemployment', *Public Interest* (Fall, 1965) pp. 17-26.
3. F. H. Hahn (ed.), *Readings in the Theory of Growth* (London: Macmillan, 1971) Introduction.
4. M. Morishima, *Marx's Economics* (Cambridge University Press, 1973) Ch. 1.
5. Ibid., Ch. 14.
6. D. Ricardo, *On Machinery: The Works and Correspondence of David Ricardo* (Cambridge University Press, 1953) vol. 1.
7. N. Rosenberg, *Perspectives on Technology* (Cambridge University Press, 1976) Ch. 1.
8. See, for instance, H. Braverman, *Labour and Monopoly Capital* (London: Monthly Review Press, 1974).

2 Technological Change, Demand and Employment[1]

DOUGLAS JONES

1 INTRODUCTION

In his seminal 1939 paper,[2] Sir Roy Harrod stressed the need
to 'think dynamically'. In this spirit, this chapter attempts
to apply the basic insights of the simple Harrod-Domar model
to an assessment of the impact of technological change on
employment. On the assumption that the demand for labour is
a function of the demand for output, the advantage of the
approach outlined is that it allows a clear theoretical
distinction to be made between, on the one hand, the direct
and indirect labour-displacing effects of new technology,
and, on the other, the factors generating compensatory demand
for labour. The latter can be divided into increases in
demand induced by new technology and increases in demand
determined independently of technological change.

The arguments presented are, as yet, in a preliminary and
underdeveloped state. They are not so concerned with
variables that might be precisely measured as with analytical
concepts that might be used for illustration. The aim of the
paper is to specify a number of aspects of the relationship
between technological change and employment that need to be
dealt with by any analysis that claims to be satisfactory.

At the outset it is necessary to explain what is meant by
the term 'technological unemployment' as used in this
chapter. The chapter is not directly concerned with what
might be termed 'structural' technological unemployment
based on changing skill requirements. This is because evidence suggests[3] that 'apparent' structural problems diminish
as growth increases; problems associated with structural
change are more likely to be as a result of slow growth
rather than a cause of it. The definition of technological
unemployment is that used by Lederer in an ILO report
written in the 1930s:

> that fraction of unemployment which being caused by
> technical progress, is not counterbalanced within a
> given period of time by the effects of technical
> progress or by the changes it produces, *or by the*

spontaneous automatic development of the economic system.[4]

Some might wish to argue that new technology, by helping Britain to remain competitive, cannot be a 'cause' of unemployment. This, however, assumes an expansion of demand which may not actually take place, possibly due to factors largely unrelated to technology such as the state of world trade. Thus, simply maintaining one's competitive position may not be enough to prevent unemployment. As Mill pointed out, 'demand for commodities is not the same as demand for men'.[5] It is, therefore, emphasised that, at a time of slow growth in total demand, one of the consequences of technological change may be to increase existing unemployment.

A further definitional distinction that needs to be made is between a partial assessment of the effect of new technology on employment and an integral assessment.[6] A partial approach studies the direct relationship between these two variables, i.e. the initial and more obvious impact only. An integral approach, which is favoured in this chapter, takes into account the effect of technological change on other factors determining employment, most notably demand.

The chapter starts by briefly examining a number of existing views. These views range from the optimistic outlook of neo-classical theory,[7] through the more guarded optimism of a recent Department of Employment Report,[8] to the 'doomsday' predictions of Colin Hines[9] and Jenkins and Sherman.[10]

It is the view in this chapter that these analyses are inadequate because they fail to emphasise the key role played by demand in the determination of the impact of new technology on employment. The Department of Employment Report, for example, tries to dismiss the argument that technological unemployment will increase in future because the introduction of microelectronics is unlikely to be any more rapid than the introduction of past technologies. Similarly, Thirwall has announced his scepticism with the argument that a high rate of post-war technological progress did not lead to high unemployment in the 1950s and 1960s. Although these views may have substance, they do not dismiss the *possibility* of future technological unemployment because they are not related to the future growth rate of the economy.

In order, therefore, to emphasise that, in addition to supply-side considerations, the growth of demand is also an important determinant of technological unemployment, the second section develops a simple explanatory model loosely based on that originally conceived by Harrod in 1939. The model postulates a growth rate that is required for full employment and then outlines ways in which technological change affects both this rate and its attainment.

The views outlined in the first section are then assessed in the light of this alongside a brief discussion of other implications of the model. Finally, conclusions are drawn.

2 THREE EXISTING VIEWS

The view of neo-classical theory is that technological un-employment cannot occur because of the mechanism of compen-sation, i.e. negative employment effects are compensated by positive employment effects.

The mechanism is supposed to work as follows. A fall in costs due to labour-saving or capital-saving new technology[11] will lead to a fall in prices due to competitive forces. If demand is elastic this will cause foreign and home demand to expand, thus workers who might have been displaced find work producing extra output. If demand for the output of the innovative industry is inelastic, then the price fall has an income effect which causes the demand for other goods to rise. Displaced workers find new jobs producing the expansion of output necessary to meet this demand. Moreover, since some new technology will lead to new products which must use labour in their production, the feeling is that, in total, techno-logical unemployment should not occur. Even if price flexi-bility does not clear the labour market, then wage flexibility should eventually lead to full employment.

Technological unemployment is thus regarded, at worst, as only a temporary or frictional problem, and is therefore not of much concern. Although an extreme has been outlined, variations on this theme are the hallmark of the traditional approach. For example, some people have recognised that a lack of flexibility may cause problems, but their analysis does not develop from here.[12]

The analysis offered by the Department of Employment Report, *The Manpower Implications of Micro-electronic Technology*, suffers because part of its purpose is to propagandarise against 'Luddites' and 'Scaremongers'. Whilst attempting to recognise certain employment hazards posed by new technology, its central aim is to stress the 'necessity' of new tech-nology. It backs this view with a shrewd comment on the logic of a trading capitalist nation by stating that:

It is important to note that it is total (not just domestic) demand which needs to expand in order to maintain full employment against a background of technological change. If other countries move faster than Great Britain in exploiting new technology

their international markets (including their share
of ours) will expand while ours will contract. Any
attempt to compensate for a decrease in overseas
demand by an increase in home demand would lead to
balance of payments difficulties. *Thus while it
cannot be said with certainty that successful
adaptation is bound to result in full employment,
it may be said with absolute certainty that failure
to keep abreast of our competitors in technological
change will lead to higher unemployment.* (My emphasis.)

The last sentence of the quotation has been emphasised
since it represents the crux of the argument pursued in the
report. The unpredictability of the future and the apparent,
possible 'beneficial' effects of new technology are relied
upon to overshadow the possible negative impact on employment.
Indeed, at times, the fairly optimistic tone of the report's
conclusion is at odds with the evidence it draws upon, which
indicates a number of activities in which jobs have been, or
are likely to be, lost.
The report comes close to assuming that new technology *will*
improve Britain's competitive position, and so increases in
demand *will* take place, and, by implication, that these
increases in demand *will* be sufficient to prevent an increase
in unemployment. Besides, they add, the exogenously-determined
level of demand is a far bigger determinant of unemployment
than new technology. Finally, it is their belief that the
future pace of technological change will be 'evolutionary'
rather than 'revolutionary'.
The report pays no attention to the effects of natural
wastage policies following technical change or the increasing
difficulties faced by new entrants to the labour market.
These do not appear to have been regarded as symptoms of the
impact of technological progress on employment.[13]
Turning now to the analyses of the pessimists, the key
differences appear to be over the assumptions made about the
demand-creating effects of new technology and about the
rapidity of diffusion. Hines notes that, because of the
current slack level of total (including world) demand and
the increasing size of the labour force, people such as the
Cambridge Economic Policy Group believe that unprecedented
rates of growth will be necessary for full employment. He
also recognises that Britain needs to remain competitive
and so must not fall behind in the adoption of new technology.
Falling behind, however, should not be a problem in his model
since the assumption is of rapid diffusion, despite the slack
level of demand. The result is high labour displacement. At
the same time, little positive benefit for demand and

especially employment is expected to follow rapid technological change. Jobs are thus expected to be squeezed from
two directions: from labour-displacing new technology on the
one hand and from slow-growing demand on the other.

3 A MODEL TO ANALYSE TECHNOLOGICAL UNEMPLOYMENT

Before outlining the model, two points need to be made.
Firstly, the possibly insuperable problems of aggregation
and measurement are acknowledged but not dealt with in
detail, since it is felt that this would only distract
attention from the chief purpose of the model as an illu-
strative device. Secondly, although explicitly a long-run
model abstracting from the trade cycle, it does give some
insights into the short run. Indeed, the original Harrod
model used the short-run demand-deficiency and multiplier
models of Keynes as its starting point. The long run is
partially determined by the short run, whilst the short run
is constrained by long-run tendencies within the system.
Following Harrod, the model to be outlined is based upon
three trend growth rates: the natural rate, the warranted
rate and the actual rate.
    The natural rate of growth, g_n, is the rate at which a
fully-employed economy needs to grow for full employment to
be maintained. It depends upon the rate of growth of the
labour force (which in this chapter is assumed to be exogenously determined and given), the rate at which labour is
displaced by technological progress (or, more strictly
speaking, by technological progress and other factors making
for an increase in productivity) and the amount of labour
required for a unit increment of output (i.e. the marginal
labour-output ratio). In simple form,

$$g_n = \frac{\ell}{L}$$

    where ℓ = the total supply of labour (including the
              employed, the under-employed and the unemployed)
              per unit of output produced (alternatively, it
              might be thought of as an average gross labour-
              output ratio)
    and L = the marginal labour-output ratio.

The marginal labour-output ratio, L, will depend upon the
summation of sectoral marginal labour-output ratios weighted
according to the size and rate of growth of each sector.
The latter will be a function of the marginal income

elasticity of demand for each sector. Thus structural shifts in demand, for example towards services, will be reflected in L.

The warranted rate of growth, g_w, is the rate of growth of capacity that is required for all savings to be utilised and which generates the growth in incomes necessary for full-capacity utilisation. The net investment involved, therefore, has both an income effect via the multiplier and a capacity effect via the accelerator.

> Let s = actual savings per unit of output (i.e. the propensity to save or the inverse of the multiplier)
>
> and C = actual accelerator (i.e. the actual value of the marginal capital-output ratio).

The marginal capital-output ratio, C, will depend upon the summation of sectoral marginal capital-output ratios weighted according to the size and rate of growth of each sector. The latter will depend upon the marginal income elasticity of demand for each sector. Thus the accelerator, C, depends upon the changes in income which actually take place.

The warranted rate, g_w, however, is achieved only when s takes on a particular value, s_w, and C takes on a particular value, C_w. Thus,

$$g_w = \frac{s_w}{C_w} \quad \text{(ex ante)}$$

> where s_w = the value of s required, given C, to generate the equilibrium growth rate, g_w
>
> and C_w = the value of C required, given s, to generate g_w.

It can be seen that g_w may take a range of values, but that it will be achieved only when s and C stand in particular relationship to one another. Since it is probable that s and C will fluctuate (over the trade cycle for example), g_w will be unstable, and so it is likely that g_w will not equal g_a, the actual growth rate, making some form of disequilibrium the norm. A difference between g_w and g_a implies a tendency to ever-increasing divergence. However, there are a number of factors to offset this, which will be dealt with later.[14]

In simple form, the actual real growth rate, g_a, is as follows:

$$g_a = \frac{s}{C} \quad \text{(ex post)}.$$

In order to take into account the role of government and
foreign trade, a more complicated multiplier of $1/\sigma$ is
assumed, whereby:

$$\sigma = s(1 - t) + (t - g) + (m - e)$$

and s = average propensity to save out of disposable income
t = average propensity of taxation
g = average propensity of government expenditure
m = average propensity to import
e = average propensity to export.

Thus,

$$g_a = \frac{\sigma}{C} \text{ (ex post).}$$

Furthermore, there are a number of variables other than
the technological changes that affect C, which may affect
the real growth of output, g_a, via their impact on real
demand growth (even when a closed economy is assumed). Thus,

$$\frac{\sigma}{C} = f (\Delta p, e_p, \Delta q)$$

where Δp = the change in final prices following a change
in costs
e_p = the price elasticity of demand (in an open
economy this will, in part, depend upon the
actions of foreign rivals)
and Δq = the change in the non-price competitiveness of
goods (this will include quality changes,
improved supply, marketing and the host of
other non-price intangibles that are a key
determinant of whether or not a good is sold;
even in a closed economy, Δq will help increase
or maintain sales via its effect on the
propensity to consume; this may be important in
overcoming any tendency to saturation; in an
open economy, Δq is more obviously important in
the maintenance or expansion of a country's
markets).

The actual growth rate will be subject to a second upper
bound in addition to g_n. This is what Thirlwall and Dixon[15]
have called the balance of payments constrained growth rate.
It is the rate of growth which, for a given set of relative
import and export elasticities and a fixed exchange rate,

will be compatible with long-term balance of payments equilibrium.[16] The balance of payments constrained growth rate, g_f, will also depend on Δp, e_p and Δq.

The g_f will also be determined by the growth of world monetary demand, because when world monetary demand is expanding, there is more likelihood that a country will be able to expand its exports even if its market share is falling. If, on the other hand, the growth of world demand is only very slow, then competitive pressure will become more acute. The only way for countries to expand their market shares will be at the expense of rivals. Thus during a world trade recession, Δp, e_p and especially Δq take on extra importance.

In this chapter we are specifically concerned with technological unemployment, i.e. the extent to which technological change causes g_n to exceed g_a. Thus we are interested in the extent to which technological change affects g_n (and any feedback effect this has on g_a), g_a and g_w (to the extent it affects g_n).

We now turn to an assessment of the factors affecting g_n, g_w and g_a, looking firstly at the nature, supply and diffusion of innovations with particular reference to their labour displacing effects, and secondly, at the tendencies likely to promote compensatory increases in demand. The advantage of this distinction is that it allows the necessary emphasis to be given to the need for an expansion of output in order to avoid either labour displacement, increased labour hoarding or increased problems in finding work for an expanding work-force.

Firstly, we need to know what kind of factor savings are being made. It is important to note that the definitions of labour- and capital-saving which follow are different from those generally associated with Harrod and Hicks. This is because the latter are designed to deal with questions of distribution under conditions of full employment equilibrium. Since this chapter is concerned with the question of unemployment and thereby disequilibrium dynamics, the following definitions have been formulated.

A labour-saving innovation (or wave of innovations) means that following a technological change, less labour is required at a given level of capacity utilisation to produce a given output. In other words a technological change raises average *potential* or full employment labour productivity. This needs to be distinguished from five other non-technical factors which will also raise average labour productivity. These are:

(a) a decrease in labour hoarding;
(b) an increase in capacity utilisation;
(c) economies of scale (not due to technological change);
(d) capital-labour substitution (not due to technological change);
(e) learning by doing and organisational changes.

A labour-saving innovation may be either labour-displacing[17] or labour-employing, depending on what happens to the compensatory demand for labour.[18] Furthermore, a labour-saving innovation is compatible with a move in either direction of the capital-labour ratio.[19] Formally speaking, therefore, a labour-saving innovation is where:

$$\frac{N_t - N_{t+1}}{\bar{Y}} > 0$$

where $\dfrac{N_t}{\bar{Y}}$ = the technologically determined labour input required to produce given output $\bar{Y}$ prior to technological change,

and $\dfrac{N_{t+1}}{\bar{Y}}$ = the labour input required to produce given output $\bar{Y}$ following a technological change.

The aggregate effect will depend upon the weighted summation of sectoral labour-saving innovations and will thus in turn depend upon which sectors introduce innovations and how labour-saving these innovations are.

Labour-saving innovations will increase g_n because ℓ will increase and L will fall. If compensatory increases in demand and output are not sufficient, then an increase in unemployment will occur. This will lower g_a through its negative multiplier effect, further increasing the gap between g_n and g_a (unless the incomes of those in employment rise by more than the loss of income experienced by the unemployed).

If technical change causes $\dfrac{N_t - N_{t+1}}{\bar{Y}} < 0$, then it is

labour-using. This definition must be distinguished from 'labour-employing', which is what happens if a technology leads to an increase in the employment of labour regardless of the effect on $\dfrac{N_t - N_{t+1}}{\bar{Y}}$.

A capital-saving innovation (or wave of innovations) is analogous to a labour-saving innovation and means that, due

to a technological change, less capital is needed to produce
a given output. Formally speaking, therefore, a capital-saving
innovation occurs when,

$$\frac{K_t - K_{t+1}}{\bar{Y}} > 0$$

where $\dfrac{K_t}{\bar{Y}}$ = the technologically-determined capital input
required to produce $\bar{Y}$ prior to the techno-
logical change,

and $\dfrac{K_{t+1}}{\bar{Y}}$ = the capital input required to produce $\bar{Y}$
following the technological change.

A capital-saving innovation will raise g_w by lowering C.
This will have the reverse effect on g_a, which will be
lowered because there will be surplus savings and thus depressed demand.

An innovation or wave of innovations, moreover, may be
both labour-saving and capital-saving. Alternatively, it may
use more of one factor and less of another, that is, a new
technology may involve what amounts to capital-labour substitution. This will provide at least some compensatory
income effects to offset the tendency for income to fall due
to the saving of one of the factors of production.

In determining the aggregate labour and capital-saving
effects of innovations, the aggregate supply of innovations
and their diffusion must be considered. For any particular
period of time, the aggregate supply of innovations will, to
a certain extent, be independent of changes in the demand
for final goods. Indeed, even when the market induces changes
in supply, these may not be in the direction that either full
employment or equilibrium require. It is useful, however, to
divide the total supply of innovations into the autonomous
supply, SS_A, and the induced supply, SS_I.[20]

The autonomous supply of innovations will enter the economy
in a rather random fashion,[21] since they will, by definition,
be developed autonomously of perceived demand. However, once
implemented, they help to create their own demand either
because of their novelty or because of their superiority
over existing techniques, goods and services. The best
example is provided by the relatively recent major developments in microelectronics and computing, the massive R & D
costs of which were met by the American Space and Defence
Programme. Subsequently, demand was found in other fields
for these developments and their spin-offs, because the

technology was superior and/or the prices and costs were lower than for existing products and processes. Potential demand does not rely on an increase in total demand, because it is profitable to produce products and utilise processes embodying the new technology whatever the level of total output.

The effect of the autonomous supply of inventions is difficult to gauge since it is difficult to predict either its quantity or its factor saving bias. However, Jenkins and Sherman suggest that in comparing the 1950s and 1960s to the 1970s (and probably the 1980s), there has been a shift from an emphasis on product innovation to process innovation, with the conclusion that process innovations are likely to create less demand and employment than product innovations.

The induced supply of innovations will, in some way, respond to signals generated by the market. Fellner[22] has suggested that if the economy is on the equilibrium growth path and shortages of a certain factor occur, then the price of this factor will rise, causing inventive activity to be directed towards overcoming these shortages and helping the economy to remain on the equilibrium growth path. There are a number of problems in applying this argument generally, particularly if the economy, as has already been argued, is more likely to be in disequilibrium than equilibrium. Furthermore, the time it takes for adjustment[23] and the fact that factor shortages will not be the only influence on factor prices, suggest that there is little reason to expect the signals generated by market forces to induce technological change that will promote a tendency towards equilibrium. Indeed, disequilibrium may be exacerbated.

This can be made clearer by way of an example. It has been suggested[24] that the high levels of employment in Britain in the 1960s led to labour shortages and increased trade union strength, which, in turn, forced up labour costs. This may have led to an emphasis on technologies using less labour and, in many cases, more capital. However, such induced changes in the capital-labour ratios and the marginal labour-output ratio took some time to feed through. By the 1970s, labour shortages (except of particular skills) were less of a problem, although union pressure on wages continued. Thus as the spectre of Keynesian demand deficiency unemployment arose, the induced tendencies working on the system were towards labour saving, which, in an unfavourable demand environment, is likely to be labour-displacing.

With respect to capital and investment, it has been suggested by Lamfalussy,[25] Sautter[26] and Gregory[27] that slow-growing demand, which leads to g_w exceeding g_a, will affect the nature of investment activity and technological change. Lamfalussy distinguishes between enterprise investment and defensive investment. Enterprise investment is aimed at an expanding market and is likely to lead to more jobs. Although defensive investment may raise the capital-output ratio, it is likely to cause job loss. Rationalisation may not involve substantial investment but, in so far as it does, it will be cost-saving. This would seem natural if market prospects are dull and existing profit margins are being squeezed.

Finally, there is a category of supply that is important as a source of innovation but difficult to classify. The only way for firms in the producer-goods industry to maintain or expand their output is to innovate. The only innovations that will be purchased by the final goods industry will be those which help them raise their profits (generally speaking by lowering their costs). This is thus a powerful force for the diffusion of cost-saving replacement capital goods. Indeed, in a sense, most innovations are of this semi-autonomous type since they are likely to come from outside the firm or even outside the country. On the other hand, they can also be considered induced for two reasons: first, as competitor firms introduce new technology, this will force other firms to adopt it; and second, supplier firms will have to have an eye for potential demand.

Therefore, following Salter, the view is taken that providing businesses believe they can benefit individually from innovations they will be introduced regardless of the macro-economic implications for employment and equilibrium. Diffusion, D, thus depends, in the main, upon the difference between the expected future profitability of using a new technology, π_f, and the expected future profitability of continuing the use of an existing technology, π_e.[28] (Some theories suggest that the latter will contain a premium for the current rate of interest.)

The implicit assumption is, therefore, of some sort of cost-plus, semi-monopolistic pricing. This is likely to slow diffusion since it allows a sufficient margin for older technologies to continue alongside newer technologies for a considerable amount of time. The work of Mansfield[29] and Nabseth and Ray suggests that quite a long time elapses even before 50 per cent take-up of innovations in any particular industry occurs. Hamburg and Schultze[30] suggest that 'it is important to avoid romantic notions about the rate of obsolescence (or Schumpeter's "creative destruction") brought about by innovations'. The view of this chapter is therefore that technological change is largely creeping and incremental rather than discrete and spectacular and that it will, to a certain extent, be immune from short-run changes in demand. The assumption remains however that:

$$D = f \; (\pi_f - \pi_e).$$

New technology might be expected to lower π_e below what it would otherwise have been, because as more firms innovate, competitive pressure increases. As Baran and Sweezy[31] point out, no firm can afford to fall too far behind. Also, as more firms introduce a new technology π_f will increase (for those who have not introduced it, but not for those who already have it, since their first-in-the-field, 'temporary monopoly' profits will gradually be eaten away by diffusion) because teething troubles will be sorted out and a learning-by-doing effect will take hold. It is important to note, therefore, that the diffusion of innovations will still continue during a recession, provided they are profitable. Indeed, π_e is likely to be lowered during a recession as the increased competition this brings will put pressure on profit margins. Against this, a recession will also lower π_f since the allowance made for risk and uncertainty will be increased.

   Given these varying influences, therefore, plus the fact that not all firms are likely to be equally depressed at the same time, it is hardly surprising that both Davies, and Nabseth and Ray found little or no relation between the trade cycle and diffusion. It remains to be conclusively seen what effect the more deep-seated recession of the 1970s had on both diffusion and the induced supply of innovations. This is an area of research which requires something more systematic and substantial than the inspired speculation now in existence.[32]

   However, periods of depression are, as already indicated, likely to affect expectations. Thus Eisner[33] has found that both replacement and net investment fall during a recession. Replacement investment, however, does not fluctuate to anything like the same degree as net investment. This will allow some diffusion to continue during a recession without there necessarily being a rise in gross investment. (NB It is a rise in gross investment that is necessary for there to be a positive income effect via the multiplier.) Only if a new technology raises replacement of existing capital over and above what it might have been in the absence of technological change can it be said to be inducing a compensatory income mechanism. Whether or not this increase will promote sufficient income effects to avert unemployment depends on the extent to which these income effects are sufficient to outweigh the labour displaced by the demise of older processes and substitute goods. The Harrod model suggests that positive income effects will, in any case, be more short-run than capacity and factor-output ratio effects. This will be discussed further, later in the chapter.

We can now briefly summarise how the displacement tendencies will be effective. In particular,

$$g_n = f \frac{(N_t - N_{t+1})}{\bar{Y}}$$

where $\dfrac{N_t - N_{t+1}}{\bar{Y}} = f(SS_A, SS_I, D)$

and $g_w = f \dfrac{(K_t - K_{t+1})}{\bar{Y}}$

where $\dfrac{K_t - K_{t+1}}{\bar{Y}} = f(SS_A, SS_I, D)$.

Having outlined the ways in which technological change can
lead to displacement both directly and via its income effects,
we are now in a position to look towards factors which might
promote compensatory increases in employment.[34] Essentially,
the question being asked is not whether or not output will
remain static, but whether or not it will rise sufficiently
to provide employment for those who do not have jobs
because of technological changes.

We can break compensatory tendencies down into five broad
categories.

(i) If new technology leads to the production of a new, as
opposed to a substitute, product it will be unequivocally
labour- and capital-employing (provided demand arises).

(ii) If a new technology needs to be capital-embodied, and
leads to an increased rate of replacement or to an expansion
of capacity, then there will be compensatory employment
creating pressures both directly via the increase in output
and indirectly via the multiplier effect on income.

(iii) A fall in production costs may improve profitability
and/or lower prices, possibly leading to an expansion of
investment and consumption. Some or all of the potentially
displaced workers will find jobs producing the expanded
output.

Whether or not an induced expansion following a cost/price
fall actually takes place depends on the elasticity of demand
for final goods. Whether or not the expansion is sufficient
will depend on the number of workers displaced and the
marginal labour-output ratio. Since labour costs form only
part of total costs, the income from expanded output will

have to be spent not only on paying labour, but also on
expanding capital and other complementary factors of
production.

Furthermore, since many firms use some sort of monopolistic
mark-up pricing, it might be assumed, *a priori*, that not all
of the benefit from reduced costs will be passed on to the
consumer. Wragg and Robertson,[35] in their follow-up study to
Salter, have found that the benefits from increased productivity are still partially reflected in final prices,
albeit to a lesser extent than during the period Salter
studied. Thus only partial compensatory demand rises are
likely from real price falls.

(iv) The fourth factor leading to compensation is the effect
on q, the quality and non-price competitiveness variable.
An improvement in q may help to open new markets or maintain
existing market shares. This will ease the balance of payments constraint, g_f, whilst it might also ease any domestic
problem of surplus savings if it raises consumption.

It is not enough, however, to simply introduce new technology because, if trading rivals are also introducing new
technology, q may not improve. Thus if the market is
expanding only slowly or not at all, compensatory rises in
demand will be insufficient. Indeed, given that technology
is only one of the factors affecting q, new technology may
not be sufficient to reverse stagnant demand or falling
market share; its only effect will be to increase job loss.

(v) In a rapidly growing economy, technological change will
enhance the growth rate by easing resource and factor constraints, lowering costs and prices and opening new markets.
These will all aid a prolongation of boom conditions and
delay the onset and the severity of the downturn. It is a
mistake, however, to assume that new technology alone can
be relied upon to set high growth in motion. It may, however,
help to prevent a tendency to ever-increasing divergence
between g_w and g_a. Hamburg and Schultze think that this may
occur if new technology brings about investment that is
autonomous of expected increases in demand.[36] Alongside other
autonomous investment, such as public expenditure, this will
help soak up savings, thus lowering g_w. Thus, in simple form,
g_w becomes

$$\frac{(s - K)_w}{C_w}$$

where w is the subscript to denote s, K and C are in some
relationship to each other such that the economy
would be on the warranted growth path if it was

> growing at g_w,
>
> and K = autonomous capital expenditure.

It must be noted, however, that unless new technology leads to a permanently higher level of autonomous capital expenditure, its positive effect (in a recession) of reducing the numerator in $g_w{}^{37}$ will only be short-run, whereas its negative effect in reducing L and C will be long-run. Thus, even if in the short run new technology appears to have positive income effects via an investment multiplier, these will be dissipated in the long run. It is, therefore, very important to determine what the long-term prospects for demand growth are (whether caused by new technology, domestic capital accumulation, expanding world trade or whatever), because these will determine whether or not a fall in C or L will cause unemployment.

The question remains, therefore, whether the rate of growth will be as high as g_n. Already there is jobless growth in agriculture, and many people[38] feel that this trend is spreading through the manufacturing sector. Unless there is a shift to the more labour-intensive service sector, L will fall, thus further raising the required growth rate g_n.

4 THREE EXISTING VIEWS IN THE LIGHT OF THE MODEL PLUS FURTHER IMPLICATIONS

We now return to an examination of the three approaches to the relationship between technological change and employment outlined earlier.

The model of orthodox neo-classical theory suffers from a large number of defects. To outline these in detail would require a chapter of its own. The areas in which the main criticisms lie are given and the reader is referred to alternative sources for more detailed comment.[39] Criticisms centre upon the degree to which prices are sufficiently flexible in an imperfect world; the question of whether price and wage flexibility are sufficient conditions for full employment anyway,[40] the lack of an investment function; the problems of marginal productivity theory; and the problems associated with a model of compensatory increases in demand which does not take into consideration the likelihood of different labour and capital-output ratios between the displacing and the compensating sectors of the economy.

These criticisms emphasise that although market forces have some role to play, their power may not be sufficient in either theory or practice to ensure equilibrium. Indeed, the Harrod-Domar model suggests that at times the market will

send signals contrary to those required for equilibrium.
The view of the critics is well summarised by the principal
conclusion of Neisser's excellent review of the classical
and neo-classical position on technological unemployment.
'There is no mechanism within the framework of rational
economic analysis that . . . would secure the full absorption
of displaced workers and render "permanent" technological
unemployment in any sense impossible.'

The Department of Employment Report would probably have
avoided a lot of its weaknesses if it had paid more attention
to how the demand for labour is determined. The analysis of
this chapter is based upon the assumption that the demand for
labour is a function of the growth of aggregate demand. At
any given time, moreover, there is a certain growth rate,
g_n, determined by technological change and the structure of
demand, that is necessary for the level of employment within
an economy to remain unchanged. The actual growth rate, g_a,
may fall below this level. This may be because new technology has caused g_n to rise or g_a to fall. However, g_a may
fall for other, non-technological reasons such as a
declining rate of capital accumulation or a world trade
recession. This will cause Keynesian unemployment to rise
but it will also raise technological unemployment, provided
$g_n > 0$ and $g_n > g_a$. This is because the displacement effects
of technological change are no longer being compensated to
the extent that they had been before. The effects of a
recession-induced fall in g_a can be divided into three.

(a) The recession-induced fall in demand may offset any
    technologically-induced positive effects on demand.
(b) The recession, especially if prolonged, may affect
    the type of new technology introduced, e.g. it may
    become more factor-saving with an emphasis on process
    innovation, rather than output expanding with an
    emphasis on product innovation.
(c) Recession may mean that autonomous compensation (i.e.
    non-technological increases in demand which prevent
    a gap between g_n and g_a appearing) does not take place
    and so any insufficiency in technologically-induced
    compensation is exposed and so technological
    unemployment appears where it was previously 'hidden'.

Although not immediately obvious, it is impossible to
conceive of the demand for a large set of goods and factor
services simply by reference to the effect of technology on
prices, costs and product characteristics alone. Even leaving
aside the effect of the overall state of the economy on the
type of technology introduced, the demand environment will

still have an impact on the effect of technology on employment via its influence on the market's response to a given
set of price and product stimuli. Thus the chance of a
successful launch of a new product diminishes during a
recession, whilst price, price elasticity of demand and
profit potential will all be affected. It is impossible to
take some fixed or given demand environment as a point of
reference because whatever demand environment you choose will
be arbitrary in any model of technological unemployment,
because ultimately it will affect the technological unemployment generated by the model. It is, therefore, essential to
have the state of aggregate demand as an explicit variable.

The importance of this realisation manifests itself when,
during a recession, people suddenly become more aware of new
technology's displacing effects. The result is that too much
attention is paid to new technology and not enough to the
output changes which are causing new technology to have the
impact it appears to be having.

In the light of this discussion it appears that the report's
arguments about whether or not the pace of technological
change is 'evolutionary' or 'revolutionary' are only half
relevant. Even if g_n remains constant but g_a falls, technological unemployment will occur. This is because without
technological change, g_n would have been lower than it
actually is. It is only if new technology causes g_a to rise
by more than the increment it adds to g_n that it can,
strictly speaking, be said that no technological unemployment
has occurred. Thus the problem of technological unemployment
is intimately linked to the problems of demand and profitable
capital accumulation. The chief criticism of the report is
that this is not acknowledged.

A second criticism is that the report does not pay attention
to either the difficulties faced by new entrants to the labour
force or to the effect of company de-manning policies based
on natural wastage. If technological change lowers L, even
without causing redundancies, it may still increase unemployment by lengthening the amount of time out of work for the
exogenously-determined increases in the labour supply (e.g.
the increased number of women seeking work). This effect can
be put down to technological change if it is the change in
the rate of technological change which makes the problems
posed by increases in the labour supply greater than they
would otherwise have been. Similarly, firms may not have to
sack workers to shed labour, but they may be able to raise
or maintain output without taking on new workers as others
leave.

The final criticism of the report centres on its discussion
of services. It reckons that continued growth of the service

sector will help soak up any labour displaced in both manufacturing and services themselves. (Services generally have
a higher L than manufacturing.)

There are a number of reasons why this may prove to be
over-optimistic. First, the growth of services is probably
highly income-elastic, thus the service sector depends on
overall economic growth in order to expand. It is not
generally regarded as a likely vehicle of growth itself.
Thus there is some doubt as to whether growth in the service
sector can solve the problems of insufficient capital
accumulation which lead to a divergence between g_w and g_a
(and in turn ensures that the gap between g_n and g_a continues). Although services are spoken of as a likely source
of growth the report does not explain how this might take
place independently of manufacturing growth, given that
much of the service sector services the manufacturing
industry.

Secondly, even if service expansion could take place based
on government expenditure, or on the so-called 'information
revolution', or even on an expansion of the leisure industry,
two questions remain. Firstly, an expansion of the 'unproductive' sector is likely to have an adverse effect on the
balance of payments, thus lowering g_f. Secondly, there is
some doubt as to whether sufficient investment would be involved to have a large-scale multiplier effect. Ironically,
if a large amount of investment did take place in the
service sector, it is likely to be to the detriment of
labour. Thus, if services did become an increasingly important part of the economy, then this should induce innovation
to keep down costs in this sector. Since labour is the chief
cost in this sector then innovation might be expected to be
directed towards labour-saving and capital-labour substitution.[41] Even ignoring the present Government's cuts in
public services, it is by no means certain that sufficient
service sector growth will take place. If this sector does
expand rapidly then the service sector L will probably fall,
making large-scale employment creation less certain.

Hines' pessimistic view may, unfortunately, be a little
nearer the mark. He lacks a general theoretical perspective,
however, which can explain periods of boom as well as periods
of recession. He concentrates too much on the supply side,
leaving himself open to the objections of the Department of
Employment's Report, which takes the view that the pace of
technological change has remained fairly constant. As has
already been indicated, it is important not to over-
emphasise the rapidity of diffusion, but Hines does not pay
heed to this. Indeed, in order to arrive at Hines' scenario
of massive unemployment it is not necessary to concentrate

on new technology. Implicit in the Harrod-Domar model and
in the work of a number of Marxist writers[42] is the need for
a certain rate of capital accumulation for the avoidance of
a tendency to stagnation and large-scale unemployment.
Unfortunately, Hines does not build such considerations into
his speculations, and thus weakens the force of his conclusions of potentially large-scale unemployment. To be fair
to Hines, if there is large-scale labour saving as a result
of technology, the possibility of increased unemployment in
the long run increases. (Given the rate of diffusion assumed
by Hines, the short-run effect is difficult to predict if
new technology is capital-embodied and has an investment
multiplier effect.) However, large-scale unemployment cannot
be inferred solely from what happens to new technology
without reference to the growth rate of the economy. Technological unemployment did not appear to be a problem in the
1950s and 1960s, not because new technology was absent or
diffusion slow, but because sufficient compensatory mechanisms were generated by the technology itself and by the
growth of the economic system as a whole. It is as likely to
be the breakdown of these compensatory mechanisms that is
causing the current discussions about technological unemployment as anything to do with the nature and diffusion of new
technology itself. Thus, although looking at the supply side
will tell us what the rate of compensation will have to be,
it will not actually tell us what will happen to technological
unemployment.

Indeed, Hines' failure to fully appreciate the mechanisms
causing technological unemployment is reflected in his rather
idealistic remedies for unemployment. He suggests that there
is no shortage of jobs that need doing, and that, furthermore,
there are possibilities for decentralised, more labour-
intensive capitalism.

However, the reason that socially-desirable jobs have not
been done in the past has never been a shortage of demand
(in the sense of need) or a shortage of labour or a shortage
of wealth. Like decentralised capitalism, they are simply
not compatible with the capitalist system's desire for
profitable capital accumulation. A similar argument applies
to the advocates of increased leisure, shorter working
weeks, more sabbaticals and the like. The question remains
of who pays for such benefits. As the problems for profitable
capital accumulation become more acute, then the solution to
this problem of the distribution of wealth becomes more
acute also.

5 CONCLUSIONS

This chapter has attempted to show that a fully-satisfactory explanation of the effects on employment of technological change must take into account both demand and supply factors. It criticises a number of existing approaches on the grounds that demand is not given enough attention. In attempting to overcome this shortcoming, a simple model loosely based on Harrod's 1939 paper was used. The model postulated a number of rather intangible variables that ought to be considered. The effect of new technology on these variables was then examined. The central conclusion of the paper is as follows. New technology will help determine a rate of growth, g_n, that is necessary for there to be no change in the rate of unemployment. It will also directly and indirectly help determine the actual growth rate, g_a. There are, however, other powerful forces which will also affect g_a and which may outweigh the effects of new technology on g_a. Thus any gap between g_n and g_a may not close sufficiently for the avoidance of an adverse effect of new technology on employment.

Some will no doubt want to argue that my rather loose and general use of the term technological unemployment is not particularly useful because superficially, in many of its manifestations, it seems to be little distinct from unemployment based on some sort of demand deficiency. This would not be a wounding criticism, however, because this is probably what is indeed the case. Furthermore, if for any reason it is on the supply side that the main cause of increased unemployment due to new technology lies then the model outlined can quite happily cope with this. The important contribution of the model is that, unlike most explanations of technological unemployment, it does not automatically look to the supply side or to the characteristics of the technologies themselves for the whole explanation. As a result of such a tendency in other papers, some of the pessimistic views of massive labour displacement have been dismissed because they rely upon unprecedented rates of diffusion. Unfortunately, this has tended to give credence by default to the more orthodox views of assorted British quasi-government reports and neo-classical theory. These latter views are also at fault, however, because of their belief that new technology will look after itself or that there is a tendency towards some mythical notion of equilibrium.

Dividing labour-displacing tendencies on the supply side from labour-employing tendencies on the demand side should make it clear that these processes are theoretically distinct. Furthermore, the division into technologically-induced and autonomous increases in demand should make it theoretically clear that automatic fully-compensatory increases in demand should not be assumed. This chapter does not make any policy recommendation other than that this should be borne in mind when considering what should be done about the employment implications of new technology.

Finally, the approach outlined does encounter one or two difficulties.

Firstly, the model does not pay explicit attention to the effect of the trade cycle.[43] Thus, in reality, the effect on g_w, g_n and g_a of new technology is not so clear cut as the trends outlined in the model might suggest.

Instead of the headlong tumble into collapse that divergence between g_w and g_a might suggest, it is more likely that persistent divergence will be reflected as a longer, slower process based on a dampening of boom and a prolongation of slumps. Blackaby[44] has already observed this creeping stagnation. The target rate of unemployment has gradually risen so that the level of unemployment in the 1970s associated with a government decision to deflate (marking the top of the boom) is greater than the level of unemployment that was deemed severe enough in the 1950s and 1960s to spark off reflationary action. Thus, although the cycle of boom and slump continues giving credence to the short- and medium-term analyses of orthodox economics, the problems associated with the cycle seem to be becoming a little more intractable, requiring increasing policy trade-offs, and giving some substance to stagnationist arguments.

Secondly, following on from this it is necessary to explain why the system has not broken down given the divergence implications of Harrod. There are, of course, a number of off-setting factors. The brief discussion of the relationship between autonomous investment and g_w provided a starting point. In addition, public expenditure has also helped soak up surplus saving.

Paul Sweezy[45] has put forward the fairly plausible view that such off-setting boosts to the system can only partially ameliorate the chronic tendency to stagnation in the advanced capitalist world. It is only if massive exogenous shocks to the system occur that this tendency will be overcome for any significant period of time. The idea is that, in the past, clusters of major technological innovations associated with steam power, the railways, the motor car and other consumer durables, have caused major structural changes which have necessitated the use of large amounts of capital and its complementary factor, labour. The investment boom which followed had a cumulative wave effect which spreads throughout the rest of the economy. Sweezy does not wish to suggest that these long-run upward swings are in any way at odds with capitalist development, only that they are not inherent or automatic to the system. Thus the long waves analysis associated with Kondratieff[46] and Schumpeter[47] may have some merit as historical description, but it is of no use as a predictive mechanism since the waves are set off by exogenous as opposed to endogenous boosts to the system.

Some have suggested that microelectronics and computing or the search for alternative sources of energy will provide the necessary boost to overcome the current tendency to stagnation. Whether innovations in these areas will have sufficient labour-creating effects via their effect on g_a remains to be seen. If they do, then the problem of technological unemployment will, at worst, have proved to have been medium-term.

Even if a major exogenous boost to the economy is not forthcoming, however, it still seems unlikely that the figures of 6-7 million unemployed being quoted by some people[48] will actually come about. Capitalism is a remarkably robust and pragmatic system; unemployment figures of six million would, however, be a threat to its continued existence. Thus a series of palliatives such as subsidised employment seem likely. The result is likely to be slow growth and greater inefficiency (the efficient paying for the inefficient) with little increase in living standards.

NOTES

1. I should like to thank members of the School of Economic Studies, University of Leeds, who commented on earlier drafts of this chapter. In particular, I should like to thank John Brothwell, John Bowers and Professor Mike Surrey. The usual disclaimer with respect to responsibility for content, of course, applies.
2. R. F. Harrod, 'An Essay in Dynamic Theory', *Economic Journal*, vol. 49 (1939) pp.14-33.
3. J. K. Bowers, 'Labour Mobility and Economic Depression', Leeds University School of Economic Studies, Discussion paper, no.28, 1975. P. Cheshire, 'Is It the Inner City Miasma that Causes Unemployment?', *Guardian*, 12 November 1979.
4. E. Lederer, *Technical Progress and Unemployment*, Studies and Reports, Series C, vols. 20-22 (Geneva: ILO, 1935-8). (My emphasis.)
5. Cited (p.50) by H. P. Nieisser, '"Permanent" Technological

Unemployment', *American Economic Review*, vol. 32 (1942)
pp. 50-71.

6. A distinction borrowed from W. Driehus, *Employment and
Technical Progress in Open Economies*, mimeo, 1979.

7. For a good summary see A. Heertje, *Economics and
Technical Change* (London: Weidenfeld and Nicolson,
1977). M. Bourniatin, 'Technical Progress and Unemployment', *International Labour Review*, vol. 27 (1933)
pp. 327-48 gives an insight to the cruder form of the
neo-classical approach.

8. J. Sleigh, B. Boatwright, P. Irwin and R. Stanyon,
Department of Employment, *The Manpower Implications of
Micro-electronic Technology* (London: HMSO, 1979).

9. C. Hines, *The Chips are Down* (London: Earth Resources
Research, 1978).

10. C. Jenkins and B. Sherman, *The Collapse of Work* (London:
Eyre Methuen, 1979).

11. These terms are explained and discussed below.

12. For example, N. Kaldor, 'A Case against Technological
Progress?', *Economica*, vol. 12, OS (1932) pp. 180-96.

13. See, below, the relevance of technological progress for
employment via its effect on job loss through natural
wastage and indirectly via the way in which it can make
it relatively more difficult for an expanding labour
force to find work.

14. See below pp. 29-30.

15. A. Thirlwall and R. J. Dixon, 'A Model of Export-led
Growth with a Balance of Payment Constraint', in J. K.
Bowers (ed.), *Inflation, Integration and Development:
Essays in Honour of A. J. Brown* (Leeds University Press,
1979).

16. I have preferred to make the balance of payments constraint explicit rather than include it in a more complex
g_w as Harrod, op. cit., has done. This is because the
Harrod model implies that the problem is simply one of
matching leakages and injections, whereas in reality the
balance of payments is a separate constraint.

17. The immediate result might merely be an increase in the
inefficient use of labour rather than actual job loss.
The technology will still be introduced provided the net
savings of innovation remain worthwhile even at less
than efficient operation. However, during periods of
expansion, such labour loading will give bigger scope
for jobless growth because non-technological increases
in average productivity will take place.

18. See below, where the assumption of fixed output is
relaxed.

19. This may be illustrated if, for example, we hold the

size (but not necessarily the content, i.e. problems of
capital measurement and aggregation are ignored) of the
capital stock constant and we introduce an innovation
that is labour-saving but that is also capital-saving.
We assume that it is relatively more capital-saving
than labour-saving. Thus output will increase, and so
will labour, but by our assumption capital is constant.
This is because the fall in the capital-output ratio was
greater than the fall in the labour-output ratio. With
output held constant, the capital-labour ratio will have
fallen, despite the fact that the innovation was partly
labour-saving. It is important to note the implications
of this since definitions based on relative distributive
shares do not take them into account.

20. For an interesting discussion of a similar distinction
    based on supply-push versus demand-pull classification,
    see N. Rosenburg, *Perspectives on Technology* (Cambridge
    University Press, 1976).

21. W. E. G. Salter, *Productivity and Technical Change*
    (Cambridge University Press, 1966), in particular,
    stresses the extent to which inventions may be autonomous
    of demand changes and how they may not contribute any
    tendency towards macro-economic equilibrium.

22. See, for example, W. Fellner, 'Two Propositions in the
    Theory of Induced Innovation', *Economic Journal*, vol. 71
    (1961) pp. 305-8 among others.

23. For some good discussion of the importance of historical
    time in models of growth and accumulation see J. Robinson,
    'History vs Equilibrium', in *Collected Economic Papers*,
    vol. V (Oxford: Basil Blackwell, 1979), and A. Bhaduri
    and J. Robinson, 'Accumulation and Exploitation: an
    Analysis in the Tradition of Marx, Sraffa and Kalecki',
    Cambridge Journal of Economics, vol. 4 (1980) pp. 103-15.

24. A number of writers in OECD, *Structural Determinants of
    Employment and Unemployment* (Paris: OECD, 1979) make the
    points which follow.

25. A Lamfalussy, *Investment and Growth in Mature Economies:
    The Case of Belgium* (London: Macmillan, 1961).

26. C. Sautter, *Investment and Employment on the Assumption
    of Slower Growth* (Paris: OECD, 1979).

27. T. Gregory, 'Rationalisation and Technological Unemploy-
    ment', *Economic Journal*, vol. 40 (1930) pp. 551-67.

28. The importance of profitability in the diffusion of new
    techniques is stressed in all of the following: S. Davies,
    The Diffusion of Process Innovations (Cambridge University
    Press, 1979); L. Nabseth and G. Ray, *The Diffusion of New
    Industrial Processes: An International Study* (Cambridge
    University Press, 1974); J. Schmookler, *Invention and*

Economic Growth (Cambridge, Mass.: Harvard University Press, 1966).

29. E. Mansfield, *The Economics of Technological Change* (London: Longmans, 1969).

30. D. Hamburg and C. L. Schultze, 'Autonomous Versus Induced Investment: the Inter-relatedness of Parameters in Growth Models', *Economic Journal*, vol. 71 (1961) pp. 53-65, in particular pp. 56-7.

31. P. A. Baran and P. M. Sweezy, *Monopoly Capital* (London: Pelican, 1968).

32. For example, C. Freeman, 'Technical Change and Unemployment', paper presented to the Conference on Science, Technology and Public Policy, University of New South Wales (1-2 December 1977). See also Hines, op. cit.

33. R. Eisner, 'Components of Capital Expenditures: Replacement and Modernisation Versus Expansion', *Review of Economics and Statistics*, vol. 54 (1972) pp. 297-305.

34. For a good discussion of such distinctions and their likely impact on employment see J. M. McLean and H. J. Rush, 'The Impact of Microelectronics on the UK: a Suggested Classification and Illustrated Case Studies', Science Policy Research Unit, Occasional Paper, no. 7 (1978).

35. R. Wragg and J. Robertson, *Britain's Industrial Performance since the War: Trends in Productivity, Employment, Output, Labour Costs and Prices by Industry in the UK 1950-73* (London: Department of Employment, Research Paper no. 3, 1978).

36. See Hamburg and Schultze, op. cit. For further discussion of this point, see Harrod, op. cit.

37. The implication in the short run will be of a replacement investment multiplier effect.

38. See, for example, C. Freeman, op. cit.

39. See Lederer, op. cit.; E. Lederer, *Technical Progress and Unemployment*, vol. 28 (Geneva: ILO, 1933); Nieisser, op. cit.; Heertje, op. cit; M. Blaug, 'A Survey of the Theory of Process Innovations', *Economica*, vol. 30, n.s. (1963) pp. 13-32.

40. For a good discussion of wage flexibility and employment see R. Simmons, 'Keynes, Effective Demand and the Real Wage', School of Economics Discussion Paper, no. 78, University of Leeds (1979).

41. Quite an interesting discussion of possible employment trends in services, particularly with reference to labour-saving technology and capital-labour substitution (e.g. the washing machines for the laundry etc.), is contained in a paper by J. Gershuny, 'The Service Sector and Unemployment: Some Speculations on Future Structural

Changes in the Developed World', presented to the Six
Countries Programme Workshop, Paris (November 1978).
42. For example, Baran and Sweezy, op. cit.
43. For an attempt to combine trend and cycle in a model of
growth see M. Kalecki, 'Trend and Business Cycle Re-
considered', *Economics Journal*, vol. 78 (1968) pp. 263-
76.
44. F. Blackaby, 'The Target Rate of Unemployment', in
G. D. N. Worswick (ed.), *The Concept and Measurement of Unemployment* (London: Allen and Unwin, 1976).
45. P. Sweezy, 'The Crisis of US Capitalism', lecture given
at the University of Leeds (May 1980).
46. N. D. Kondratieff, 'The Long Waves in Economic Life',
reprinted in *Lloyds Bank Review* (July 1978).
47. J. Schumpeter, *Business Cycles: A Theoretical, Historical
and Statistical Analysis of the Capitalist Process*
(London: McGraw-Hill, 1939).
48. University of Cambridge Department of Applied Economics,
Economic Policy Review, no. 4 (March 1978); see also
Hines, op. cit.

3   The Nature of Unemployment under Technical Progress

DAVID DEATON and PETER NOLAN

1 INTRODUCTION

Many contributors to the debate on the impact of micro-electronics on employment[1] seem to have implicitly adopted a notion of technological unemployment, for they place little faith in the conventional policies designed to combat structural and demand-deficient unemployment for dealing with the displacement effects of microelectronics technology. They call instead for direct government intervention to create jobs, various measures designed to reduce labour supply and even a new social attitude to work and leisure.

The question to which this paper is addressed is whether it is useful to distinguish a category of unemployment which we can label as technological. Technical progress can clearly contribute towards structural unemployment when the demand for new skills is not matched by the obsolescent skills of those displaced by the new technology, but it is not apparent that such unemployment is different in kind rather than degree from the structural unemployment which arises from relative shifts in demand.

Unemployment may also arise which is not accompanied by new vacancies if technical progress increases labour productivity without being accompanied by increased demand. Again, however, it is not obvious that a new category of technological unemployment is called for. Is this not simply a form of demand-deficient unemployment which happens to have been initiated by technical progress rather than a fall in aggregate demand?

The object of this paper is to explore whether technical progress can give rise to unemployment in an aggregate model which is not simply removed by the expansion of demand. We consider two rather different models: first, a neo-classical growth model in which demand is always forthcoming, and second, a model in which unemployment can arise either because of a deficiency of demand or because of a lack of capacity.

In the first instance, we use Solow's model of neo-classical growth with a CES production function.[2] Usually in such a model full employment is ensured by a combination of factor-price flexibility and capital/labour substitution. Here we introduce downward real wage rigidity and consider under what other conditions unemployment will result from technical progress.

2 SOLOW MODEL

It is a well-known finding that in neo-classical growth models, steady-state growth is possible only if technical progress is Harrod neutral.[3] If technical progress is labour-saving, the share of national income going to labour will decline. What is not clear are the circumstances in which the wage rate declines. To consider this question, we examine Solow's model with a CES production function:

$$Y = \{a(Ke^{gt})^{\alpha} + b(Le^{nt})^{\alpha}\}^{1/\alpha}.$$

Technical progress has two components: a capital-augmenting element at rate g, and a labour-augmenting element at rate n. For the purposes of illustration, we assume zero population growth, no depreciation, and a constant savings ratio, and hence the investment-savings equality gives

$$\dot{K} = sY.$$

To simplify the mathematics, consider the case where $\alpha = \frac{1}{2}$, $a = \frac{1}{2}$, $b = 1$:

$$Y = (\tfrac{1}{2}\sqrt{Ke^{gt}} + \sqrt{Le^{nt}})^2.$$

To ensure full employment, the wage rate adjusts to the marginal product of labour, therefore

$$w = \frac{dY}{dL} = \tfrac{1}{2}e^{\frac{1}{2}nt}L^{-\frac{1}{2}}(\tfrac{1}{2}\sqrt{Ke^{gt}} + \sqrt{Le^{nt}}) \; . \; 2,$$

therefore

$$w = e^{nt} + \tfrac{1}{2}\sqrt{\frac{K}{L}}\,e^{\frac{1}{2}(g+n)t} \; .$$

Translating the model into discrete time:

$$Y_t = (\tfrac{1}{2}\sqrt{K(1+g)^t} + \sqrt{L(1+n)^t})^2,$$

$$K_{t+1} = K_t + sY_t,$$

$$w_t = (1+n)^t + \tfrac{1}{2}\sqrt{\frac{K_t}{L_t}(1+n)^t(1+g)^t}.$$

One steady-state model compatible with this production function is given when

$$s = 0.02, \qquad K_0 = 100,$$
$$n = 0.045,$$
$$g = 0 \qquad\qquad L_0 = 100.$$

This generates $w_0 = 1.5$, $Y_0 = 225$, $K_1 = 104.5$. The shares going to labour and capital remain constant and the wage rate rises at 4.5 per cent per period. This is what we should expect from Harrod neutral technical progress.

If we maintain the same rate of technical progress but allow it to take a labour-saving form, then

$$\tfrac{2}{3}n + \tfrac{1}{3}g = 0.03 \quad \text{and} \quad g > 0.$$

Consider the case where $g = 0.09$ and $n = 0$. The simulation in Table 3.1 shows that the wage rate rises in each period even though the relative share of labour declines. This happens because the absolute share of labour is rising as a result of the increased productivity due to technical change.

TABLE 3.1 *Simulation of Solow's model: I (with $\alpha = \tfrac{1}{2}$, $g = 0.09$, $n = 0$)*

t	Capital stock	Output	Wages	Labour's share
0	100.0	225.0	1.50	66.7
1	104.5	235.2	1.53	65.2
2	109.2	246.3	1.57	63.7
3	114.1	258.5	1.61	62.2
4	119.3	271.9	1.65	60.6
5	124.7	286.5	1.69	59.1
6	130.5	302.6	1.74	57.5
7	136.5	320.4	1.79	55.9
8	142.9	340.0	1.84	54.2
9	149.7	361.6	1.90	52.6
10	157.0	385.7	1.96	50.9

To achieve a declining real wage rate, it proved necessary to assume more extreme rates of factor augmentation. The

simulation in Table 3.2, for example, assumes augmentation
rates[4] of $g = 0.21$ and $n = -0.06$. Initially, both the wage
rate and the relative share of labour decline. After period
3, however, the wage rate begins to rise again, indicating

TABLE 3.2 *Simulation of Solow's model: II (with* $\alpha = \frac{1}{2}$,
$g = 0.21$, $n = -0.06$)

t	Capital stock	Output	Wages	Labour's share
0	100.0	225.0	1.50	66.7
1	104.5	234.6	1.49	63.3
2	109.2	247.2	1.48	59.8
3	114.1	263.2	1.48	56.2
4	119.4	283.4	1.49	52.5
5	125.1	308.8	1.51	48.8
6	131.2	340.5	1.53	45.0
7	138.1	380.3	1.57	41.3
8	145.7	430.3	1.62	37.6
9	154.3	493.4	1.68	34.1
10	164.1	573.8	1.76	30.6

that the increase in output per period, raising labour's
absolute level of income, is sufficient to support an increasing wage rate. Table 3.3 shows what happens if the
wage rate is fixed at a minimum level of 1.5. Unemployment
emerges in period 1, but disappears by period 5 as the
market-clearing wage rate rises above the 1.5 minimum level.

TABLE 3.3 *Simulation of Solow's model: III (with* $\alpha = \frac{1}{2}$,
$g = 0.21$, $n = -0.06$; *wage subject to a minimum of* 1.5)

t	Capital stock	Output	Wages	Unemployment	Labour's share
0	100.0	225.0	1.50	0.0	66.7
1	104.5	226.8	1.50	5.2	62.7
2	109.0	236.3	1.50	7.2	58.9
3	113.8	253.0	1.50	6.6	55.4
4	118.8	277.0	1.50	3.9	52.0
5	124.4	307.9	1.50	0.0	48.8
6	130.5	339.5	1.53	0.0	45.1
7	137.3	379.1	1.57	0.0	41.4
8	144.9	428.9	1.62	0.0	37.7
9	153.5	491.7	1.68	0.0	34.1
10	163.3	571.8	1.76	0.0	30.7

So far we have considered only the case where the
elasticity of substitution is equal to 2. What happens when

it is less than 1? If we set $\alpha = -1$ in the original CES function, the elasticity of substitution is $\frac{1}{2}$, $a = \frac{1}{2}$ and $b = 1$, then

$$Y = (\tfrac{1}{2} K^{-1} e^{-gt} + L^{-1} e^{-nt})^{-1}.$$

With this production function, steady-state growth is compatible with labour augmenting technical progress at $n = 0.045$ if $s = 0.0675$ and the initial values are

$$L_0 = 100, \quad K_0 = 100, \quad Y_0 = 66.67.$$

Simulating the model gives steady-state growth with wages rising from an initial value of 0.444 at 4.5 per cent per period.

When the elasticity of substitution is less than unity, labour-saving technical progress is represented by higher rates of labour augmentation and negative rates of capital augmentation. To achieve falling wage rates, it proved necessary to assume fairly extreme augmentation rates such as

$$n = 0.09, \quad g = -0.09,$$

which represents a superior technology only whilst labour's share is greater than a half. The results of simulating this model are given in Table 3.4. Here the wage rate declines as the result of technical progress, though this system of augmentation represents progress only up to period 5.

TABLE 3.4 *Simulation of Solow's model: IV (with $\alpha = -1$, $n = 0.09$, $g = -0.09$)*

t	Capital stock	Output	Wages	Labour's share
0	100.0	66.67	0.444	66.7
1	104.5	69.28	0.440	63.5
2	109.2	71.70	0.433	59.9
3	114.0	73.90	0.422	57.1
4	118.0	75.69	0.406	53.6
5	124.1	77.17	0.387	50.1
6	129.3	78.29	0.365	46.6
7	134.6	78.97	0.341	43.2
8	139.9	79.25	0.315	39.7
9	145.2	79.09	0.288	35.4
10	150.5	78.46	0.260	33.1

We now consider what happens if we impose a minimum value
of $w = 0.444$. The simulation is given in Table 3.5. Labour
demand, which was initially at 100, declines, and unemployment grows, reaching nearly 23 per cent by period 7. However,

TABLE 3.5 *Simulation of Solow's model: V (with* $\alpha = -1$,
$n = 0.09$, $g = -0.09$; *wages subject to a minimum of 0.444*)

t	Capital stock	Output	Unemployment	Labour's share
0	100.0	66.67	0.00	66.7
1	104.5	68.75	1.22	63.9
2	109.1	70.26	3.39	61.1
3	113.8	71.27	6.23	58.5
4	118.6	71.37	9.85	56.1
5	123.4	71.28	13.84	53.7
6	128.2	70.74	18.14	51.4
7	133.0	69.74	22.67	49.3
8	137.7	68.27	27.41	47.2
9	142.3	66.69	32.09	45.2
10	146.8	64.92	36.74	43.3
if technical progress stops after period 7, then we have:				
8	137.7	72.22	19.02	49.3
9	142.6	74.77	17.08	49.2
10	147.6	77.43	14.13	49.3

by period 7, the share going to labour is less than a half,
and this system of augmentation is no longer progress. One
would expect technical progress to stop at that point, but
for capital accumulation to continue. At the foot of the
table, we show what happens if this is the case. Labour
demand begins to grow again, though, at a fairly slow rate.

Thus within Solow's growth model it is possible to generate
technological unemployment by holding the wage rate constant
if suitable values of capital and labour augmentation are
selected. However, the process does not continue without
limit. When the elasticity of substitution is greater than
one, the decline in labour share means that increasing
weight is given to positive capital augmentation and labour
productivity starts to rise again. When the elasticity of
substitution is less than one, the decline in labour share
gives less weight to positive labour augmentation and
technical progress tends to stop.

We have not sought in this paper to examine whether
particular forms of technical progress (such as the new
microelectronic technology) are, in fact, labour-saving in
the Harrod sense. Indeed, some authors, such as Kennedy and

Weizsäcker,[5] have argued the case for a mechanism which
ensures Harrod neutrality. Our argument would be that, in
the normal course of events, firms do create their own
technical progress and that it may be legitimate to argue
that induced technical progress ensures Harrod neutrality.
However, some technological advances such as steam power
and silicon chips are exogenous to firms and have widespread
applications, and may be biased in a labour-saving way.
These, in the presence of downward real wage rigidity, may
not give rise to permanent unemployment but perhaps to
unemployment which lasts for longer than the normal cycle.

3 MALINVAUD MODEL

The second model we explore is Malinvaud's dynamic model.[6]
This is essentially a medium-term model around a stationary
state of Walrasian equilibrium. However, we can amend it
to allow for technical progress by incorporating changes in
labour productivity. In Malinvaud's model, three sorts of
departure from general equilibrium are possible: inflation,
Keynesian unemployment and classical unemployment. The
simple incorporation of technical progress, in the form of
labour productivity growth, will, in the absence of anything
to promote growth in demand, lead simply to Keynesian
unemployment. However, if technological unemployment is to
be other than a sub-class of Keynesian unemployment, it
must appear in the Malinvaud model in the form of classical
unemployment which arises from technical progress.

Malinvaud's model is one of fixed factor proportions, with
non-instantaneous adjustment of wages and prices. The three
short-run disequilibrium states give rise to different wage
and price adjustments. Net output (y) is the minimum of
demand (d), full employment output of labour (βL) and the
productive capacity of capital ($\bar{y}$). The labour force (L)
and the productivity of labour (β) are constant, demand is
the sum of consumption (c), investment (i) and government
expenditure (g). Productivity capacity is augmented by
investment times the output/capital ratio (γ).

$$\bar{y}_{t+1} = \bar{y}_t + \gamma i_t$$
$$c = f(w, m, u)$$
$$w = \text{real wage}$$
$$m = \text{real wealth}$$
$$u = \text{unemployment.}$$

This level of planned consumption is realised only if

output is demand-determined. Under classical unemployment or inflation, actual consumption is less than planned. Investment is governed by the relationships between wages and labour productivity and between existing capacity and the minimum of demand and the productive capacity of labour:

$$i_t = a(\beta - e - w_{t-1}) + b(\hat{y}_{t-1} - \bar{y}_{t-1})$$

where $\hat{y}_t = \min\,[\,\beta L,\ d\,]$

and a, e, b are parameters.

The following values produce a steady state:

$\beta = 1$	$w = 0.9$
$L = 1000$	$P = 1$
$\underline{i} = 0$	$g = 100$
$\bar{y} = 1000$	$c = 900$
$m = 900$	$u = 0$

The real wage (w) and the price level (P) are adjusted depending on the relationship between d, $\bar{y}$ and βL. In the case of Keynesian unemployment, real wages are unchanged. The real wealth of consumers is affected by the balance of income and consumption and changes in the price level. The full simulation model with Malinvaud's parameter values are given in the Appendix to this chapter.

We represent the introduction of a new technology by a shock increase in labour productivity of 20 per cent at the end of the first period. Technical progress is entirely disembodied, and its introduction creates no extra demand by itself. Table 3.6 shows the path of the variables in the system as a result of this shock. As expected, Keynesian unemployment emerges and grows if the Government takes no steps to expand demand.

What happens if the Government does intervene to expand demand? Let us assume that the Government can correctly forecast planned investment and consumption and makes up demand to the full employment output level of 1200. The consequence of this is that both full-employment output and demand exceed capacity and classical unemployment results. The shortage of capacity means that not all planned expenditure is realised. In the simulation reported in Table 3.7 we assume that the shortage of output resulting from the capacity constraint is shared proportionately by the three forms of expenditure (rather than just consumption, as in the original model). Although actual investment is therefore less than planned, it is sufficient to remove the capacity

TABLE 3.6 *Malinvaud model with shock increase in* β

t	β	d	y	State	u	c	i	g	P	w	$\bar{y}$	m
1	1.0	1000.0	1000.0	W	0.00	900.0	0.00	100	1.000	0.900	1000.0	900.0
2	1.2	857.1	857.1	K	0.29	757.1	0.00	100	0.937	0.900	1000.0	846.1
3	1.2	923.9	923.9	K	0.23	779.6	44.28	100	0.897	0.900	1000.0	793.3
4	1.2	943.9	943.9	K	0.21	782.6	60.98	100	0.860	0.900	1022.1	751.4
5	1.2	935.3	935.3	K	0.22	775.1	60.44	100	0.817	0.900	1052.6	713.4
6	1.2	918.3	918.3	K	0.24	761.3	50.67	100	0.777	0.900	1082.9	673.9
7	1.2	895.0	895.0	K	0.25	752.4	38.86	100	0.720	0.900	1108.2	639.7
8	1.2	869.2	869.2	K	0.28	733.9	26.70	100	0.659	0.900	1127.6	609.3
9	1.2	843.4	843.4	K	0.30	722.4	15.40	100	0.596	0.900	1140.9	574.4
10	1.2	818.4	818.4	K	0.32	707.4	5.61	100	0.534	0.900	1148.7	536.6
11	1.2	795.4	795.4	K	0.34	695.1	-2.57	100	0.474	0.900	1151.5	493.5
12	1.2	774.2	774.2	K	0.36	681.9	-9.02	100	0.418	0.900	1150.2	444.8

TABLE 3.7 *Malinvaud model with shock increase in β and government providing sufficient demand, shortage borne proportionately by all sectors*

t	β	d	y	State	u	c	i	g	P	w	ȳ	m
1	1.0	1000	1000.0	W	0.000	900.0	0.0	100.0	1.000	0.900	1000.0	900.0
2	1.2	1200	1000.0	C	0.167	680.6	0.0	319.4	1.180	0.867	1000.0	821.5
3	1.2	1200	1000.0	C	0.167	649.2	108.3	242.5	1.392	0.834	1054.2	758.5
4	1.2	1200	1054.2	C	0.122	672.7	137.4	244.1	1.575	0.810	1122.9	723.4
5	1.2	1200	1122.9	C	0.064	719.8	142.7	260.4	1.684	0.797	1194.3	713.1
6	1.2	1200	1194.3	C	0.005	782.5	122.0	289.8	1.693	0.796	1253.3	709.3
7	1.2	1200	1200.0	K/I	0.000	787.3	107.8	304.9	1.693	0.796	1309.2	718.0
8	1.2	1200	1200.0	K/I	0.000	788.2	94.3	317.5	1.693	0.796	1356.3	725.0
9	1.2	1200	1200.0	K/I	0.000	788.9	82.5	328.6	1.693	0.796	1397.6	732.1
10	1.2	1200	1200.0	K/I	0.000	789.6	72.2	338.2	1.693	0.796	1433.7	738.5
11	1.2	1200	1200.0	K/I	0.000	790.3	63.2	346.6	1.693	0.796	1456.3	744.2

which tends to an equilibrium at

	β	d	y	State	u	c	i	g	P	w	ȳ	m
	1.2	1200	1200.0	K/I	0.000	796.0	0.0	404.0	1.693	0.796	1686.4	796.0

constraint by period 7 and the level of unemployment drops
sharply from the initial level of 17 per cent. However, the
system converges on a new non-Walrasian equilibrium with
government expenditure supporting demand and preventing
Keynesian unemployment.[7]

An alternative assumption is made in the simulation presented in Table 3.8 - namely that the supply constraint
results in investment being crowded out. The effect of this
is that no investment is realised until the real wage has
fallen sufficiently to push planned investment over the
200 threshold. Once this level has been achieved, classical
unemployment falls quite quickly, but again the system converges on a non-Walrasian equilibrium with government
expenditure permanently propping up demand.

4 CONCLUSIONS

In this chapter we have posed the question of whether there
is a type of technological unemployment which is essentially
different from demand deficient and structural unemployment.
We have looked at the problem in two ways: first, within an
orthodox growth model, and second, by using the framework
outlined in Malinvaud (1980). In the first example, we have
seen that unemployment can emerge if we impose downward
rigidity in the real wage, but only if fairly extreme
assumptions are made about rates of factor augmentation. The
second model, with its focus on non-Walrasian disequilibrium
states, provides, in some ways, a more satisfactory approach
to this problem. We have seen above that technical progress
- in the presence of government demand support - gives rise
to Malinvaud's classical unemployment state in which productive capacity is deficient with respect to the full
employment requirements of the economy. However, such
unemployment has a tendency to disappear. Thus neither model
generates long-term unemployment, but both, under certain
conditions, generate medium-term non-Keynesian unemployment.
The concept of technological unemployment has been neither
firmly established nor shown to be dispensable. Two questions,
in particular, require further consideration: first, whether
the new microelectronic technology is of such a different
kind that these special conditions apply, and second, if we
conclude that technical progress leads simply to Keynesian
or structural unemployment, whether technological unemployment
is a useful or trivial sub-class of such unemployment.

TABLE 3.8 *Malinvaud model with shock increase in β and government providing sufficient demand, shortage borne first by investment and then consumption*

t	β	d	y	State	u	C	i	g	P	w	$\bar{y}$	m
1	1.0	1000	1000.0	W	0.000	900.0	0.0	100.0	1.000	0.900	1000.0	900.0
2	1.2	1200	1000.0	C	0.167	616.7	0.0	383.3	1.180	0.867	1000.0	875.7
3	1.2	1200	1000.0	C	0.167	714.4	0.0	285.6	1.392	0.834	1000.0	748.9
4	1.2	1200	1000.0	C	0.167	685.2	0.0	314.8	1.643	0.801	1000.0	643.0
5	1.2	1200	1000.0	C	0.167	658.1	0.0	341.9	1.939	0.768	1000.0	552.9
6	1.2	1200	1000.0	C	0.167	633.0	0.0	367.0	2.288	0.735	1000.0	474.5
7	1.2	1200	1000.0	C	0.167	621.4	0.0	378.6	2.700	0.701	1000.0	394.6
8	1.2	1200	1000.0	C	0.167	586.9	9.6	403.5	3.186	0.667	1004.8	322.1
9	1.2	1200	1004.8	C	0.163	552.0	26.8	426.0	3.746	0.634	1018.2	288.0
10	1.2	1200	1018.2	C	0.152	523.4	49.9	444.9	4.359	0.604	1043.2	268.4
11	1.2	1200	1043.2	C	0.131	494.4	80.9	467.9	5.042	0.578	1083.6	258.6
12	1.2	1200	1083.6	C	0.097	497.5	121.6	464.5	5.570	0.559	1144.4	256.2
13	1.2	1200	1144.4	C	0.046	505.7	174.9	463.8	5.849	0.559	1231.9	270.1
14	1.2	1200	1200.0	K/I	0.000	522.1	212.0	465.9	5.849	0.550	1337.9	300.0
15	1.2	1200	1200.0	K/I	0.000	525.0	185.5	489.5	5.849	0.550	1430.7	325.0

which tends to an equilibrium at

	β	d	y	State	u	C	i	g	P	w	$\bar{y}$	m
	1.2	1200	1200.0	K/I	0.000	550.0	0.0	650.0	5.849	0.550	2080.0	550.0

APPENDIX: MALINVAUD'S MODEL

Malinvaud's model (1980), written in a form suitable for simulation, is as follows.

```
1   Enter initial values of β, L, i, ȳ, m, w, P, g
2   Begin loop to run for n periods
3   X = (900w + 0.1m + i + g - 500)/(1 - 500/βL)
4   If (X ≥ βL or X ≥ ȳ) go to 12
5   If (X < βL and X < ȳ) state = 1 (Keynesian unemployment)
6       d = X
7       y = X
8       u = 1 - y/βL
9       c = 900w + 0.1m - 500u
10      P = P - P(0.2(ȳ - y) + 0.1(βL - y))/1000
11      Go to 27
12  If (βL ≥ ȳ) go to 20
13  If (βL < ȳ) and (βL < X) state = 2 (inflation) y = βL
14      u = 0
15      c = 900w + 0.1m
16      d = c + i + g
17      P = P + P((d - y) + 0.5(ȳ - βL))/1000
18      W = W + 0.2(min [d, ȳ] - βL)/1000
19      Go to 27
20  If (ȳ ≤ X and y ≤ βL) state = 3 (Classical unemployment)
21      y = ȳ
22      u = 1 - y/βL
23      c = 900w + 0.1m - 500u
24      d = c + i + g
25      P = P + P(d - y - 0.1(βL - y))/1000
26      w = w - 0.2u
27  ȳ = min [d, βL]
28  ȳ₋₁ = ȳ
29  ȳ = ȳ + 0.5i
30  c = y - i - g
31  i = 400 (β - 0.1 - w) + 0.25 (ŷ - ȳ₋₁)
32  w₋₁ = w
33  m = m + P₋₁(w₋₁y/β - c - m(P - P₋₁)/P₋₁)/P
34  Write values of variables
35  P₋₁ = P
36  Continue loop
```

Key to Variables

β labour productivity
L labour force
i investment
y output
$\underline{y}$ output capacity of capital stock
m money stock held by consumers (real)
g government expenditure (real)
w real wages
P price level
u unemployment rate
d effective demand
X notional demand if $u = 0$

NOTES

1. See C. Jenkins and B. Sherman, *The Collapse of Work* (London: Eyre Methuen, 1979); C. Hines and G. Searle, *Automatic Unemployment* (London: Earth Resources Research, 1979); T. Stonier, 'The Impact of Microprocessors on Employment' and C. Freeman, 'Unemployment and Government', in Tom Forester (ed.), *The Microelectronics Revolution* (Oxford: Blackwell, 1980).
2. See R. M. Solow, 'A Contribution to the Theory of Economic Growth', *Quarterly Journal of Economics*, vol. LXX (1956) pp. 65-94.
3. Although this is often quoted in textbooks, it is not strictly true, as pointed out by A. Chilosi and S. Gomulka, 'Technological Condition for Balanced Growth: a Criticism and Restatement', *Journal of Economic Theory*, vol. IX (1974) pp. 171-84.
4. The negative rate of labour augmentation means that this is not necessarily technical progress for all combinations of K and L.
5. C. Kennedy, 'Induced Bias in Innovation and the Theory of Distribution', *Economic Journal*, vol. LXXXIV (1964) pp. 541-7; C. C. von Weizsäcker, 'Tentative Notes on a Two-Sector Model with Induced Technical Progress', *Review of Economic Studies*, vol. XXXIII (1966) pp. 245-51.
6. See E. Malinvaud, *Profitability and Unemployment* (Cambridge University Press, 1980).
7. The system converges to a non-Walrasian equilibrium because there are no wage or price adjustments on the borderline between two disequilibrium states. See Malinvaud, ibid., pp. 55-6.

4 Employment Policy for Balanced Growth under an Input Constraint

DANIEL WEISERBS, A. KERVYN and
ALAN INGHAM

1 INTRODUCTION

We consider a vintage model in which an economy combines
labour, capital and an imported resource (raw material) to
produce a single manufactured good. The purpose of this
chapter is to study the behaviour of the system when it is
shocked out of its 'golden rule' path by the sudden imposition
of a constraint on the volume of imports of the resource,
while the relative price of the resource grows at a rate
determined exogenously. A 'capitalist' and a 'socialist'
solution are presented. The capitalist solution retains the
constraint that the wage rate is equal to labour productivity
on the oldest vintage in use. The socialist solution chooses
the path on which consumption per capita is maximised and then
examines various policies such that all of the labour force is
employed.

2 THE MODEL

2.1 *The Goods Market*

(a) *Supply*: Output serves as the numeraire, and the capital
coefficient is constant. A 'machine' is defined either in
terms of its opportunity cost in production (one unit of
output), or in terms of the output it produces, v; output per
machine is thus constant, both over the life of a single
machine, and over all vintages of machines. Technical progress
appears as a reduction in the labour crew and in the inputs of
raw materials associated with successive vintages to produce
the same output.

The stock of machines, K_t, is determined by past investment.
k_θ machines built at time θ yield at period $t(t > \theta)$ an output
of $q_{t,\theta}$,

$$q_{t,\theta} = vk_\theta. \tag{1}$$

The useful life of a machine, s, is endogenous, that is, the machine is scrapped on economic grounds before it breaks down. Then the oldest vintage in operation at time t is $t-s$, and the useful stock of machines at t is:

$$K_t = \sum_{\theta=t-s}^{t-1} k_\theta, \tag{2}$$

so that total output is simply given by:

$$Q_t = \sum_{\theta=t-s}^{t-1} q_{t,\theta} = vK_t. \tag{3}$$

(b) *Demand*: Assuming that no stockpiling may occur in the economy (any stock of output or input evaporates at the end of the period), current output is either consumed (C_t), invested (k_t) or exported (X_t). Thus, denoting total demand for the good by D_t, we have

$$D_t = C_t + k_t + X_t. \tag{4}$$

Under the classical assumption that the economy's saving ratio is equal to the share of profit in the value added – or, equivalently, that all wages are consumed and all profits are invested – consumption is determined by

$$C_t = w_t L_t, \tag{5}$$

where w_t is the wage rate and L_t the volume of labour employed at period t.

If M_t is the quantity of the resource imported at a (relative) price p_t and X_t is the value of output exported in return, the external debt, B_t, evolves according to

$$B_t = (1 + r_{t-1})B_{t-1} + p_t M_t - X_t, \tag{6}$$

where r_t is the rate of interest on foreign debt.

For simplicity, in the present chapter we shall impose equilibrium in the balance of trade at every period t:

$$X_t = p_t M_t. \tag{7}$$

This implicitly assumes that exporters of the resource purchase $p_t M_t$ of the manufactured good regardless of its competitiveness on the world market.

2.2 *The Labour Market*

(a) *Demand*: The number of workers required to operate one machine of vintage θ is

$$\ell_\theta = \frac{1}{1+\mu} \ell_{\theta-1} = (1+\mu)^{-\theta} \ell_o, \tag{8}$$

where ℓ_o is the amount of labour required to operate one machine of the oldest vintage utilised at the beginning of the plan and μ the coefficient of Harrod neutral technical progress. Thus, at time t, the volume of labour demanded in the economy is

$$L_t = \ell_o \sum_{\theta=t-s}^{t-1} (1+\mu)^{-\theta} k_\theta. \tag{9}$$

(b) *Supply*: The labour force, N_t, grows at a constant rate λ,

$$N_t = (1+\lambda)N_{t-1} = (1+\lambda)^t N_o, \tag{10}$$

so that u_t, the unemployment rate, is

$$u_t = 1 - \frac{L_t}{N_t} = 1 - \frac{\ell_o}{N_o} (1+\lambda)^{-t} \sum_{\theta=t-s}^{t-1} (1+\mu)^{-\theta} k_\theta \geqslant 0. \tag{11}$$

If labour demand, L_t, exceeds labour supply, N_t, then some machines, presumably of the oldest vintage, must be scrapped (machines cannot lie idle).

(c) *Wages*: The real wage rate, w_t, is determined endogen-ously: (i) by the profitability condition (equation (15) below) in a 'capitalist' system or (ii) by the maximisation of a welfare function in a 'socialist system'.

2.3   *The Resource Market*

(a)   *Demand*: Similarly, the resource requirement for a machine of age θ is defined as

$$m_\theta = \frac{1}{1+\nu} \, m_{\theta-1} = (1+\nu)^{-\theta} m_o, \tag{12}$$

where ν expresses resource-saving technical progress (if $\nu > 0$) analogous to the Harrod neutral type. Total demand for the resource is thus determined by

$$M_t = m_o \sum_{\theta=t-s}^{t-1} (1+\nu)^{-\theta} k_\theta. \tag{13}$$

(b)   *Supply*: The economy receives a share of the world market which covers its needs up to period $t = \tau-1$. From period $t = \tau$ onward, its demand is rationed at the level of the previous period,

$$M_t = \bar{M} = M_{\tau-1} \tag{14}$$

for $t > \tau$. If M_t as determined by (13) exceeds $\bar{M}$, then some machines must be scrapped.

(c)   *Price*: We consider that the economy is too small to influence the price of the resource, p_t. We shall further assume that p_t grows exponentially at the rate $1+\nu$. In other words, the price of the resource remains constant in terms of efficiency units. The monopolist controlling the resource is in a position to capture all the gains derived from growing efficiency in its use. In terms of output prices, there is a continuing deterioration in the terms of trade of our economy.

2.4   *Profitability*

A necessary condition to maintain in operation at time t a vintage of age $t-\theta$, is that it covers its costs. Thus, for $t-s$, the oldest vintage producing at time t, we have

$$v = w_t \ell_{t-s} + p_t m_{t-s}, \tag{15}$$

or

$$v = w_t \ell_o (1+\mu)^{s-t} + p_t m_o (1+\upsilon)^{s-t}.$$

However, as we shall see later, in a 'socialist system' where the economy is fully controlled, the planner will decide to keep a machine operating as long as its net social marginal utility is non-negative.

3   SCOPE OF THE INVESTIGATION

The disequilibrium regimes à *la Malinvaud* arising from the model are analysed in another paper.[1] In order to avoid the difficulties posed by a three-input vintage production structure in an inter-temporal maximisation framework, we shall confine ourselves to a balanced growth path in the following contexts:

  (a) no rationing, so that full employment prevails
      ('Walrasian golden age');
  (b) resource rationing as defined by (14) under (i) profit
      maximisation ('capitalist system') and (ii) maximisation
      of a social welfare function whose arguments are con-
      sumption per capita and the rate of employment
      ('socialist system').

4   GOLDEN AGE

It is well known for this kind of model that the Walrasian Golden Age is characterised by (a)-(e) below.

(a) Supply equals demand on each market (full employment is
    assumed).

$$Q_t = D_t \tag{16.1}$$

$$N_t = L_t \tag{16.2}$$

$$X_t = p_t M_t \tag{16.3}$$

(b) Investment grows at a constant rate (denoted by ρ),
    determined by the rate of Harrod neutral technical progress
    and the rate of growth of the labour force,

$$k_t = (1+\rho)k_{t-1} = (1+\rho)^t k_o \tag{17}$$

where

$$1+\rho = (1+\mu)(1+\lambda). \tag{18}$$

(c) The wage rate grows at the rate of Harrod neutral technical progress.

$$w_t = (1+\mu)w_{t-1} = (1+\mu)^t w_o \tag{19}$$

(d) The price of the resource grows (declines if ν happens to be negative) at the rate of progress (or inefficiency) in resource use.

$$p_t = (1+\nu)p_{t-1} = (1+\nu)^t p_o \tag{20}$$

(e) The useful life of equipment is constant and the oldest vintage just covers its costs.

$$v = w_t \ell_{t-s} + p_t m_{t-s} = w_t \ell_o (1+\mu)^{s-t} + p_t m_o (1+\nu)^{s-t} \tag{21}$$

A sufficient condition for $t-s$ to be constant is, of course, (19) and (20). Then it follows that

$$v = w_o \ell_o (1+\mu)^s + p_o m_o (1+\nu)^s. \tag{22}$$

The total number of machines operating at time t is

$$K_t = \sum_{\theta=t-s}^{t-1} k_\theta = (1+\rho)^t \left[1 - (1+\rho)^{-s} \right] \frac{k_o}{\rho}. \tag{23}$$

Hence supply for the good is defined by

$$Q_t = (1+\rho)^t \left[1 - (1+\rho)^{-s} \right] \frac{k_o v}{\rho}. \tag{24}$$

From (8), (12) and (19), we deduce the evolution of demand for labour and the resource:

$$L_t = \sum_{\theta=t-s}^{t-1} \ell_\theta k_\theta = (1+\rho)^t (1+\mu)^{-t} \left[1 - \left(\frac{1+\rho}{1+\mu} \right)^{-s} \right]$$

$$\frac{\ell_o k_o (1+\mu)}{(\rho-\mu)} \tag{25}$$

and

$$M_t = \sum_{\theta=t-s}^{t-1} m_\theta k_\theta = (1+\rho)^t (1+\nu)^{-t} \left[1 - \left(\frac{1+\rho}{1+\nu}\right)^{-s} \right]$$

$$\frac{m_o k_o (1+\nu)}{(\rho-\nu)} . \tag{26}$$

Labour supply is exogenously determined by (10). Then full employment implies (18), since

$$L_t = \frac{1+\rho}{1+\mu} L_{t-1} \quad \text{and} \quad N_t = (1+\lambda)N_{t-1}. \tag{27}$$

Since consumption equals $w_t L_t$, by assumption (cf. (6) and (7)), and exports equal $p_t M_t$, total demand in the goods market is given by the sum of

$$C_t = (1+\rho)^t \left[1 - \left(\frac{1+\rho}{1+\mu}\right)^{-s} \right] w_o \ell_o k_o \left(\frac{1+\mu}{\rho-\mu}\right), \tag{28}$$

$$X_t = (1+\rho)^t \left[1 - \left(\frac{1+\rho}{1+\nu}\right)^{-s} \right] p_o m_o k_o \left(\frac{1+\nu}{\rho-\nu}\right) \tag{29}$$

and

$$k_t = (1+\rho)^t k_o. \tag{30}$$

A numerical illustration is presented in Table 4.1. This example has been constructed with parameter values $\mu = 0.05$, $w = 0.02$, $\lambda = 0.01$, $v = 0.7569$; and initial conditions at $\tau-1$: $k = 100$, $w = 1$, $p = 1$. As a result, equipment is used during 10 periods.

Along this golden-age path, output grows at 6.05 per cent per period, consumption per capita, c_t $(= w_t)$, grows at 5 per cent per period, while labour's share in value added is 0.769.

5   THE CAPITALIST SOLUTION

We now turn to the behaviour of the economy when rationing is imposed in the use of the resource. With the volume of imported resource constrained to a maximum value $\bar{M} = M_{\tau-1}$,

TABLE 4.1 *Numerical example I: Walrasian Golden Age*

t	k	C	X	$Q=D$	$\overline{M}$	w	p	u	s
$\tau-2$	94.295	313.835	115.932	524.062	118.251	0.952	0.980	0	10.0
$\tau-1$	100.000	332.822	122.946	555.768	122.946	1.000	1.000	0	10.0
τ	106.050	352.958	130.384	589.392	127.827	1.050	1.020	0	10.0
$\tau+1$	112.466	374.312	138.272	625.050	132.903	1.102	1.040	0	10.0
$\tau+2$	119.270	396.957	146.638	662.865	138.180	1.158	1.061	0	10.0
$\tau+3$	126.486	420.973	155.509	702.969	143.667	1.216	1.082	0	10.0
$\tau+5$	142.254	473.452	174.895	790.601	155.302	1.340	1.126	0	10.0
$\tau+8$	169.666	564.687	208.598	942.952	174.545	1.551	1.195	0	10.0
$\tau+15$	255.959	851.888	314.691	1422.539	229.235	2.183	1.373	0	10.0

the maximum rate of growth becomes the rate of technical
progress in resource use. We shall first examine the steady-
rate and then briefly discuss the transition period.

Since no stockpiling is allowed in our economy, profit
maximisation implies that firms will not produce more than
they can sell. Therefore, investment (= profits), denoted by
k_t^C, along the capitalist path follows the highest possible
rate of growth:

$$k_t^C = (1+\nu)k_{t-1}^C = (1+\nu)^{t-\tau}k_\tau^C, \quad t \geqslant \tau. \tag{31}$$

It follows (cf. (3)) that supply on the goods market evolves
according to

$$Q_t = (1+\nu)^{t-\tau}k_\tau^C \frac{v}{\nu}\left[1 - (1+\nu)^{-s}\right]. \tag{32}$$

As we shall see below, from equation (39), k_τ^C depends on $\overline{M}$
while the useful life of the equipment is simultaneously determined by the level of total demand on the goods market.

By assumption, total demand is defined as

$$D_t = C_t + k_t^C + X_t = w_t L_t + k_t^C + p_t \overline{M}, \quad t \geqslant \tau. \tag{33}$$

The wage rate is determined by the profitability condition:

$$w_t = (1+\mu)^{t-s-\tau}\left[v - p_\tau m_\tau(1+\nu)^s\right]\frac{1}{\ell_\tau}; \tag{34}$$

and, since labour demand evolves according to

$$L_t = \left(\frac{1+\nu}{1+\mu}\right)^{t-\tau}\left[1 - \left(\frac{1+\nu}{1+\mu}\right)^{-s}\right]\left(\frac{1+\mu}{1+\nu}\right)\ell_\tau k_\tau^C, \tag{35}$$

consumption is given by:

$$C_t = (1+\nu)^{t-\tau}(1+\mu)^{-s}\left[\nu - p_\tau m_\tau(1+\nu)^s\right]$$

$$\left[1 - \left(\frac{1+\nu}{1+\mu}\right)^{-s}\right]\left(\frac{1+\mu}{\mu-\nu}\right)k_\tau^C. \tag{36}$$

Since $M_t = \overline{M}$ ($t \geqslant \tau$), exports continue to grow at the same
rate as p, or

$$X_t = p_t\overline{M} = (1+\nu)^{t-\tau}p_\tau\overline{M}. \tag{37}$$

However, demand for the resource is

$$M_t = \sum_{t-s}^{t-1} m_\theta k_\theta^C = s\ m_\tau k_\tau^C , \tag{38}$$

and therefore

$$k_\tau^C = \frac{\overline{M}}{sm_\tau} = \frac{X_\tau}{sp_\tau m_\tau} . \tag{39}$$

Substituting (36) and (39) in (33) yields total demand on the goods market:

$$D_t = (1+\nu)^{t-\tau} k_\tau^C \left[\left(\frac{1+\mu}{\mu-\ell}\right) (1+\mu)^{-s} \left[v - p_\tau m_\tau (1+\nu)^s \right] \right.$$
$$\left. \left[1 - \left(\frac{1+\nu}{1+\mu}\right)^{-s} \right] + 1 + sp_\tau m_\tau \right] . \tag{40}$$

Then, the optimal value for s is given by the equilibrium condition (40) = (32). In our numerical simulation, we find $s = 9.2869$.

It is worth noticing that if the system was somehow forced to be on this new balanced growth path right from period τ, (i) investment would drop by 12.5 per cent with respect to its $\tau-1$ level (instead of increasing by 6 per cent along the golden age path); (ii) the wage rate would increase by 9 per cent (instead of 5 per cent) because the oldest vintage is $\tau - 9.2869$ (instead of $\tau-10$); (iii) the unemployment rate grows by approximately 4 per cent per period (output grows at a 2 per cent rate, while the labour force grows by 1 per cent and labour productivity by 5 per cent). Also notice that the labour share in value added is now 0.798 (instead of 0.769). This results from a shortening of the useful life of equipment.

This steady-state programme could be initiated at period τ only if some of our initial assumptions were relaxed, to allow firms to accumulate cash balances arising out of an export surplus. Without such an export surplus, insufficient demand along the new golden-rule path (during the transition period) would make the appropriate investment decisions incompatible with profit maximisation.

Under the hypothesis of instantaneous profit maximisation, as illustrated in Table 4.2, the system oscillates around the optimal path and converges only for $t\to\infty$.

TABLE 4.2   *Numerical example II: profit maximisation*

t	k	C	X	$Q=D$	$\bar{M}$	w	p	u	s
$\tau-2$	94.2951	313.8349	115.9319	524.0619	118.2505	0.9524	0.9804	0	10.0000
$\tau-1$	100.0000	332.8219	122.9458	555.7677	122.9458	1.0000	1.0000	0	10.0000
τ	97.4209	346.1394	125.4047	568.9650	122.9458	1.0768	1.0200	0.0438	9.5421
$\tau+1$	95.3256	358.2476	127.9128	581.4860	122.9458	1.1511	1.0404	0.0833	9.2172
$\tau+2$	93.7540	369.2450	130.4710	593.4700	122.9458	1.2228	1.0612	0.1194	9.0056
$\tau+3$	92.5907	379.2711	133.0804	604.9422	122.9458	1.2919	1.0824	0.1523	8.8937
$\tau+5$	92.5430	396.4674	138.4568	627.4671	122.9458	1.4247	1.1262	0.2123	8.8890
$\tau+8$	99.1442	416.3592	146.9315	662.4348	122.9458	1.6188	1.1951	0.2934	9.2280
$\tau+15$	124.1622	471.1791	168.7781	764.1195	122.9458	2.2575	1.3728	0.4652	9.3902

6 THE SOCIALIST SOLUTION

In a socialist system, the 'capitalist' constraint, that no
equipment will be operated at a loss, is no longer binding.
Provided that they are socially desirable, negative rents are
acceptable as long as macro-economic balances are respected.
In other words, the wage rate is no longer constrained by the
profitability conditions. The production constraint originated
by the limited volume of resource available links the investment and scrapping decisions, which, in turn, determine the
level of capacity. The wage rate is chosen such that it
guarantees equality between demand and supply on the goods
market.

The standard social objective is to maximise consumption per
capita. However, the planner may also take into consideration
the rate of unemployment. Thus the social welfare function can
be written:

$$J_t = j \, [\, J_1(c_t) \, , \, J_2(-u_t) \,] \, . \tag{41}$$

First, we consider the case where $J_2 = 0$, i.e. the maximisation
of consumption per capita with no regard to employment.

The natural growth rate is the rate of productivity increase
in terms of resource use. Denoting by k_t^s investment along the
'socialist balanced growth path', we have

$$k_t^s = (1+v)^{t-\tau} \, \frac{\overline{M}}{sm_\tau} \quad (t \geqslant \tau). \tag{42}$$

Since, along this path, demand for the resource is

$$M_t = \sum_{t-s}^{t-1} m_\theta k_\theta^s = s \, m_\tau k_\tau^s = \overline{M}, \tag{43}$$

it follows that output evolves according to

$$Q_t = vK_t = \frac{v}{v}[1 - (1-v)^{-s}]k_\tau^s(1+v)^{t-\tau} \tag{44}$$

while exports grow according to (37).

Now, total consumption is defined by

$$C_t = Q_t - k_t - X_t = (1+v)^{t-\tau} \, \frac{\overline{M}}{sm_\tau}$$

$$\left[\frac{v}{v} \, [(1-(1+v)^{-s} \,] - 1 - s \, p_\tau m_\tau \right] \tag{45}$$

yielding consumption per capita of

$$c_t = \left(\frac{1+\nu}{1+\lambda}\right)^{t-\tau} \frac{\overline{M}}{sm_\tau N_\tau} \left[\frac{\nu}{\nu}\left[\,1-(1+\nu)^{-s}\right]-1\right] - \left(\frac{1+\nu}{1+\lambda}\right)^{t-\tau} \frac{\overline{}}{M} \frac{p_\tau}{N_\tau}, \quad (46)$$

since $c_t = C_t/N_t$. Differentiating (46) with respect to s gives

$$\frac{\partial c_t}{\partial s} = 0 = \frac{v}{\nu}\,(1+\nu)^{-s}\,\ln\,(1+\nu) - \frac{1}{s}\left[\frac{v}{\nu}[\,1\,-\,(1+\nu)^{-s}]-1\right] \quad (47)$$

and

$$(1+\nu)^s\left(\frac{\nu}{v}-1\right) + s\,\ln\,(1+\nu)\, +\, 1 = 0 \qquad\qquad (48)$$

which yields $s = 12.605005$ in our simulation exercise reported in Table 4.3. This implies that the transition period is in effect from τ to $\tau + 12$.

At period τ, investment drops drastically (by 34 per cent) making room for an immediate wage increase (of almost 18 per cent). Along the balanced growth path, investment (as well as Q, C and X) grows by 2 per cent ($=\nu$), wages by 5 per cent and consumption per capita by 1 per cent [2 per cent (c) - 1 per cent (N)] . Employment declines by almost 3 per cent. However, labour's share in value added becomes 0.85. This solution is superior to the capitalist one both in terms of employment and, of course, consumption per capita.

Let us now consider the case where the planner is primarily concerned with the level of employment ($J_1 = 0$, $J_2 > 0$). The older rather than newer technologies appear preferable. In terms of employment, a single machine of vintage t-1 provides $1+\mu$ the number of jobs supplied by a machine of vintage t. In terms of resource use, the trade-off is one machine of vintage t-1 against $1+\nu$ machines of vintage t.

This situation defines an appropriate technology where full employment can be maintained by replacing existing machines by older vintages. Among all possible solutions of this type insuring full employment, we suppose that the planner chooses the one which minimises consumption losses, i.e. minimises investment. The optimal solution could then be determined as follows.

(a) Since some investment is necessary to provide jobs for the increase in the labour force, one machine of vintage t-n is built at any period t.

TABLE 4.3 *Numerical example III: maximisation of social welfare*

t	k	C	X	Q=D	$\overline{M}$	w	p	u	s
τ-2	94.2951	313.8349	115.9319	524.0619	118.2505	0.9524	0.9804	0	10.0000
τ-1	100.0000	332.8219	122.9458	555.7677	122.9458	1.0000	1.0000	0	10.0000
τ	65.7298	377.8304	125.4046	568.9648	122.9458	1.1754	1.0200	0.0438	9.5421
τ+1	67.0444	382.6131	127.9128	577.5703	122.9458	1.2170	1.0404	0.0740	9.6415
τ+2	68.3852	387.6047	130.4709	586.4608	122.9458	1.2608	1.0612	0.1035	9.7707
τ+3	69.7530	392.8503	133.0801	595.6835	122.9458	1.3073	1.0824	0.1323	9.9272
τ+5	72.5710	403.9364	138.4569	614.9642	122.9458	1.4073	1.1262	0.1876	10.3260
τ+8	77.0129	423.1780	146.9315	647.1225	122.9458	1.5860	1.1951	0.2670	11.1112
τ+15	88.4636	482.1786	168.7782	739.4204	122.9458	2.1925	1.3728	0.4365	12.6050

(b) Simultaneously, machines of the oldest vintage are
    scrapped in order to meet the resource constraint (this
    seems more realistic than scrapping the most recent
    vintages).
(c) n is chosen to maintain full employment.

In our numerical simulation, the planner's decision at
period τ in this context is to build one machine of vintage
τ-58, while a period τ technology will still be operating at
τ+200. This, of course, does not sound very reasonable, and
additional constraints ought to be imposed. For instance, one
might specify: the maximum life of a machine of vintage t;
the reverse technology frontier (what is the oldest vintage
that can be built at time t?).

The quasi-stoppage of investment permits a large increase
in consumption at period τ: the wage rate rises at once by
almost 30 per cent. However, at period τ+1, it is reduced by
approximately 2 per cent (a negative rate of growth of the
economy) and by a slightly growing fraction in each subsequent
period.

The question becomes: 'Is it possible for the planner to do
better in terms of consumption per capita, or (with respect to
the solution where c_t is maximised) in terms of employment?'
For the latter case, the answer is yes, and simple on paper.

Consider the case where the planner's objective was to maximise consumption per capita (Section 6.2). In such a system,
the wage rate no longer depends on labour productivity. Indeed,
wages are growing at the same rate as C/N (1 per cent per
period) while labour productivity is rising by μ (5 per cent).
In terms of social policy, we could go one step further and
distinguish productive from unproductive (services) employment.
Ignoring the latter, full employment can still be achieved by
distributing labour demand between the total labour force, for
instance by continuously reducing working hours (work sharing)
or by continuously augmenting the number of workers per machine.
Alternatively, it is possible to provide 'unproductive' employment for excess labour (i.e. caring for the sick and elderly,
educating the young, revitalising cities or improving their
cultural and artistic level, doing research, and so on). Such
an altruistic combination would provide an agreeable solution
far better than technological regression with full employment,
or to the capitalist solution with the wage rate equal to marginal labour productivity.

Of course, such a utopian scheme is possible only within the
limited framework of our model. In the real world, do we imagine the Government levying taxes on firms and workers in
order to redistribute these revenues respectively: (i) in the
form of subsidies to those plants which fail to cover their

production costs as long as their 'social marginal utility' is non-negative; and (ii) to provide jobs for and pay wages to labour which would otherwise be unemployed? While this solution satisfies the requirements of both internal and external balances, it raises problems of social consensus and incentives: labour would have to accept real wages growing at 1 per cent per period, while its productivity (the output of goods) rises by 5 per cent and profits by 2 per cent; and firms would have to maintain steady-state investment while the Government confiscates most of the quasi-rent on new machines.

NOTES

The authors are grateful to F. Melese for research assistance.
1. A. Ingham, D. Weiserbs and F. Melese, 'Unemployment Equilibria in a Small Resource Importing Economy with a Vintage Production Structure', Department of Economics, University of Southampton.

5 New Technology, Demand and Employment

PAUL STONEMAN

1 INTRODUCTION

In the analysis of the impact of new technology on employment there are six major modelling decisions to make:

(i) How should technology be represented? One needs a representation of technology that allows for the multiplier effects that are present in real world technology, e.g. the expansion of output in one sector requires increased levels of intermediate inputs from other sectors. In this chapter we consider a two-sector economy which allows such multiplier effects to exist, but does not prevent a reasonably simple derivation of conclusions.

(ii) How does the economy react to disequilibrium? If one specifies, in a Walrasian manner, that prices react instantaneously to notional disequilibria, then there will be no unemployment resulting from new technology (see Neisser, 1942). In this chapter prices are assumed to not so react, and thus we may specify that our model is Keynesian in character. Given this Keynesian character, we now need to decide on (iii) and (iv).

(iii) How do wages and prices move over time? We will specify that, subject to the condition of complementary slackness (see below), wages will remain constant over time, and that prices will then be determined by the usual two-sector model price relations (see Hicks, 1965).

(iv) How is demand behaviour to be modelled? In this chapter we shall allow:

(a) that consumption is determined by a classical savings function, whereby all profits are invested, all wages consumed;
(b) that investment is just sufficient to meet, in each period, the demand for increased capacity in the economy; and
(c) there is no government.

(v) How is the trade sector to be modelled? Worlds with fixed and floating exchange rates will typically behave differently.

We shall assume a closed economy.

(vi) How fast is the new technology taken up? A prime purpose of this chapter is to analyse how the speed of take up (or diffusion) will affect employment. We have chosen to consider this speed as exogenous to the macro-economy, and we wish to analyse the effects of varying the speed.

The impact of new technology on employment will then depend on the labour-saving nature of the technology and the automatic response of demand in creating new job opportunities. If demand increases quickly relative to the labour saving, then there will not be unemployment; if it does not, there may be unemployment. However, demand is endogenous to the system.

We might note that the model worked out here is concerned with the traverse or the transition path. Given the time taken for an economy to change technology (say a minimum of 20 years), comparative statics results hold little interest. The transition path is of overriding importance.

We turn, then, to the formal modelling of the system.

2 THE MODEL

As one of the key impacts to be analysed is the extra demands on the capital goods sector generated by new technology, the model is a two-sector one with a consumption goods and a capital goods sector. We shall consider only process innovations, and we shall assume that all process innovations are wholly embodied. Thus, to change technology, a whole new set of capital goods is required.

We consider two technologies, labelled 1 and 2, that are the old and new respectively. Both capital goods are made wholly by labour (although circulating capital could be allowed), but consumption goods are made by capital and labour. The technology of capital goods production is considered in this manner for it yields considerable simplification; however, the omission of a capital goods input from capital goods production will bias any compensation effects we find. We represent the quantity relations of the two technologies as follows:

$$K_{it} = \alpha_i C_{it}, \qquad i = 1, 2, \tag{1}$$

$$L_{it} = \beta_i C_{it} + b_i x_{it}, \qquad i = 1, 2, \tag{2}$$

$$x_{it} = \frac{dK_{it}}{dt}, \qquad i = 1, 2, \tag{3}$$

where K_{it} = stock of capital good i in time t,

C_{it} = output of consumption goods on capital good i in time t,

L_{it} = labour employed producing or using capital good i in time t,

x_{it} = output of capital good i in time t.

We shall consider that capital has an infinitely long physical life and there is thus no depreciation. Total labour supply will be given by (4):

$$L_t^s = L_0 e^{nt}. \tag{4}$$

We shall consider that, at time t, the economy is in the process of making the transition from using technology 1 to using technology 2, and at any moment in time the two technologies are used in consumption goods production in the proportions $1 - \theta_t : \theta_t$. We specify that θ_t is the result of a diffusion process, the time profile of which can be represented by a logistic curve. This curve is assumed to be the result of forces outside the model. The logistic diffusion curve has, in fact, merited much empirical support in the diffusion literature, and the justification for its existence (or the existence of other sigmoid diffusion curves) is primarily based on either epidemic or learning mechanisms operating across entrepreneurs at the micro level (cf. Mansfield, 1968). Thus we have (5):

$$\theta_t = \frac{1}{1 + \exp(-\eta - yt)} \tag{5}$$

We shall assume that, at any time t, the output of the relevant capital good is just sufficient to meet the demands of the consumer goods industry, subject only to $x_1 \geqslant 0$ $(i = 1, 2)$. Thus we have (6):

$$x_i = \alpha_i \frac{dC_i}{dt} \tag{6}$$

Defining $C \equiv C_1 + C_2$, and $\frac{dC}{dt} \cdot \frac{1}{C} \equiv g_t$, we may state

$$x_1 \geqslant 0 \text{ if } g_t \geqslant \frac{d\theta}{dt} \cdot \frac{1}{1-\theta} = y\theta_t, \tag{7}$$

$$x_2 \geqslant 0 \text{ if } g_t \geqslant y(\theta_{t-1}) \leqslant 0.$$

We shall be considering the transition process in two stages:

Stage 1: where $g_t > y\theta_t$, implying $x_1 > 0$, $x_2 > 0$;

Stage 2: where $g_t < y\theta_t$, implying $x_1 = 0$.

We can show that Stage 1 always precedes Stage 2. We define T as that time t at which $g_t = y\theta_t$.

Consider now the price relations: we require, if the diffusion is to be rational, that the switch to technology 2 must yield a higher profit for the entrepreneur. In Stage 1 we may specify, assuming the same wage is paid to all workers, that (see <u>Hicks</u>, 1965)

$$p_i = wb_i, \qquad i = 1, 2, \tag{8}$$

$$\Pi = r_i p_i \alpha_i + w\beta_i, \quad i = 1, 2, \tag{9}$$

where p_i = price of capital good i,

w = wage rate,

r_i = rate of profit on capital good i,

Π = price of the consumption good.

Setting $\Pi = 1$, technology 2 will be superior if it can yield a higher profit at wage rate w than can technology 1, i.e. if

$$\frac{1 - w\beta_2}{wb_2\alpha_2} > \frac{1 - w\beta_1}{wb_1\alpha_1},$$

implying (10):

$$\frac{b_1\alpha_1}{b_2\alpha_2} > \frac{1 - w\beta_1}{1 - w\beta_2}. \tag{10}$$

At times, it is useful to state this condition as that technology 2 can yield a higher w at profit rate $r \geqslant 0$ than can technology 1, i.e. that

$$\frac{1}{rb_2\alpha_2 + \beta_2} > \frac{1}{rb_1\alpha_1 + \beta_1}.$$

This reduces to (11):

$$r(\alpha_1 b_1 - \alpha_2 b_2) > \beta_2 - \beta_1. \tag{11}$$

In Stage 2, the price relations are slightly different. Given that $x_1 = 0$, because there is an excess supply of the old capital good, we should expect $p_1 = 0$ in a linear model such as this, through complementary slackness. In which case, if (9) is to hold for $i = 1$, we must have $w = 1/\beta_1$. If technology 2 is still to be preferred to technology 1, and thus the diffusion to proceed, technology 2 must still be able to yield a positive return for $w = 1/\beta_1$, i.e. (12) must hold:

$$\hat{r} = \frac{\beta_1 - \beta_2}{b_2 \alpha_2} > 0, \tag{12}$$

where $\hat{r}$ is the rate of profit generated by technology 2 when $w = \dfrac{1}{\beta_1}$. For (12) to hold, we must have $\beta_1 > \beta_2$. Given $\beta_1 > \beta_2$ if (11) is to hold for all r, we must have $\alpha_1 b_1 > \alpha_2 b_2$, although without this condition (11) may still hold for some r. Most of our results will refer to the 'absolutely' labour-saving case.

The internal consistency of the model requires that, during Stage 2, $w = \dfrac{1}{\beta_1}$. As we are working in an environment without flexible wages and prices, we shall consider that w remains constant at $\dfrac{1}{\beta_1}$ for the whole of Stage 2. This determination of w will determine all prices in Stage 2. In Stage 1, we shall assume that the wage will remain at the level it was prior to the start of the transition process. As we shall consider that the economy prior to the introduction of the new technology was growing on a full-employment steady-state growth path, we shall, given the savings function, be able to determine the wages, and thus prices, in Stage 1.

The main concern of this chapter is with aggregate labour demand. We ignore skill or locational differences in the labour force. We shall be making comparisons of labour demand on the transition path relative to labour supply. Labour supply is given by (4), but we may also specify that if, at time t, $\overline{C}_t$ is the level of consumption that would involve full employment using just technology 1, then (13) will hold:

$$L_t^S = \overline{C}_t (\beta_1 + \alpha_1 b_1 n).$$ (13)

In general, labour demand is given by (14) (for $x_i \geqslant 0$, $i = 1, 2$):

$$L_t^D = \beta_1 C_{1t} + \beta_2 C_{2t} + b_1 x_{1t} + b_2 x_{2t},$$ (14)

which we may reduce to (15) and (16) below.

Stage 1:

$$L_t^D = C_t \left[\beta_1(1-\theta_t) + \theta_t(\beta_2 + b_2\alpha_2 g_t) + (1-\theta_t)(b_1\alpha_1 g_t) \right. $$
$$\left. + \frac{d\theta}{dt}(b_2\alpha_2 - b_1\alpha_1) \right]$$ (15)

Stage 2:

$$L_t^D = C_t \left[\beta_1(1-\theta_t) + \theta_t(\beta_2 + b_2\alpha_2 g_t) + b_2\alpha_2 \frac{d\theta}{dt} \right]$$ (16)

Defining $\gamma_t \equiv L_t^D / L_t^S$, we can now specify (17) and (18):

Stage 1:

$$\gamma_t = \frac{C_t}{\overline{C}_t} \cdot \frac{\left[\beta_1(1-\theta_t) + \theta_t(\beta_2 + b_2\alpha_2 g_t) + (1-\theta_t)(b_1\alpha_1 g_t) + \frac{d\theta}{dt}(b_2\alpha_2 - b_1\alpha_1) \right]}{\beta_1 + b_1\alpha_1 n};$$ (17)

Stage 2:

$$\gamma_t = \frac{C_t}{\overline{C}_t} \cdot \frac{\left[\beta_1(1-\theta) + \theta_t(\beta_2 + b_2\alpha_2 g_t) + b_2\alpha_2 \frac{d\theta}{dt} \right]}{\beta_1 + b_1\alpha_1 n}.$$ (18)

Equations (15)-(18) illustrate that the time path of labour demand depends upon:

(i)   the time path of consumption;
(ii) the time path of θ_t, i.e. the diffusion process;
(iii) the input coefficients of the two technologies.

We have already specified that θ_t is logistic. However, we have not specified y, the speed of diffusion. A prime purpose of this chapter is to investigate how the time path of employment will

vary as the speed of diffusion varies, i.e. we ask, will a
faster spread of the new technology mean higher employment in
some, all or no years during the transition phase? For these
purposes, we shall consider that y is determined exogenously
to the model and can be manipulated almost as a control variable. One might object to this because in the diffusion literature y is often considered as a function of (among other
things) the profitability of the new technology relative to
the old, and this ought to be treated as an endogenous variable. However, we argue that as y can be manipulated by, for
example, appropriate changes in the information spreading
mechanism, any variation in y introduced because of this endo-
geneity can be offset. We might well be asking the question,
ought the government to opt for high or low diffusion speeds
if its prime consideration is the employment level?

Given that we are treating y as exogenous, we shall then
model the economy on its transition path from using only technology 1 to using only technology 2. We shall make C_t endogenous using a classical savings function. We define $t = 0$
as the start of the transition process, and, at that date,
θ_0 is given exogenously as the proportion of consumption
goods output produced on the new technology. We assume that
θ_0 has been achieved without any impact on the economy.

3   THE PROPERTIES OF THE MODEL

We shall consider separately the time path of employment in
the two stages.

Stage 1

Given that all wages are consumed and all profits saved, we
may specify that in Stage 1, (19) holds.

$$(1-w\beta_1)\ (1-\theta)C + (1-w\beta_2)\theta C = wb_2\alpha_2\theta\frac{dC}{dt} + wb_2\alpha_2 C\frac{d\theta}{dt}$$

$$+ wb_1\alpha_1(1-\theta)\frac{dC}{dt} - wb_1\alpha_1 C\frac{d\theta}{dt}, \tag{19}$$

which yields (20):

$$\frac{dC}{dt}\frac{1}{C} = g_t = \frac{(1-w\beta_1)(1-\theta_t) + (1-w\beta_2)\theta_t - (wb_2\alpha_2-wb_1\alpha_1)\frac{d\theta}{dt}}{wb_2\alpha_2\theta_t + wb_1\alpha_1(1-\theta_t)}. \tag{20}$$

From this we may derive (21):

$$\theta_T = \frac{1 - w\beta_1}{ywb_2\alpha_2 + w(\beta_2 - \beta_1)}, \tag{21}$$

and thus $\partial\theta_T/\partial y < 0$. We can also determine that $\partial T/\partial y < 0$.

First, we need to ensure that a Stage 1 exists. One can show that if $\theta_0 < \theta_T$, then in time period 0 we are in Stage 1. We also need to know whether a Stage 2 exists. We may show that for $\theta_T < 1$, we need $y > r_2$ where r_2 is the rate of profit on technology 2 when $\frac{1}{w} = nb_1\alpha_1 + \beta_1$. However, we also need to show that Stage 2 will come about. Given that $\theta_0 < \theta_T$, we have for $t < T$ that $\frac{g_t}{y} > \theta_t$. If we can show that $\frac{g_t}{y} - \theta_t$ declines with t, then Stage 2 will come about. A sufficient condition for this is that $r_2 - n < y$. Thus, if $\theta_T < 1$, because this implies $r_2 < y$, it must be the case that θ_T is reached as t increases, and therefore a Stage 2 exists. We shall assume $\theta_0 < \theta_T$, but if this does not hold then we shall have only a Stage 2. If $r_2 > y$, only a Stage 1 exists. We may specify (22) in Stages 1 and 2 which implies (23) if w is constant over time (i.e. within a stage):

$$\gamma_t = \frac{c_t}{\bar{C}_t(\beta_1 + b_1\alpha_1 n)} \cdot \frac{1}{w}, \tag{22}$$

$$\frac{d\gamma}{dt} \cdot \frac{1}{\gamma} = g_t - n. \tag{23}$$

We are assuming that, in Stage 1, w stays at the level in time period 0. Given the savings function, in time period 0, $r_1 = n$; thus we have that $\frac{1}{w} = nb_1\alpha_1 + \beta_1$ from the price relations. Substituting into (20), we generate (24):

$$g_t = \frac{b_2\alpha_2\theta_t(r_2 - y(1-\theta)) + b_1\alpha_1(1-\theta_t)(n+y\theta)}{b_2\alpha_2\theta_t + b_1\alpha_1(1-\theta_t)},$$

where r_2 is the rate of profit on the new technology when $\frac{1}{w} = nb_1\alpha_1 + \beta_1$.

Now, from (23), $\frac{d\gamma}{dt} \cdot \frac{1}{t} > 0$ if $g > n$, which, using (24), we may reduce to the condition that (25) holds:

$$b_2\alpha_2(r_2 - n) > (b_1\alpha_1 - b_2\alpha_2)(\theta_t - 1)y. \tag{25}$$

As $r_2 > n$ (given technology 2 is more profitable) and $\theta_t \leqslant 1$, then if $b_1\alpha_1 \geqslant b_2\alpha_2$, (25) will hold.

To investigate the effect of y on γ_t, we can note that, from (22), if w is constant then (26) holds for all t:

$$\frac{\partial\gamma}{\partial y} \cdot \frac{y}{\gamma} = \frac{\partial C}{\partial y} \cdot \frac{y}{C}. \tag{26}$$

From (26) we can derive (27):

$$\log C_t - \log C_0 = \int_0^t \frac{\gamma_1 e^{-yt} + \gamma_2}{\delta_1 e^{-yt} + \delta_2}dt - \left[\log wb_2\alpha_2\theta_t + wb_1\alpha_1(1-\theta_t)\right]$$
$$+ \log\left[wb_2\alpha_2\theta_0 + wb_1\alpha_1(1-\theta_0)\right], \tag{27}$$

where $\delta_1 = wb_1\alpha_1 e^{-\eta}$,

$\delta_2 = wb_2\alpha_2$,

$\gamma_1 = 1 - w\beta_2$,

$\gamma_2 = (1 - w\beta_1)e^{-\eta}$.

From (27), we obtain (28):

$$\frac{\partial\log C_t}{\partial y} = \int_0^t \frac{(-\delta_2\gamma_1 + \delta_1\gamma_2)te^{-yt}}{\left[\delta_1 e^{-yt} + \delta_2\right]^2} dt - \frac{(b_2\alpha_2 - b_1\alpha_1)\frac{\partial\theta_t}{\partial y}}{wb_2\alpha_2\theta + wb_1\alpha_1(1-\theta_t)}. \tag{28}$$

If $b_2\alpha_2 < b_1\alpha_1$, given $\partial\theta_t/\partial y > 0$, the second term is positive. The first term is positive if $\delta_1\gamma_2 > \delta_2\gamma_1$, i.e. if (29) holds:

$$\frac{b_1\alpha_1}{b_2\alpha_2} > \frac{1 - w\beta_1}{1 - w\beta_2}. \tag{29}$$

Finally, we can look at γ_T. From (26), $\frac{\partial\gamma_T}{\partial y} \cdot \frac{y}{\gamma_T} = \partial C_T/\partial y \cdot y/C_T$

From (29), we can derive (30):

$$\log C_T - \log C_0 = \frac{\gamma_1}{y\delta_1} \log \left[\frac{\dfrac{b_1\alpha_1}{b_2\alpha_2} \cdot \dfrac{1 - \theta_0}{\theta_0} + 1}{\dfrac{b_1\alpha_1}{b_2\alpha_2} \cdot \dfrac{1 - \theta_T}{\theta_T} + 1} \right]$$

$$+ \frac{\gamma_2}{y\delta_2} \log \left[\frac{\dfrac{b_1\alpha_1}{b_2\alpha_2} \cdot \dfrac{1 - \theta_0}{\theta_0} + \dfrac{\theta_T}{1 - \theta_T}}{\dfrac{b_1\alpha_1}{b_2\alpha_2} \cdot \dfrac{1 - \theta_0}{\theta_0} + 1} \right]$$

$$- \log \left[\frac{wb_2\alpha_2\theta_T + wb_1\alpha_1(1 - \theta_T)}{wb_2\alpha_2\theta_0 + wb_1\alpha_1(1 - \theta_0)} \right] \quad (30)$$

Without explicit derivation, we know that $\dfrac{\partial \theta_T}{\partial y} < 0$ and thus $\partial\left(\dfrac{\theta_T}{1 - \theta_T}\right) / \partial y < 0$. We may then, by inspection, derive that if $b_1\alpha_1 > b_2\alpha_2$, all terms in (30) decline with an increase in y.

Thus, from (25), (28) and (29), we have that if $1 \geqslant \dfrac{b_1\alpha_1}{b_2\alpha_2} > \dfrac{1 - w\beta_1}{1 - w\beta_2}$, then $\dfrac{d\gamma}{dt} > 0$, $\dfrac{\partial \gamma}{\partial y} > 0$ and $\dfrac{\partial \gamma_T}{\partial y} < 0$. It is also the case that $\dfrac{\partial T}{\partial y} < 0$.

We may state first, from (10), that $\dfrac{b_1\alpha_1}{b_2\alpha_2} > \dfrac{1 - w\beta_1}{1 - w\beta_2}$ if technology 2 is to be superior in Stage 1. Secondly, if we consider that technology 2 is superior for all $r \geqslant 0$, then, from (11), $b_1\alpha_1 > b_2\alpha_2$ and thus $\dfrac{d\gamma}{dt} > 0$, $\dfrac{\partial \gamma}{\partial y} > 0$ and $\dfrac{\partial \gamma_T}{\partial y} < 0$, producing time profiles for γ_t as in Figure 5.1. In Figure 5.1, curve B has a higher diffusion speed than has curve A.

Given that, in Stage 1, $\dfrac{1}{w} = nb_1\alpha_1 + \beta_1$, we may reduce the condition for superiority of technology 2 to the condition that

$$b_1\alpha_1 - b_2\alpha_2 > \frac{\beta_2 - \beta_1}{n}.$$

We have shown the time path of γ_t for $b_1\alpha_1 > b_2\alpha_2$ in Figure 5.1 (although the curvature is not clear (see below)). If $0 > b_1\alpha_1 - b_2\alpha_2 > \frac{\beta_2 - \beta_1}{n}$, and thus $b_2\alpha_2 > b_1\alpha_1$, it is possible that one would have $\frac{d\gamma}{dt} < 0$, $\frac{\partial\gamma}{\partial y} < 0$ and $\frac{\partial\gamma_T}{\partial y} > 0$. We can thus state that, given $\beta_1 > \beta_2$:

   (a) if $b_1\alpha_1 > b_2\alpha_2$, and thus the new technology is labour-
       saving in both direct and indirect use, then labour
       demand will increase in Stage 1;

   (b) if $0 > b_1\alpha_1 - b_2\alpha_2 > \frac{\beta_2 - \beta_1}{n}$, and thus the new tech-
       nology saves labour in direct use but is labour-using
       indirectly, then labour demand may decrease in Stage 1.

From above, we know that $\frac{d\gamma}{dt} \cdot \frac{1}{\gamma}$ has the same sign as $g_t - n$. As $g_t - n$ tells us how consumption per head moves over time,

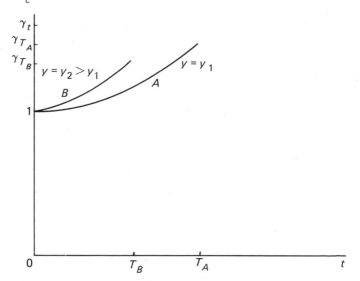

FIGURE 5.1 *Employment and time: Stage 1:*
absolutely labour-saving technology

our results on the path of γ_t also tell us of the time path of consumption per head.

Stage 2

In Stage 2, only capital good 2 is being produced. As we have argued before, this means that w will rise to $\frac{1}{\beta_1}$. We may then write (31) if all wages are consumed, all savings invested:

$$g_t \equiv \frac{dC}{dt} \cdot \frac{1}{C} = \frac{\beta_1 - \beta_2}{b_2 \alpha_2} - \frac{d\theta}{dt} \cdot \frac{1}{\theta} = \hat{r} - y(1 - \theta). \qquad (31)$$

Given (31), $g_t > y\theta - y$, thus $x_2 > 0$ for all of Stage 2.

We have argued above that we shall enter Stage 2 if $r_2 - n < y$, but also $r_2 < y$. We now wish to know whether, if we enter Stage 2, there is any chance of reverting back to Stage 1, i.e. back to a position where $g_t/y > \theta_t$. From (31), we see that (32) holds:

$$\frac{g_t}{y} - \theta_t = \frac{\hat{r}}{y} - 1. \qquad (32)$$

We know that $r_2 > \hat{r}$ and $r_2 < y$, thus $y > \hat{r}$ and $g_t/y - \theta_t < 0$ for all $t > T$. Thus if we enter Stage 2, we never leave it.

The next thing we wish to know is whether γ_t will increase or decrease with time in Stage 2. From (31) we may derive (33):

$$\log C_t = \hat{r}(t - T) - \log \theta_t + \log \theta_T + \log C_T. \qquad (33)$$

From (22) we may derive (34):

$$\log \gamma_t - \log \gamma_T = \log C_t - \log C_T - n(t-T)$$

$$- \log w_t + \log w_T \qquad (34)$$

Interpreting w_t as that appropriate to Stage 2 $\left(\frac{1}{\beta_1}\right)$, and w_T as that appropriate to Stage 1 $\left(\frac{1}{\beta_1 + b_1 \alpha_1 n}\right)$, we may see that there is a discontinuity in γ_t at time T. From (33) and (34) we derive (35):

$$\log \gamma_t - \log \gamma_T = (\hat{r}-n)(t - T) - \log \theta_t + \log \theta_T$$
$$+ \log \left(\frac{\beta_1}{\beta_1 + b_1 \alpha_1 n} \right). \tag{35}$$

The last term in (35) suggests that when w rises to $\frac{1}{\beta_1}$ at time T, γ_t will fall, the extent of the fall being dependent on the characteristics of the technology and n, but independent of the diffusion speed.

From (35) we can see that if $\hat{r} < n$, $\gamma_t < \gamma_T$ for all $t > T$. However, if $\hat{r} < n$, the economy cannot support a full-employment growth path with $w = \frac{1}{\beta_1}$. If $\hat{r} > n$, $d\gamma/dt \cdot \frac{1}{\gamma} > 0$ when (36) holds:

$$\theta_t > 1 + \frac{n - \hat{r}}{y}. \tag{36}$$

To investigate the impact of a change in the diffusion speed, we can derive (37) from (35):

$$\frac{\partial \log \gamma_t}{\partial y} = \frac{\partial \log \theta_T}{\partial y} - \frac{\partial \log \theta_t}{\partial y} - (\hat{r} - n) \frac{\partial T}{\partial y}$$
$$+ \frac{\partial \log \gamma_T}{\partial y}. \tag{37}$$

If $\hat{r} < n$, all these terms are negative. If $\hat{r} > n$, $\partial \log \gamma_t/\partial y$ may be positive for some higher values of t, for as t increases, $\partial \log \theta_t/\partial y$ declines.

To summarise, we can show two curves for our transition path, as in Figure 5.2. In this diagram we allow that technology 2 is superior for all w and $\hat{r} < n$. Curve B is drawn with a higher y than curve A. If $\hat{r} > n$, then the curves will rise again for t such that $\theta_t > \frac{1 + n - \hat{r}}{y}$. The curvature is derived from (38), which holds in Stage 2:

$$\frac{d^2\gamma}{dt^2} = (g_t - n)^2 + y\frac{d\theta}{dt} > 0. \tag{38}$$

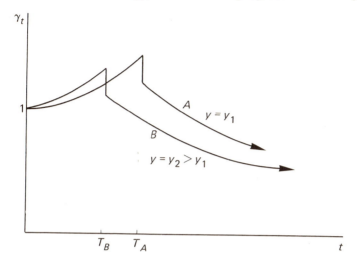

FIGURE 5.2 *Employment and time: Stages 1 and 2:
absolutely labour-saving technology* ($\hat{r} < n$)

In Stage 1 there is no clear way to determine curvature.

4 CONCLUSIONS

We have investigated the time path of employment in a two-
sector model during a period in which the economy is changing
technology. In a closed-economy semi-fixed-price environment,
we have shown that, if the economy has a classical savings
function, then if the new technology is absolutely labour-
saving, the time profile of labour demand relative to labour
supply will at first increase and then decline, with a possible upturn in labour demand for higher values of t. This
conclusion may be modified for a technology that is only
directly labour-saving. The higher the diffusion speed, the
higher will be the employment ratio in early years. In this
model also, consumption per head will follow the same time
path as labour demand.

These results are calculated for a closed economy. To extend
them to an open economy would require another paper. However,
we might note that the expansions in labour demand essentially
arise from the expansion of the capital goods sector and increases in consumer demand. To the extent that capital goods
are imported, no such expansion could arise. The important

point, however, is that, in contrast to alternative approaches to the modelling of technological unemployment, we have here a methodology that is yielding much richer and more interesting conclusions than have been available previously.

NOTE

I wish to thank the members of the Warwick Economic Theory Workshop, especially Avinash Dixit, for their useful comments on and criticisms of an early draft of this paper, consideration of which has led to a considerable improvement.

REFERENCES

Hicks, Sir J. R. (1965) *Capital and Growth* (Oxford University Press).
Mansfield, R. (1968) *Industrial Research and Technological Innovation* (London: Longmans).
Neisser, N. (1942) 'Permanent Technological Unemployment', *American Economic Review*, vol. 32 (March) pp. 50-71.

6 The Diffusion of Microelectronic Technology in South-East England

TOM BOURNER, HOWARD DAVIES,

VAL LINTNER, A. WOODS and M. WOODS

1 INTRODUCTION

It is widely held that the employment consequences of micro-electronic technology depend significantly upon the extent of application and the speed of diffusion of this range of innovations.

On the one hand, there is the view that the new technology will result in substantial structural unemployment because of the unprecedented speed with which it is feared it will be introduced. Those who hold this view (see, for example, Rothwell and Zegfeld, 1979) are presumably sceptical of the ability of labour markets to re-allocate manpower smoothly, and would argue that the more rapidly the technology is introduced, the more traumatic is the structural change and the greater is the consequent unemployment.[1]

On the other hand, there is the opposite view, implicit in the thinking of the Central Policy Review Staff (1978) and expressed by others who adopt an international perspective (e.g. Boatwright et al., 1980), that structural unemployment will result from a loss of international competitiveness if Britain adopts the new technology more slowly than its competitors. Britain is particularly vulnerable to unemployment from this source since a high proportion of its labour force is employed in the traded goods sector. Moreover, insofar as sales of North Sea oil sustain the value of sterling in the 1980s, these employment consequences are unlikely to be substantially mitigated by movements in the sterling exchange rate.[2] From this point of view, therefore, it becomes particularly important to identify and remove the impediments to rapid introduction of the new technology.

This debate is obviously important, but it has been conducted in something of an empirical vacuum. This chapter seeks to partially fill that vacuum by reporting some recent results from a pilot survey of manufacturing firms in the South-East of England (including London). The chapter is in three sections. The first deals with the extent to which microelectronic technology had diffused through firms in June 1980. The

second section examines executives' views on the impediments
to diffusion, and the third covers the relationships between
the adoption of silicon chip-based technology and employment
in the responding firms. The questions concerning microelectronics were added to the final section of the 'Sixteenth
London and South East Manufacturing Trend Survey' carried out
in June 1980 for the London Chamber of Commerce and Industry.
The questionnaires were sent to a total of 1500 firms, and a
total of 379 forms were returned. In addition to the questions
directly related to the new technology, the standard part of
the survey sought information concerning the main activity of
the company, the number of employees and the firms' investment
and employment plans.

2   THE EXTENT OF DIFFUSION

The potential ubiquity of microelectronic technology poses a
number of problems for survey work in this area. Unlike most
studies of technological diffusion (see, for instance, Nabseth
and Ray, 1974), in this it is not possible to identify a
single, highly specific innovation, and it is possible that
any firm with an electronic calculator on the premises would
classify itself as having adopted the new technology. Even
with a much more detailed questionnaire, it is much more difficult to differentiate between a significant and a trivial
application of the new technology, and, as a result, executives were, in effect, asked to make their own judgement on
whether or not they had, in fact, adopted microelectronics.[3]
  Of the 379 firms responding to the questionnaire, over two-
thirds (255) claimed to have adopted micros in at least one
area. Table 6.1 shows the basic data.

TABLE 6.1   *The diffusion of microelectronic technology*
            by activity (London and South-East England
            manufacturing firms at June 1980)

	Percentage of respondents to questionnaire	Number of firms
Embodied in products	22.7	86
Used in production processes	21.6	82
Used in clerical/secretarial work	29.3	111
Used in managerial methods	43.3	164
Others	2.1	8

Table 6.1 appears to confirm some elements of the conventional wisdom surrounding the effects of the new technology in that:

(a) the new technology is more widely adopted in work methods than in products;

(b) its introduction is most rapid in those functions where trade union organisation is weakest. As Table 6.1 suggests, the impact is greatest on managerial methods, with less impact on clerical/secretarial work and least impact on the shop floor.

Needless to say, any such interpretations need to be qualified. It may be the case, for example, that new microelectronic products are frequently developed within new firms (which would be under-represented in the Chamber of Commerce Survey), and this would tend to invalidate (a). The plausibility of inference (b) will be examined later, in the light of responses to other parts of the questionnaire.

If the more pessimistic prognostications of the employment effects of the new technology prove correct, then Table 6.1 suggests that the first impact is on managerial employment, with the least impact on the employment of production workers. Since the mobility of managers is typically greater than that of production workers, this could be interpreted as a factor tending to minimise any structural unemployment which might arise.

A question which arises directly out of Table 6.1 concerns the extent to which firms that had introduced microelectronic technology into one area of their operations had also introduced it into other areas. The responses showed that, in fact, a majority of the 255 'adopters' had applied the technology in more than one area. This raises an interesting new dimension to the question of technology diffusion if it is possible to identify patterns of diffusion within, as well as between, organisations. Table 6.2 displays some further information from the survey which is relevant to these questions.

The first column of Table 6.1 may be compared with each of the rows of Table 6.2 to see whether the introduction of microtechnology in one area of activity enhances a firm's propensity to introduce it in other areas.

Row 1 of Table 6.2 shows that firms which had embodied the new technology into their products were more likely to have introduced it into production processes, but no more likely to have introduced it into clerical or managerial methods than firms in the sample as a whole. The second row shows that firms that had introduced micros into production processes were more likely to have introduced it into all other areas.

Employment and Technological Change

TABLE 6.2   *The diffusion of microelectronic technology across business activities (London and South East manufacturing companies at June 1980)*

	Embodied in products		Used in production		Used in clerical work		Used in managerial methods	
	%	No.	%	No.	%	No.	%	No.
Embodied in products	100.0	86	30.2*	26	26.7	23	43.0	37
Used in production	31.7*	26	100.0	82	52.4**	43	63.4**	52
Used in clerical work	20.7	23	38.7**	43	100.0	111	72.1**	80
Used in managerial methods	22.6	37	31.7*	52	48.8**	80	100.0	164

** and * indicate that the value shown is significantly different from the Table 6.1, column 1 value at the 1% and 10% levels respectively.

From row 3 it can be seen that in firms where the technology
has been applied to clerical or secretarial work, it is more
likely to have been applied to the other areas, except embodiment into the firm's products. Finally, a similar conclusion
can be drawn from the fourth row, regarding those firms which
had applied micros to their managerial methods.

As a broad generalisation, the data displayed in Table 6.2
suggest that microtechnology spreads swiftly between clerical/
secretarial work and managerial work, but that these activities
are isolated from product development, a finding that may support the belief that there exists a cultural, social and even
physical distance between British engineers and managers. It
should also be noted that on the evidence of Table 6.2, the
introduction of micros in the production process seems to
offer a bridge for the spread of new technology between these
different aspects of industrial activity.

One of the most distinctive features of the new technology
is that it makes accessible to small firms techniques which
were previously available only to large firms, mini- and micro-
computers being the most obvious example. In that case it might
be hypothesised that small firms may have seized upon microtechnology more readily than have large firms.[4] Table 6.3 distinguishes between 'small' firms, having less than 200 employees at the address surveyed, and 'large' firms, having
more than 200 employees.

TABLE 6.3   *The diffusion of microelectronic
technology by firm size*

	Less than 200 employees		More than 200 employees	
	%	No.	%	No.
Embodied in products	20.7	57	28.2	29
Used in production	16.3**	45	35.9	37
Used in clerical work	26.4*	73	36.9	38
Used in managerial methods	36.6**	101	61.2	63
Other	2.5	7	1.0	1
Total number of firms		276		103

** and * indicate that the value is significantly different
from the percentage in the following column at the 1% and 10%
level respectively.

The results presented in Table 6.3 offer a clear refutation of this hypothesis concerning firm size. In most areas of business activity, a significantly greater proportion of the large firms had introduced the new technology. In view of this conclusion, it is particularly useful in the next section of the chapter to examine for systematic differences perceived by large and small firms in the impediments to the adoption of micros.

Table 6.4 provides evidence on the industrial pattern of the results on the extent of diffusion.

The first row of Table 6.4 shows the percentage of firms which had already embodied micros in their products. The wide range in this proportion, from 83.3 per cent in instrument engineering to zero in several other sectors, is probably a simple reflection of the fact that some types of product are amenable to the introduction of micros whereas others are not.

The second row of Table 6.4 shows that the penetration of the silicon chip technology into production processes is much more even than in the case of products, but that the difference is still significant. Comparing the first two rows, it is surprising to note that there is no correspondence across industrial sectors between penetration of micros into products and into processes.

The third and fourth rows of the table relate to clerical and managerial uses of micros. No statistically significant variation across the industrial sectors is evident, and it would seem that in these functions, where micros are most widespread, all industrial sectors have similar adoption rates.

It may be noted that the sectoral analysis of Table 6.4 confirms the conclusion noted above that the application of microtechnology to product development is largely independent of its application in the clerical and managerial areas. An extreme example of this is to be found in instrument engineering, where penetration into products is far more marked than in other sectors, but where penetration into clerical and managerial methods is significantly behind the other sectors.

3   IMPEDIMENTS TO THE APPLICATION OF MICROELECTRONIC TECHNOLOGY

Having outlined the extent of diffusion, attention may be shifted to an examination of the factors affecting its rate. In particular, the survey collected evidence on executives' own perceptions of the major impediments to the adoption of the new technology. This raises a major methodological issue, in that businessmen's own explanations of their conduct have

TABLE 6.4 *The adoption of microelectronic technology by industry and area of operation*

Area of adoption	Chemicals and metals % / No.	Mechanical engineering % / No.	Electrical engineering % / No.	Instrument engineering % / No.	Other metal goods % / No.	Food and drink % / No.	Footwear and clothing % / No.	Timber and furniture % / No.	Paper and publishing % / No.	Rubber and Plastics % / No.	Other % / No.
Products	0 / 0	17.1 / 12	59.1 / 39	83.3 / 15	10.7 / 3	0 / 0	0 / 0	0 / 0	5.6 / 1	0 / 0	15.9 / 14
Production	28.0 / 7	22.9 / 16	33.3 / 22	16.7 / 3	14.3 / 4	22.2 / 4	6.7 / 1	9.1 / 1	22.2 / 4	40.9 / 9	12.5 / 11
Clerical	48.0 / 12	31.4 / 22	33.3 / 22	11.1 / 2	21.4 / 6	27.8 / 5	40.0 / 6	27.3 / 3	22.2 / 4	22.7 / 5	26.1 / 23
Managerial	40.0 / 10	37.1 / 26	51.5 / 34	38.9 / 7	42.9 / 12	27.8 / 5	40.0 / 6	45.5 / 5	55.6 / 10	50.0 / 11	42.0 / 37
Other	0 / 0	1.4 / 1	9.1 / 5	0 / 0	0 / 0	0 / 0	0 / 0	0 / 0	0 / 0	0 / 0	0 / 0
Total number of firms	25	70	66	18	28	18	15	11	18	22	88

been viewed as rather dubious evidence, at least since the
debates on pricing policy in the immediate post-war period.
Nevertheless, the value of such opinions may be defended
(see Blaug, 1980), and it is hoped to cast light upon the
relative importance of various impediments.

Of the organisations returning questionnaires, 239 identified at least one impediment. Table 6.5 shows the results.

TABLE 6.5   *Perceived impediments to the
introduction of microelectronics*

Perceived impediment	Percentage of respondents	Number of respondents
No known relevant applications	26.6	101
Finance unavailable	7.1	27
Skills unavailable	11.3	43
Labour relations problems	3.7	14
Excessive cost	9.8	37
Inappropriate general economic climate	12.4	47
Other	4.2	16

Perhaps the most striking feature of the data presented in
Table 6.5 is the finding that labour relations problems were
mentioned by fewer firms than any other impediment listed -
despite the extensive publicity that has been given to this
factor. In the light of this response, it is difficult to
sustain the belief that the relatively slow introduction of
micro-technology into production processes results from labour
resistance. It seems that the rather positive response of the
TUC (1979) to the new technology might be more typical of
labour attitudes than some much publicised cases of union
resistance. Perhaps the trade unions have been unjustly criti-
cised in this respect.

The most commonly cited impediment was 'no known applications'. This might indicate that there are significant areas
of manufacturing where microtechnology is inappropriate, or
it might indicate executives' ignorance about existing opportunities. Since there are some techniques of very wide application, like word-processors and accounting systems, there
must be a strong suspicion that the latter explanation
carries a good deal of weight.

Of the remaining impediments covered by the survey, the
most often cited were 'inappropriate general economic climate'
(12.4 per cent), 'skills unavailable' (11.3 per cent) and
'excessive cost' (9.8 per cent). As these proportions are all

relatively small, they seem to cast doubt on the popular
hypotheses that current macro-economic policy, skill shortages,
or the cost of equipment form substantial barriers to the
adoption of micros. However, it should also be borne in mind
that more than a third of the respondents were unable to
identify any impediments at all, which is perhaps an indication of the very great element of uncertainty surrounding
micro-technology in 1980.

Table 6.5 refers to the impediments perceived by all the
respondents to the survey, whether or not they themselves had
adopted micros. Table 6.6 disaggregates these totals in order
to see if the perceived impediments differ for firms which
actually had experience of the adoption process.

TABLE 6.6 *Perceived impediments by adoption/*
non-adoption of microelectronics

Perceived impediment	Respondents who had adopted micros		Others	
	%	No.	%	No.
No known relevant applica-tions	18.4**	47	43.5	54
Finance unavailable	6.3*	16	8.9	11
Skills unavailable	14.1*	36	5.6	7
Labour relations problems	2.4	6	6.5	8
Excessive cost	9.4	24	10.5	13
Inappropriate general economic climate	12.5	32	12.1	15
Other	5.5*	14	1.6	2
Total number of firms		255		124

** and * indicate a significant difference between the
percentages at the 1% and 10% levels respectively.

Of the organisations with no experience of the application
of microelectronic technology, almost half mentioned 'no
known relevant applications', a finding which would tend to
support the view expressed above that ignorance is a very
important factor retarding adoption. Further examination of
Table 6.6 suggests that, compared to the 'adopters', firms
which had not yet had experience of introducing the new
technology were inclined to over-emphasise the potential
labour problems and under-emphasise the difficulty of securing
the necessary skills. This might, of course, reflect genuinely
greater labour relations problems in 'non-adopting' firms, but
it might also be noted that the proportions concerned are, in

any event, very small indeed (2.4 and 6.5 per cent).

At this point it is worth noting that Table 6.3 showed substantial differences in the rate of adoption between large and small firms. As a result, the findings in Table 6.6 might be accounted for by differences in the impediments perceived by firms of different sizes. Table 6.7 examines this possibility.

TABLE 6.7   *Perceived impediments by firm size*

	Less than 200 employees		More than 200 employees	
	%	No.	%	No.
No known relevant applications	27.2*	75	25.2	26
Finance unavailable	9.1	25	1.9	2
Skills unavailable	10.9	30	12.6	13
Labour relations problems	3.6	10	3.9	4
Excessive cost	10.1	28	8.7	9
Inappropriate general economic conditions	12.3	34	12.6	13
Other	4.7	13	2.9	3
Total number of firms		276		103

* indicates significant differences in percentages at the 1% level.

The most obvious feature of Table 6.7 is the similarity in the proportions of firms of different sizes mentioning each of the identified impediments. This is somewhat surprising in the case of labour relations problems, given that it is generally assumed that large firms experience these kinds of problems to a larger extent than do small firms. Again, the conclusion that labour relations form no substantial impediment to the adoption of micros seems to be borne out.

The only exception to the rule that small and large firms perceive the same impediments comes (unsurprisingly) in the case of finance, where a much larger proportion of small firms (9.1 per cent) felt that the lack of finance formed a major impediment. Over the years, a number of government reports, including that of the Wilson Committee (1980, Appendix 2, p. 388), have concluded that large firms enjoy easier access to funds than small firms.

Whilst Table 6.6 shows a slight tendency for a smaller

proportion of adopters to view finance as a major impediment, it is clear from Table 6.7 that the difference in firm size between adopters and other firms cannot, in general, explain the differences in the pattern of perceived impediments.

4 MICROELECTRONICS AND EMPLOYMENT PLANS

In addition to the issues covered above, executives were asked about their plans for employment over the four months following June 1980 (this is a standard part of the Trend Survey). Table 6.8 shows the results.

The general impression gained from Table 6.8 is that the pattern of labour market intentions does not differ dramatically between 'adopters' and other firms. In most cases, there are no significant differences in the proportions of firms adopting a particular stance. However, there are a number of exceptions in some areas. In every skill category, 'adopters' were more frequently reducing their labour force through recruitment cut-backs than were the other firms. In the managerial category, 'adopters' were more frequently resorting to voluntary redundancy. In each of these cases, the relationship between the use of micros and employment prospects seems consistent with the pessimistic view of future developments. On the other hand, the opposite view receives some small support from the only other significant difference in Table 6.8, which shows that in the 'skilled' category, a smaller proportion of 'adopters' were putting workers on short time.

5 CONCLUSIONS

This pilot survey has shed limited light upon empirical aspects of the so-called Microelectronic Revolution, and, in so doing, has reinforced the conventional wisdom in some respects, but weakened it in others. Nevertheless, it is plain that a good deal of work, both theoretical and empirical, remains to be done before we can even formulate the appropriate questions on which to base an informed judgement on the net effect of the new technology.

NOTES

1. The Department of Employment has attempted to counter this fear by claiming that the speed of diffusion of the silicon chip technology is unlikely to be rapid, since the cost of hardware and software associated with the relatively cheap electronic components is still high (*Employment News*,

TABLE 6.8 *Employment expectations and the adoption of microelectronics*

Employment plans for the four months following June 1980	Labour categories							
	Unskilled		Skilled		Managerial		Other office	
	Adopters %	Others %	Adopters %	Others %	Adopters %	Others %	Adopters %	Others %
Increase work-force through								
increased numbers	8.2	10.5	13.3	9.7	7.1	7.3	7.5	6.5
extra overtime	3.1	3.2	7.5	4.8	1.6	2.4	1.2	1.6
Reduce work-force through								
forced redundancy	7.5	8.2	3.9*	5.6	4.3	4.8	7.1	8.9
short time	8.6	9.7	5.5*	10.5	0.4	0.8	1.6	1.6
voluntary redundancy	3.1	0.8	2.4	1.6	3.9*	0.8	3.1	0.8
recruitment cut-back	12.2*	6.5	8.2*	3.2	8.8**	0.8	11.8**	2.4

** and * indicate that the differences are significant at the 1% and 10% levels respectively.

Dec./Jan. 1980). However, Table 6.5 of this chapter suggests that excessive cost of adoption is not often seen as an impediment to the introduction of micros.
2. Adherents to 'neo-technology' theories of trade would probably go further, and argue that countries which lead in the adoption of micros will acquire a dynamic comparative advantage, enjoying employment benefits from the new technology, while slow adopters suffer the negative employment effects.
3. The questionnaire asked, 'Do microelectronics (silicon chips) feature in your company's operations in any of the following ways: (a) embodied in the products you sell; (b) used in your production processes; (c) used in your clerical/secretarial work; (d) used in your managerial methods (e.g. accounting systems, personnel records, etc.); (e) others - please specify?'.
4. This hypothesis may be extended in a number of ways. If large firms exist in a less competitive environment, then X-inefficiency may take the form of slow adoption rates for micros.

REFERENCES

Blaug, M. (1980) 'Economic Methodology in One Easy Lesson', *British Review of Economic Issues*, vol. 12, no. 6, pp. 1-16.
Boatwright, B., P. Irwin, J. Sleigh and R. Stanyon (1980) *The Manpower Implications of Microelectronic Technology*, Department of Employment (London: HMSO).
Central Policy Review Staff (1978) 'Social and Employment Implications of Microelectronics', mimeo.
Nabseth, L. and G. Ray (eds) (1974) *The Diffusion of New Industrial Processes* (Cambridge University Press).
Rothwell, R. and W. Zegfeld (1979) *Technical Change and Employment* (London: Francis Pinter).
Trades Union Congress (1979) *Employment and Technology: Report of the TUC General Council to the 1979 Congress,* rev. edn (London: TUC).
Wilson Committee (1980) *Report of the Committee to Review the Functioning of Financial Institutions*, Cmnd 7939 (London: HMSO).

7 Employment Projections and Structural Change

JOHN CLARK

1 INTRODUCTION

Some recent econometric projections have given rise to pessimistic conclusions about likely future levels of unemployment
in the UK and have suggested the necessity for radical economic or social measures to avert, or make acceptable, a decline in demand for labour. The discussion below is intended
to help to clarify the historical trends which underlie these
prognoses, with a view to assessing the robustness of the
results obtained and to contribute to the debate on whether
the policy prescriptions proposed are appropriate.

The best-publicised of the recent studies, and the work
most frequently referred to here, is that of the Cambridge
Economic Policy Group (1978). A major conclusion of this work
was that very high rates of economic growth will, in future,
be required to substantially reduce UK unemployment; and
further, arguing that such growth rates cannot be achieved
under current conditions and policies owing to balance of
payments constraints, the group advocate the introduction of
import controls. Leicester (1977a, 1977b) of the Institute of
Manpower Studies (IMS) and the Warwick Manpower Research Group
(1978) also foresee a substantial increase in unemployment if
present trends continue.

These studies share certain common elements. First, they
involve a process of 'extrapolation', in that no major changes
in the form of the equations used are expected to occur without major policy intervention. Also, the Cambridge and IMS
studies, while differing in detail, are both based on the
estimation of an assumed historical relationship between output and employment. Hence, to understand the results of these
analyses, it is useful to begin with an examination of equations used and the historical data behind them.

2 THE VERDOORN LAW AND ITS DESCENDANTS

A widely used version of the 'Verdoorn Law' (Verdoorn, 1949)
asserts the existence of a positive linear association

between the (exponential) growth rates of labour productivity, P, and output, Q:

$$\frac{\dot{P}}{P} = a + b \frac{\dot{Q}}{Q} . \qquad (1)$$

Since P is here defined as $P = Q/E$, where E is employment,

$$\frac{\dot{E}}{E} = \frac{\dot{Q}}{Q} - \frac{\dot{P}}{P} , \qquad (2)$$

so that equation (1) can be written

$$\frac{\dot{E}}{E} = \alpha + \beta \frac{\dot{Q}}{Q} , \qquad (3)$$

relating employment growth to output growth, where $\alpha = -a$ and $\beta = 1-b$.

It is not difficult to suggest causal interpretations of an observed strong association between output growth and productivity growth. Rapidly rising output may enable productivity-increasing scale economies to be achieved, and is likely to be associated with a high level of investment in modern, labour-saving machinery. Conversely, productivity increases may give rise to relative price reductions which stimulate increased demand and output, as is suggested by some of the neo-classical 'compensation' theories of employment and technical change (see Kaldor, 1966, 1975; Rowthorn, 1975a, 1975b).

Equation (3) can be easily integrated to give

$$\ln E_t = \theta + at + \beta \ln Q_t . \qquad (4)$$

The actual equation used by the Cambridge Economic Policy Group is

$$\ln E_t = \theta + at + \beta \ln Q_t + \phi \ln Q_{t-1} , \qquad (5)$$

i.e. essentially of the form of equation (4), but with an extra term allowing for lags in the employment effects of changes in output. This equation is estimated for each of three sectors (manufacturing, 'other industries' and private services) and employment projections to 1985 are made for each of these sectors given assumptions regarding the growth rate of output. Hence 'exogenous' changes in employment (i.e. those resulting from productivity changes not associated with changes in output) are assumed to follow a linear time trend, while 'output-induced' changes are represented by the constants β and φ.

The Institute of Manpower Studies model essentially re-
verses these assumptions; specifically, the employment function in this case is

$$E = \phi' + (\alpha' + \beta't)Q, \tag{6}$$

so that the time trend is incorporated in the output multiplier, the 'exogenous' term being constant. In the Cambridge
formulation, equation (5), a constant output Q implies a
change in employment at a steady *rate* of 100α per cent per
annum, while with constant output, the IMS relationship
(equation (6)) implies a constant *absolute difference* in employment from year to year of $\beta'Q$. In the IMS work, equation
(6) is estimated using historical data and, with a slight
modification in the treatment of the trend term, $\alpha'+\beta't$, the
equation is used to project employment to the year 2001,
under four different assumptions of future growth rates.

Other studies, apart from that of the Warwick group mentioned above, have opted for similar representations. The
Treasury medium-term model (McLean, 1974) incorporates an
equation similar to equation (4), with three elaborations.
Terms representing lagged employment and working hours are
included, and two (rather than one) time trends representing
change in labour productivity are incorporated. The employment equation is used as an integral part of the overall
econometric model.

Because of the wide use of Verdoorn-type relationships as
a basis of employment projections, the expression is tested
in the following section with respect to time-series data on
the UK manufacturing industry. The choice of manufacturing is
based on the belief that this sector plays a central role in
determining the welfare of the economy as a whole. Several
studies (see, for example, Cornwall, 1977) have reported that
a close correlation exists between the growth rate of the
manufacturing sector and that of GDP; for the data obtained
from the sources cited in Appendix 1, for the 1950-77 period,
the following linear relationship was fitted:

$$\frac{\dot{Q}_m}{Q_m} = -1.81 + 1.93 \frac{\dot{Q}}{Q}, \quad R^2 = 0.93, \tag{7}$$
$$(0.11)$$

where Q is GDP and Q_m is net manufacturing output. Cripps and
Tarling (1973) show that the correlation with GDP growth is
closer in the case of manufacturing than for any other sector,

and Kaldor (1975) indicates that the correlation does not
come about simply because manufacturing output forms a large
proportion of GDP.

Equation (7) implies that when the growth rate of GDP is
above a certain level (about 2 per cent), the growth rate of
manufacturing is higher still; and, similarly, that low GDP
growth is associated with yet lower manufacturing sector
growth. Thus manufacturing appears to provide a kind of ex-
aggerated reflection of the health of the total economy.

Several mechanisms are likely to be responsible for this
relationship. First, manufacturing industry is closely linked
to other sectors of the economy-producer services, for example
- so that an expansion of manufacturing would be expected to
induce expansion elsewhere.[2] Secondly, manufactured goods form
the major component of UK exports, and a booming manufacturing
sector may be expected to be closely associated with 'export-
led growth'. Thirdly, manufacturing - unlike, say, publicly
provided services - generates tax revenue from profits, which
can be used to finance government-sponsored activities.

3   TRENDS IN PRODUCTIVITY AND OUTPUT IN THE UK MANUFACTURING INDUSTRY

First, the data derived from the sources cited in Appendix 1
will be used to estimate the basic Verdoorn relationship
(equation (1)). The questions being considered are: firstly,
whether the expression provides a good 'fit' to the data over
particular time periods; and secondly, whether the parameters
a and b have remained constant over different historical
periods.

The methodology adopted involves estimating the equation
over successive 10-year periods. Thus, for the period 1921-30,
the 'best' (least-squares) fit to equation (1), i.e.

$$\frac{\dot{P}}{P} = a + b \frac{\dot{Q}}{Q},$$

is determined, yielding values for a and b and the coefficient
of determination R^2. The procedure is then repeated for the
period 1922-31 and subsequently for each rolling 10-year
period over the time span covered by the data.

If employment were maintained at a constant level in each
10-year period ($\dot{E}$=0), then, from equation (2),

$$\frac{\dot{P}}{P} = \frac{\dot{Q}}{Q}.$$

Substituting this into equation (1) gives the 'implicit' rate of output growth in each period required to just maintain the level of employment; this value of output growth is

$$\gamma = \frac{a}{1-b}, \tag{8}$$

which can also be interpreted as the 'underlying' rate of productivity growth which would have been achieved *if* employment had remained constant.

The values obtained from a, b and R^2 are shown in Tables 7.1 and 7.2, together with the calculated value of the parameter γ. The results show that the Verdoorn relationship

TABLE 7.1   *Results of regression equation (1),*
1920-38[a]

Period	a	b	R^2	γ
1921-30	2.77	0.33	0.55	4.13
1922-31	1.59	0.49	0.70	3.12
1923-32	1.53	0.41	0.60	2.59
1924-33	1.65	0.42	0.65	2.84
1925-34	1.33	0.31	0.75	1.93
1926-35	1.29	0.32	0.77	1.90
1927-36	1.15	0.32	0.74	1.69
1928-37	1.03	0.31	0.64	1.49
1929-38	1.08	0.31	0.64	1.57

[a]   Production industries; for data sources, see Appendix 1.

appears, in general, to provide a useful fit to the data presented, apparently confirming the existence of a statistically significant association between output growth and productivity growth within each period. Of greater interest, however, is the clear way in which the structure of the relationship seems to have been changing over time. The regression coefficient, b (a measure of the percentage increase in productivity associated with a given percentage increase in output), is systematically higher post-war than in the pre-war period, and shows no clear pattern of variation within each period. The coefficient a (a measure of the 'exogenous' component of productivity increase) shows a general decline over the earlier period and an increase in the later period. The parameter γ shows an even clearer pattern of behaviour; again there is a pre-war decline followed by an upward movement, which is suggestive of a cycle covering the entire period from 1920.[3]

These results suggest the possibility that, in the UK

TABLE 7.2 *Results of regression equation (1),*
1949-79[a]

Period	a	b	R^2	γ
1949-58	-0.126	0.672	0.925	-0.38
1950-59	-0.016	0.716	0.857	-0.06
1951-60	0.006	0.661	0.801	0.02
1952-61	-0.082	0.693	0.822	-0.27
1953-62	0.186	0.652	0.744	0.53
1954-63	0.413	0.632	0.652	1.12
1955-64	0.350	0.707	0.740	1.23
1956-65	0.281	0.744	0.755	1.10
1957-66	0.519	0.705	0.730	1.76
1958-67	0.978	0.643	0.637	2.74
1959-68	1.048	0.695	0.606	3.44
1960-69	0.882	0.661	0.582	2.60
1961-70	0.538	0.841	0.734	3.38
1962-71	1.473	0.682	0.656	4.63
1963-72	1.942	0.637	0.539	5.35
1964-73	1.804	0.664	0.637	5.37
1965-74	1.086	0.842	0.684	6.87
1966-75	1.720	0.734	0.736	6.47
1967-76	2.086	0.746	0.733	8.21
1968-77	1.643	0.752	0.701	6.63
1969-78	1.493	0.711	0.637	5.16
1970-79	1.651	0.753	0.677	6.69

[a] Manufacturing industries; for data sources, see Appendix 1.

manufacturing sector, important structural changes have
occurred which warrant further consideration. Possible causes
for the observed trends are discussed below. An immediate
implication, however, is that the Verdoorn relationship, or
similar representations, needs to be applied with care for
medium- to long-term projections of employment of the type
considered in Section 2 above. As an example, a growth rate
of manufacturing output of 2 per cent per annum implies, over
five years, an increase in employment of about 3 per cent in
manufacturing on the basis of the 1950-9 regression line, but
a decline of about 6 per cent on the basis of the 1968-77 line.
The significance of this kind of disparity for unemployment
is clearly enormous.

Of course, the structure of the equation has not been
changing as dramatically as this in the short term; there is
no reason to suppose that analyses of the Cambridge type are
subject to this magnitude of uncertainty. To obtain an

indication of the sensitivity of the Cambridge expression to
the period of estimation, the data of Appendix 1 was used to
estimate the equation

$$\left[\frac{\dot{E}}{E}\right]_t = \hat{\alpha} + \hat{\beta}\left[\frac{\dot{Q}}{Q}\right]_t + \hat{\phi}\left[\frac{\dot{Q}}{Q}\right]_{t-1} \tag{9}$$

(which is a close approximation to the Cambridge expression,
equation (5)) for each of the periods 1950-68, 1955-73, and
1963-77. The second of these periods was that actually used
by the Cambridge group.

The results are shown in Table 7.3. The Cambridge group do

TABLE 7.3 *Results of regression equation (9)*

Period	$\hat{\alpha}$	$\hat{\beta}$	$\hat{\phi}$	R^2	$\hat{\gamma} = \frac{-\hat{\alpha}}{\hat{\beta}+\hat{\phi}}$
1950-68	-1.46	0.28	0.31	0.73	2.47
1955-73	-2.27	0.28	0.43	0.76	3.20
1963-77	-2.24	0.23	0.40	0.78	3.56

not present the data on which their estimates are based, but
for the period 1955-73, the coefficient values they derive
for manufacturing are close to those given above for this
period; in the notation used here, they find $\hat{\alpha} = 2.2$, $\hat{\beta} = 0.24$,
$\hat{\phi} = 0.43$, $R^2 = 0.84$ and $\gamma = 3.28$.

From the above results, it seems probable that, had the
Cambridge group estimated their equation over a more recent
period, they would have reached even more pessimistic conclusions concerning output growth rates required to generate
employment. Indeed, it is arguably more consistent to include
a term in the employment function which would include the
effects of the apparent temporal increase in γ, which would
imply the necessity for still higher rates of output growth
in the future.

It appears, then, that over the entire post-war period,
employment creation has been becoming 'more difficult', in
the sense of being associated with, or requiring, an increasingly rapid rate of output growth.

4 INTERPRETATION OF THE RESULTS

4.1 *Changes in Investment Patterns*

There are, of course, several possible explanations for the
observed trend. The phenomenon may be due primarily to re-

organisation within industry, leading, for example, to an
increasing rate of displacement of under-employed people,
possibly in response to increasing wage pressures.[4] However,
it is suggested here that changes in the structure of the
capital stock, and in investment patterns in particular,
have had a significant influence.

Estimates of capital stock are notoriously unreliable,
perhaps the major problem being the lack of data on discards.
This is particularly unfortunate, since a plausible explanation of the rise in the 'latent' rate of productivity growth,
γ, is that old, relatively unproductive equipment has been
scrapped at an increasing rate. It seems likely that pressures
of foreign competition have forced the least efficient UK
firms out of business on an increasing scale, yielding a
rising overall rate of productivity growth. The method by
which the stock of capital in the UK is estimated,[5] however,
makes it impossible to test this hypothesis with the data at
hand.

Turning to the question of investment patterns, it is useful in some circumstances to differentiate between 'expansion'
and 'rationalisation' investments. Although the distinction
is far from perfect and has yet to be subject to rigorous
definition, it is invoked here partly to help illustrate the
different supply-side effects that investment in fixed capital
can have, and partly because these categories have been used
in survey research on investment patterns in the post-war
period. The notion is that expansion investment (such as a new
factory) is motivated by a desire to increase productive capacity, while rationalisation (e.g. the installation of a computer system to 'replace' clerical personnel) is motivated
primarily by a desire to reduce costs. While both kinds of
investment will tend to increase income and demand through
the multiplier, only expansion investment will have significant supply-side effects. Thus, if there is a supply-side
constraint on the attainment of full employment, in the form
of insufficiency of profitable capital, rationalisation will
tend to exacerbate this constraint, while expansion will tend
to relieve it. In situations where potentially profitable
spare capacity is available but is not utilised because of a
deficiency of aggregate demand, both types of investment expenditure may increase employment through their demand-side
effects; in the case of rationalisation, the realisation of
this outcome depends on whether the initial job-displacing
effects are outweighed by the positive 'second order' effects
on output and employment generated by the multiplier process.

The apparent shift in the Verdoorn relationship is consistent with an increase in the relative contribution of the
rationalising component of investment at the expense of the

expansionary component. The principal difference between
these components of investment lies in their effect on employment: expansion investment increases employment; rationalisation investment reduces it.

It therefore seems natural to examine the trend in the
annual change of manufacturing employment, ΔE, per unit of
investment, I.[6] To reduce the effects of short-term cycles,
the employment and investment series are smoothed by taking
5-year moving averages, from which the ratio $\Delta E/I$ is plotted
against time in Figure 7.1.

From an apparently increasing tendency during the 1930s,
there has been a steady decline in the change in employment
per unit of investment since 1950, the ratio becoming negative after 1966. It is, of course, recognised that the attri-
bution of causality to this result remains only a hypothesis;
in particular, it is possible that variations in rates at
which capital equipment is scrapped without replacement, or
in rates of disembodied technical change, account for all the
variation in employment, leaving nothing to be explained by a
changing nature of investment activity. Nevertheless, the
result is consistent with the contention that a change in
investment patterns towards rationalisation could be an important contributory factor in explaining the shift in the
productivity/output relationship.

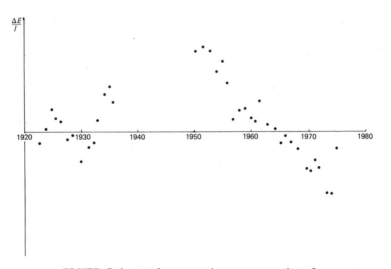

FIGURE 7.1 *Employment change per unit of
investment (smoothed), UK manufacturing*

Surveys of manufacturing industries in Germany[7] indicate
a trend in the post-war period of an increasing proportion
of investment expenditure being devoted to rationalisation.
Further evidence for this trend is provided by OECD data
indicating a decline in the share of investment devoted to
non-residential construction in most Western industrialised
nations (OECD, 1978).

It would, perhaps, be expected that, in times of low total
(gross) investment, the rationalisation component would be
relatively high - producers may always be interested in
cutting costs, and the act of replacing and updating the
capital stock is a relatively low-risk decision, being independent of uncertain expectations of market growth. Thus,
this activity may plausibly occur at a roughly constant rate,
and hence form a higher (lower) proportion of total investment as the latter falls (rises). This pattern would be expected if the type of investment activity were determined
by general economic conditions rather than being biased by
a significant 'technology push' whereby producers may be
induced to spend a 'disproportionate' fraction of their in-
vestable resources on rationalisation in the light of a
greater or lesser availability of profitable investment
opportunities in that direction. The evidence suggests that
technology may well have influenced investment decisions in
this way, but further research is needed.

4.2 *Evidence for 'Long Waves'?*

Although the interpretation must be a very tentative one,
the results presented here provide some support for the
existence of long waves in economic development of the type
suggested by Kondratieff (1935). He proposed that prices,
interest rates, wages, foreign trade and production (with
the limited time-series data then available) all exhibited
long-term cyclic behaviour, the cycles being of 45-60 years
duration. Schumpeter (1939) argued that the emergence of
radical new technologies every fifty years or so was responsible for the cycles;[8] Freeman (1977b) has articulated
Schumpeter's ideas, and extended them by suggesting that
electronics-based technologies were to a great extent responsible for the post-war boom and the subsequent (current)
recession.[9] In terms of the current discussion, the post-war
period of sustained rapid growth has apparently been accompanied by a steady increase in the potential for, and ex-
ploitation of, rationalisation.

One may speculate that, in general, a period of Kondratieff
'upswing' is characterised by a rising trend in the under-

lying rate of productivity growth, γ. Data on industrial
production and productivity for periods prior to World War
I must necessarily be treated with caution. However, estimation of equations (1) and (9) for the 30-year period prior
to World War I has been carried out. The equations are less
well satisfied in this period, but, in so far as the results
do have validity, a cyclical trend in γ is suggested. In
particular, γ appears to have been positive and decreasing
towards the end of the nineteenth century, and to have been
negative in the first decade of the twentieth.

4.3   *An International or UK-Specific Phenomenon?*

Results obtained from a similar analysis applied to other
countries are, as yet, preliminary and incomplete, but the
available evidence does imply that the structural changes
proposed above are not peculiar to the UK. In the USA, similar long swings in the value of the parameter γ appear to
have occurred between 1900 and the late 1950s; since then, γ
seems to have remained roughly constant. It is possible that
a high level of space- and defence-related innovative activity and investment has tended to counteract the employment-
displacing effects of rationalisation in the USA over the past
two decades. In West Germany, a trend in γ similar to that of
the UK is observed over the post-war period. The period immediately after the war is characterised by a large and negative value of γ, which may be explained in terms of the employment-generating effects of large-scale reconstruction.
Data on investment behaviour and capital productivity, al-
luded to earlier, also suggests a fairly general trend towards rationalisation and capital/labour substitution in the
post-war period.

Thus, although further work needs to be (and is being)
undertaken, it appears that the results obtained here do not
illustrate a situation unique to the UK. Clearly, the UK does
have special problems compared with many other OECD countries
- its long-term productivity record, for example, is very poor
by international standards. Such problems exacerbate the detri-
mental effects of the common structural trend.

5   CONCLUSIONS

The dangers of 'determinism' - i.e. the assumption that
relationships which have held in the past are immutable, and
can safely be extrapolated into the future - are, of course,
well known to forecasters. It has been suggested here that

these dangers are particularly acute in the case of employment forecasts made on the basis of a time-invariant pro-
ductivity/output relationship, since there is considerable
evidence that the form of such relationships has been changing in the past; this suggests that one should have even less
confidence about them retaining a constant form in the future.
What is required is an understanding of the forces underlying
the observed trends, both as a guide to possible future developments and as an aid to developing appropriate policies.
Some evidence has been presented to support the hypothesis
that changes in investment behaviour have been at least
partially responsible for the apparently increasing constraints on employment generation in manufacturing.

There is currently considerable debate about whether the
current economic problems faced by the UK are 'cyclical' or
'structural'. Those holding the former view argue that the
post-1973 recession is a particularly severe example of the
well-known business cycle, and that current unemployment can,
in principle, be expected to largely disappear when the expected recovery in output occurs. On this view, the persis-
tence of the recession is due to an 'inflationary psychology'
which inhibits the application of reflationary policies -
until inflation is brought under control, and business confidence re-established, any governmental attempt to expand
the economy is likely to result mainly in rising prices
rather than increased output. The 'structuralist' argument,
on the other hand, is that this is by no means the whole
story; long-term shifts in the structure of the economy are
as important, if not more important, factors to take into
account in any diagnosis of the current malaise.

The discussion here lends support to the structural view.
It seems that, over the post-war period, there has been a
fairly systematic trend, exemplified in the reduction of the
employment-generating effects of rapid output growth. In so
far as there *has* been, over this period, a significant positive relationship between output growth and employment growth,
it is reasonable to suppose that rapid output growth would
create jobs and reduce unemployment. But to rely on this
process as a means of reducing unemployment to 'acceptably'
low levels would seem to involve an unjustified act of faith.
Over the last century, there have been periods when very low,
even zero, output growth has been 'sufficient' to generate
employment. It is hoped that this chapter is a contribution
to an understanding of the other factors on which employment
generation depends.

APPENDIX 1

Data Sources

London & Cambridge Economic Service (n.d.) *The British
  Economy - Key Statistics 1900-1970* (London: Times
  Newspapers Ltd).
C. J. F. Brown and T. Sheriff (1978) 'Deindustrialisation
  in the UK: Background Statistics', Discussion Paper 23,
  National Institute of Economic and Social Research, London.
UK Central Statistical Office, *Annual Abstract of Statistics*
  (London: HMSO) various years.
UK Central Statistical Office (1971) *Historical Abstract of
  UK Labour Statistics* (London: HMSO).
UK Central Statistical Office, *National Income and Expenditure*
  (London: HMSO) various years.
Organisation for Economic Co-operation and Development (1978)
  'Revised Study on Past and Present Trends in Industrial
  Investment', mimeo (Paris).
B. R. Mitchell and P. Deane (1971) *Abstract of British
  Historical Statistics* (Cambridge University Press).
E. H. Phelps Brown and M. N. Browne (1973) 'Levels and
  Movements of Industrial Productivity and Real Wages
  Internationally Compared', *Economic Journal*, vol. 83 (March)
  pp. 58-71.

APPENDIX 2

TABLE 7.A1   *Results for the whole economy*

Period	a	b	R^2	γ
1921-30	1.35	0.28	0.47	1.88
1922-31	0.29	0.55	0.79	0.64
1923-32	0.13	0.47	0.82	0.25
1924-33	0.24	0.47	0.86	0.45
1925-34	0.16	0.43	0.88	0.28
1926-35	0.06	0.41	0.90	0.10
1927-36	0.07	0.45	0.88	0.15
1928-37	-0.29	0.50	0.70	-0.58
1929-38	-0.29	0.50	0.70	-0.58
1951-60	0.17	0.66	0.86	0.50
1952-61	0.17	0.67	0.87	0.52
1953-62	0.21	0.65	0.85	0.59

Period	a	b	R^2	γ
1954-63	0.31	0.63	0.80	0.83
1955-64	0.24	0.68	0.85	0.75
1956-65	0.23	0.69	0.86	0.75
1957-66	0.43	0.65	0.86	1.23
1958-67	0.71	0.60	0.73	1.75
1959-68	0.59	0.67	0.64	1.81
1960-69	0.63	0.66	0.62	1.87
1961-70	0.49	0.76	0.64	2.04
1962-71	1.15	0.61	0.51	2.96
1963-72	1.43	0.52	0.43	2.97
1964-73	1.63	0.42	0.41	2.80
1965-74	0.88	0.63	0.52	2.40
1966-75	0.69	0.73	0.70	2.56
1967-76	0.74	0.73	0.70	2.72

NOTES

1. Thanks are due to the UK Social Science Research Council for financial support, and to Chris Freeman, Dan Jones, Roy Turner, Keith Pavitt, Jay Gershuny, Luc Soete, Don Scott-Kemmis and other colleagues for helpful comments and discussions.
2. Using input/output data, Cornwall (1977) illustrates the strength of the links between manufacturing and other sectors.
3. A similar procedure applied to data covering the whole economy shows the same trends. See Appendix 2.
4. Taylor (1972), for example, argues that the large increases in labour productivity which occurred in 1967 and 1968 were caused by a 'shake-out' of previously hoarded labour. This argument and that developed here are not, however, necessarily mutually exclusive.
5. See Griffin (1975).
6. Evidence for a change in the relative contribution of expansion investment is usually sought by assuming that this contribution is reflected in the share of non-residential construction in total investment. This measure is more direct than the approach used here, but it is open to the obvious criticism that an increase in capacity does not necessarily require an increase in factory space.
7. The surveys for West Germany carried out by IFO (Institute for Economic Research, Munich) are particularly useful in that they have been carried out for several years. Commenting on their data, Freeman (1977a) observes that:

'In 1960 over half of German manufacturing companies
(53 per cent) gave expansion of capacity as their
principal reason for investment, but by 1970 this proportion had fallen to 40 per cent, and by 1977 to 15 per
cent.'

8. Schumpeter suggested that the first Kondratieff cycle
(1787-1842) was associated with the introduction of steam
power, the second (1843-97) with railways, and the third
with electric power and automobiles (Schumpeter, 1939;
Kuznets, 1940).

9. Freeman argues that a period of expansion is one in which
the technology leads to a 'bandwagon' of R & D activity,
with new products having a 'demand-creating' effect and
generating employment. The technology thus has a significant positive impact on the economy, but at this stage is
still localised within relatively specialised sectors.
Later, however, it begins to diffuse out to other economic
sectors, leading in many cases to radical changes in the
means of production; this is a period characterised by
'process' rather than 'product' innovation. The period
of recession begins - labour is displaced, competing
industries producing equipment under the older processes
decline, and stagnation results. On this view, the con-
flicting tendencies of labour absorption (through capital
accumulation) and labour displacement operate in such a
way that each is alternately predominant (Freeman, 1977b).

REFERENCES

Cambridge Economic Policy Group (1978) *Economic Policy
  Review*, University of Cambridge, Department of Applied
  Economics, March.
Cornwall, J. (1977) *Modern Capitalism* (London: Martin
  Robertson).
Cripps, F. and R. J. Tarling (1973) *Growth in Advanced
  Capitalist Economies 1950-1970*, University of Cambridge,
  Department of Applied Economics, Occasional Paper no. 40
  (Cambridge University Press).
Freeman, C. (1977a) 'Technical Change and Unemployment',
  paper presented at the Conference on Science, Technology
  and Public Policy: an International Perspective, University
  of New South Wales (1-2 December).
Freeman, C. (1977b) 'The Kondratieff Long Waves, Technical
  Change and Unemployment', paper presented to OECD Paris,
  mimeo.
Griffin, T. (1975) 'Revised Estimates of the Consumption
  and Stock of Fixed Capital', *Economic Trends* (London:

Central Statistical Office, HMSO) pp. 126-9.

Kaldor, N. (1966) *Causes of the Slow Rate of Growth of the United Kingdom* (Cambridge University Press).

Kaldor, N. (1975) 'Economic Growth and the Verdoorn Law', *Economic Journal*, vol. 85, pp. 891-6.

Kondratieff, N. D. (1935) 'The Long Waves of Economic Life', *Review of Economic Statistics*, vol. xvii, no. 6, pp. 105-15.

Kuznets, S. (1940) 'Review of "Business Cycles"', *American Economic Review*, vol. 30, pp. 250-71.

Leicester, C. (1977a) 'Unemployment 2001 AD', Institute of Manpower Studies Report CN120, University of Sussex.

Leicester, C. (1977b) 'Re-running the Employment Function of Model 2001', Institute of Manpower Studies Report IN155, University of Sussex.

McLean, A. A. (1974) 'The Treasury Model', in Worswick, G. D. N. and Blackaby, F. T. (eds), *The Medium Term* (London: Heinemann, 1974).

Organisation for Economic Co-operation and Development (1978) 'Revised Study on Past and Present Trends of Industrial Investment', OECD, DSTI Industry Committee, Paris, mimeo (June).

Rowthorn, R. (1975a) 'What Remains of Kaldor's Law?', *Economic Journal*, vol. 85, pp. 10-19.

Rowthorn, R. (1975b) 'A Reply to Lord Kaldor's Comment', *Economic Journal*, vol. 85, pp. 897-901.

Schumpeter, J. (1935) *Business Cycles* (New York: McGraw Hill).

Taylor, J. (1972) 'The Behaviour of Unemployment and Unfilled Vacancies: Great Britain 1958-1971, an Alternative View', *Economic Journal*, vol. 82, pp. 1352-64.

Verdoorn, P. J. (1949) 'Fattori Che Regolano lo Sviluppo della Productivita del Lavoro', *L'industria*.

Warwick Manpower Research Group (1978) *Britain's Medium-Term Employment Prospects*, ed. by R. Lindley (University of Warwick).

8 Embodied Technical Change and the Age of Capital: Empirical Evidence for Manufacturing Establishments

STUART WABE and DEREK L. BOSWORTH

1 INTRODUCTION

The early work on vintage capital models marked an important departure from the traditional lines of development in the study of production. Embodied technical change became widely accepted as an intuitively plausible concept, and this resulted in a large volume of theoretical and empirical literature. Data used to test the validity of the vintage hypothesis was often unsatisfactory, however, because of its high level of aggregation. Through a lack of incisive evidence, the 'new view' of the world failed to cause the expected demise of the neo-classical theories of production and both have developed, side-by-side. The two theories are, nevertheless, largely competitive, and there have been a number of attempts to establish which approach provides the superior description of the real world.

Tests of alternative models on the basis of macro information are unlikely to reveal distinct differences in the empirical performances of the vintage and non-vintage specifications.[1] The clearest evidence is most likely to come from studies of technical change within particular industries and, for this reason, the research reported by Gregory and James (1973) represents a major contribution, even though their analysis has its problems.[2] Their approach was to compare labour productivity in a sample of new factories with the average for the industry. The results were unfavourable towards the vintage hypothesis for a large number of the Australian manufacturing industries in their sample. In contrast, Gomulka (1976) concluded that the data available for Polish factories gave fairly strong support for the vintage hypothesis. This conclusion is made suspect, however, by the failure to take directly into account the greater capital intensity of new factories. Further evidence of the importance of this omission is provided by our analysis in Section 4, and the implications for the Gomulka conclusions are drawn in Section 5.

Results of simple tests of the vintage hypothesis, along similar lines to those undertaken by Gregory and James (1973), are reported in Section 3. Our work extends the earlier analysis in a number of important ways. First, evidence is provided for a number of economies, including France, India, Israel, Japan and Yugoslavia. Second, with this broader data base it is possible to test whether there are technical reasons why vintage effects appear in particular industries, because such effects should be observed in each of the countries for which data is available. Third, the results reported below are derived by comparing the productivity of plants that own equipment of different ages. This should prove superior to the comparisons of new factory productivity with the average for the industry, used by Gregory and James (1973) and by Gomulka (1976), if only because it avoids any problems arising from the purchase of second-hand equipment for use in new factories.[3]

The simple regression results reported at the end of Section 3 explain labour productivity using an average age and a scale variable. These results give a clear indication that it would be wrong to attribute all of the variation in labour productivity across plants to the effects of embodied technical change. The other authors were also aware of this: Gregory and James (1973, pp. 1144-5), for example, recognised variations in the scale of plant as one of a number of possible influences on labour productivity; Gomulka (1976, p. 861) pointed to the capital intensity of production as a further factor. The earlier authors were unable to take any of these factors directly into account. In contrast, however, the estimates of the vintage effect reported in Section 4 allow for the impact of such additional factors as scale, capital intensity, the level of usage and quality of the inputs. The regression results are for cement and grain milling, two industries for which there were sufficient data.

2 THE SAMPLE OF FACTORIES: DATA SOURCES

The empirical work reported below uses data from a sample of establishments that fall within the 48, 3-digit ISIC manufacturing groups.[4] The data represent 'snap-shots' of individual establishments centred on the mid-1960s. The observations are not a random sample of plants from the total population in each industry and country: UNIDO's intention was to make the sample as relevant as possible in a development planning

context. There is not, however, any reason to believe that
the sampling procedure has introduced any sort of bias in
terms of the analysis reported below.[5]

The UNIDO data is classified by well-defined and homogeneous
product groups, but there is still the problem that a given
establishment can produce more than one product. The description of the product mix and of the relationships between inputs and outputs should, ideally, be based on a well established classification of commodities, but this is not the
case in the present data.[6] The problems of product mix are
very much smaller in the UNIDO data than in most other sources
because the establishment, rather than the enterprise, is used
as the sampling unit. The data are also ideal insofar as the
emphasis is on engineering information and the technology of
production.

In order to retain as much theoretical rigour as possible,
the simple tests of the vintage hypothesis, similar to those
of Gregory and James (1973), use data from a particular industry for one country. As only a small number of observations
are generally available at this level of detail, the form of
the analysis reported in Section 3 is restricted. In order to
carry out the more rigorous tests of the vintage hypothesis
reported in Section 4, it was necessary to pool data across
countries for a given industry. Multiple regression analysis
was applied to the enlarged samples for the cement and grain
milling industries in an attempt to account for a variety of
influences, including the effects of embodied technical change.

There are very real dangers in pooling data from different
countries, but some of the more obvious problems are avoided.
Firstly, we do not have to translate values from different
countries into common units of currency: where comparisons
are made using values, they are restricted to a particular
country; where data for more than one country are pooled, the
information is in physical units. Secondly, a single classi-
ficatory scheme was used to compile the whole body of data,
making the information from different industries and from
different countries as consistent as possible. The construction of the data and the design of the analysis does not,
however, remove all the problems. Pooling data for a number
of countries, even when holding the industry constant, raises
the problem that we implicitly assume plants in a number of
countries choose their new technologies from the same *ex ante*
function.

3   SIMPLE TESTS OF THE VINTAGE HYPOTHESIS

If embodied technical change is the only important influence
on labour productivity, then the simple vintage hypothesis

suggests that, in a situation of rising real wages, factories
with newer equipment should, generally, have a higher labour
productivity than factories with older capital. In order to
facilitate comparisons, the UNIDO sample of plants is divided
into two sets within each industry and country, according to
the age of capital. Where there are an odd number of establishments, then the middle factory, when ranked by its average
age of capital, is allocated to both the 'newer' and 'older'
subsets. Labour productivity in plants with newer capital is
then compared with the productivity in plants with older
capital.

Value added appears to be the most appropriate measure of
output for each plant, and labour productivity is measured
as valued added per worker. The average age of machinery in
an establishment was estimated on the basis of a weighted
average of individual machine ages, weights being either the
replacement or book values of individual machines.[7] As the
observations reported in the UNIDO *Profiles* span a period of
two to three years, the average age of capital is adjusted
to a common, 1964 base (i.e. a two-year-old piece of capital
observed in 1965 was considered to be of the same vintage as
the equivalent one-year-old capital observed in 1964).

The simplest test of the vintage hypothesis is reported in
Tables 8.1-8.5. The results are set out to facilitate comparison between labour productivities associated with the
newer and older plants. Table 8.1 provides information for
France. In the French dairy products industry, for example,
there are four factories, and value added per worker in the
most productive plant was 3.5 times larger than in the least
productive plant. The two dairy product factories with the
newest equipment had an average age of capital of 3.4 years
and average output per employee of 29,670 francs. This com-
pares with an average age of capital of 6.2 years and labour
productivity of 26,054 francs in the sample of old factories.
Thus, in the French dairy products industry, value added per
worker was highest in those factories with the newest capital.
Over all industries, however, Table 8.1 indicates that in
exactly half of the twelve ISICs the factories with the oldest capital had the highest level of labour productivity.

Table 8.2 shows that Japanese industry was working with
relatively new capital. Establishments with the newest capital
had the highest labour productivity in 9 of the 13 industries.
Using the binomial distribution and assuming the outcome is
random (i.e. the probability of each event is 0.5), the probability of recording 4 or fewer instances where the oldest
capital has the highest labour productivity, when considering
13 industries, is 0.133. This indicates that the observed
outcome may well be a chance result and it does not provide

TABLE 8.1   *Labour productivity and age of capital: France*

ISIC[a]	Number of establishments	Productivity range [b]	Average age		Value added per worker[c]	
			Newest	Oldest	Newest	Oldest
202	4	3.49	3.4	6.2	29670	26054
231	4	2.71	6.1	14.6	12575	14900
232	2	1.31	2.8	6.5	9230	12089
251	2	1.07	1.0	8.0	17974	16772
271	2	1.21	8.0	18.0	19400	16100
311	3	2.38	3.5	6.7	58285	36220
334	2	2.03	1.0	14.0	87707	43099
339	3	1.44	3.0	6.0	23175	28770
342	6	1.57	5.5	13.3	22430	27247
350	12	2.86	4.7	12.9	18935	20843
360	8	1.86	5.1	11.0	27418	27621
370	2	1.29	5.0	10.0	22975	17800

a   The industry titles corresponding to the ISIC numbers are given in the Appendix.

b   Highest value divided by lowest value.

c   Francs.

TABLE 8.2 *Labour productivity and age of capital: Japan*

ISIC[a]	Number of establishments	Productivity range[b]	Average age		Value added per worker[c]	
			Newest	Oldest	Newest	Oldest
203	3	1.23	5.4	5.9	468	421
205	2	1.17	4.0	8.0	1416	1214
231	2	1.52	3.0	8.3	1075	706
232	5	1.96	4.4	5.8	628	562
251	2	1.44	5.6	6.0	808	1167
311	3	1.89	4.1	5.5	1815	2447
312	3	1.15	8.3	8.9	1908	1879
313	2	1.22	4.0	6.0	1090	1333
319	2	1.40	1.9	2.2	526	738
341	7	3.49	2.9	6.3	1430	1009
350	15	3.46	3.2	6.2	974	923
360	6	2.04	3.9	7.4	1049	902
385	3	1.47	3.0	6.7	1410	1299

a and b See Table 8.1.

c Thousand yen.

TABLE 8.3 Labour productivity and age of capital: India

ISIC[a]	Number of establishments	Productivity range[b]	Average age		Value added per worker[c]	
			Newest	Oldest	Newest	Oldest
205	2	1.34	14.0	20.0	3460	2582
207	2	1.12	19.2	23.3	1173	1318
231	11	3.71	9.4	26.0	3331	3198
232	2	4.36	4.5	32.0	6770	1554
251	2	1.99	5.0	14.0	6220	3120
300	5	7.24	5.3	11.7	15900	10251
311	8	8.06	4.0	13.0	9254	12715
319	10	6.64	7.0	19.3	8468	5986
331	4	1.42	5.5	8.0	2330	2480
334	4	2.46	8.0	14.5	12580	10097
339	3	1.21	13.0	18.5	7612	7012
341	4	13.56	9.2	22.5	10522	3503
342	2	7.21	2.0	13.0	26456	3670
350	9	5.19	5.7	12.3	4146	4682
360	14	4.84	5.3	8.7	4099	4477
370	9	4.93	2.6	7.2	11543	5335
385	4	2.12	7.1	11.2	4831	6344

[a] and [b] See Table 8.1.

[c] Rupees.

TABLE 8.4 *Labour productivity and age of capital: Israel*

ISIC[a]	Number of establishments	Productivity range [b]	Average age		Value added per worker[c]	
			Newest	Oldest	Newest	Oldest
202	3	1.79	4.5	8.5	10416	10986
203	2	1.84	4.0	5.0	10031	5453
205	4	1.61	10.5	15.5	18980	21075
231	10	3.13	3.3	7.6	10989	8489
251	3	1.84	2.6	3.6	8450	10716
311	6	4.44	1.7	6.5	19836	10497
319	4	3.22	6.7	9.5	16250	10731
334	2	2.10	10.0	17.0	10525	22066
350	4	1.92	5.2	17.7	9271	11941
360	4	2.82	7.2	12.5	16120	14925
383	2	3.13	1.0	10.0	7288	22831

a and b   See Table 8.1

c   Israel £s.

TABLE 8.5　Labour productivity and the age of capital: Yugoslavia

ISIC[a]	Number of establishments	Productivity range[b]	Average age		Value added per worker[c]	
			Newest	Oldest	Newest	Oldest
202	4	1.33	6.0	7.4	1080	922
203	3	1.88	7.4	9.2	728	812
205	4	2.42	4.2	7.6	2154	1510
207	6	3.98	5.1	7.9	2264	1490
231	16	2.31	6.4	9.0	1380	1144
232	13	2.35	4.3	7.0	976	1138
251	10	2.29	6.1	7.7	1031	864
271	3	1.66	5.4	6.9	2090	2170
291	5	1.34	8.2	9.2	1214	1190
300	3	1.40	6.0	6.7	1785	1835
311	9	8.39	4.4	8.9	5136	3256
312	3	1.45	6.5	7.4	2035	1950
319	6	2.18	5.5	7.5	2298	1415
331	7	2.01	6.5	7.8	1167	1175
334	4	1.52	5.5	6.8	1960	2420
339	4	2.22	5.5	6.9	985	1257
342	4	2.32	5.9	8.7	1902	3190
350	16	2.60	6.2	8.7	1174	1285
360	9	2.13	4.9	8.4	1603	1442
370	7	2.73	5.7	7.2	1795	1632
385	3	2.01	6.8	9.8	2050	1360

a　and　b　See Table 8.1.

c　Thousand dinars.

overwhelming support for the vintage hypothesis. It must be
pointed out, however, that in the industries where the oldest
capital was more productive, there was little difference between the average ages of the newest and oldest capital. This
is particularly true for wood products (ISIC 251), chemicals
(311) and other chemical products (319). Of the five countries
for which the data have been analysed, Japan shows most evidence in support of the vintage hypothesis.

The results of the same analysis for 17 Indian industries
are given in Table 8.3. In comparison with France, for example,
Indian factories exhibit a much greater range in their labour
productivities. There is also clear evidence that Indian
factories work with substantially older capital than that employed in France or Japan. Establishments with the newest
capital had the highest level of labour productivity in 11 out
of the 17 industries. The probability of recording 6 or fewer
instances where the oldest capital has the highest labour
productivity, when considering 17 industries, is 0.166, if it
is assumed that both outcomes are equally likely. Again we
cannot be confident that we have found unequivocal evidence
in favour of the vintage hypothesis.

The results for Israel, in Table 8.4, indicate that, in the
majority of industries (6 out of 11), establishments with the
oldest capital had the highest level of value added per worker.
Table 8.5 presents the results for Yugoslavia. There was a
wide spread in the values of labour productivity for establishments in chemicals (ISIC 311) and, to a lesser extent, in
sugar refining (207). In the remaining 19 industries, there
was a relatively narrow range of productivity values. Capital
was relatively modern and there was little variation in the
age of capital between plants in the same industry. Establishments with the newest capital had the highest value added
per worker in 12 of the 21 Yugoslavian industries.

Gregory and James (1973) suggested that the vintage effect
may be unique to particular industries. This can be investigated by considering the results for a particular industry in
each of the countries. Unfortunately, for most industries,
observations are available for only a minority of the countries.
For those industries where there are observations of labour
productivity and the age of capital in all five countries: 4
observations support the vintage hypothesis in textiles (ISIC
231); 3 provide support in wood products (251), chemicals (311)
and non-electrical machinery (360); but only one observation
in the metal products industry (350) provides support for the
vintage hypothesis. Again, there is no instance where overwhelming evidence is found that labour productivity is higher
for the newest capital. Similar comparisons of industries
where observations are available for four countries reinforce

this rather negative conclusion.

Whenever there were eight or more observations for a given industry in one country, an attempt was made to establish the existence of embodied technical change using a naive regression model. Sufficient observations were available for sixteen industries: two in France; one each in Japan and Israel; and six each in India and Yugoslavia. Regressions were estimated[8] where the logarithm of labour productivity appeared as the dependent variable, measured in terms of both value added per worker and value added per man-hour. In the first equation for each industry, labour productivity was regressed on the average age of capital. In a second regression equation, we allow for any scale effects arising from the size of the plant by the inclusion of the logarithm of total employment as an additional explanatory variable.

In the regressions where the age of capital is the sole explanatory variable, only half the coefficients have the expected negative sign, and only two of these coefficients are significantly less than zero. In the second regression, where both the average age of capital and a scale effect appear, the age variable does not perform any better, and, in addition, the coefficients on employment are significantly different from zero in only 6 of the 32 cases. The significant scale parameters are implausibly large and appear to be the result of extreme observations. In conclusion, this further analysis has revealed almost no support for the hypothesis that labour productivity is greater for newer capital. Furthermore, the values of R^2 were usually low, and we can be confident that there are other important variables, in addition to any scale effects, that, so far, have been omitted from the analysis. In the light of these results, a more rigorous explanation for the variation in labour productivity is reported in the next section.

4   VINTAGE EFFECTS: A DETAILED STUDY OF TWO INDUSTRIES

Our final attempt to isolate the vintage effect uses data from the cement (ISIC 334) and grain milling (205) industries. In this study, the outputs can be measured meaningfully in physical units and, because this avoids any problems of conversion between currencies, it is possible to undertake a cross-country analysis with some degree of confidence. The basic hypothesis is that labour productivity, measured as tons per worker, will be related to: the capital intensity of production; the levels of capital and labour usage; the quality of the labour input; the size of the plant (scale effect); and, finally, the age of the capital stock (vintage effect).

The most general function estimated is of the log-linear
form[9]

$$\log\left(\frac{Y}{L}\right) = a + b \log\left(\frac{K}{L^*}\right) + c \log (KU) + d \log (LQ)$$
$$+ e \log (LU) + f \log (L) + g V + u$$

where; Y denotes output; K is the stock of capital and KU a
measure of capital usage; L is the total input of labour and
L^* is total employment on the first shift; LU is a measure of
labour usage and LQ denotes the quality of the labour input;
V denotes the average age of capital; u is a random error
term.

Capital intensity, K/L^*, is measured as the installed
capacity of electric motors, in kilowatts, divided by the
number employed on the first shift. The extent to which capital is utilised, KU, is measured as actual electricity consumption divided by the theoretical maximum, assuming con-
tinuous working of the plant.

The cross-section includes such diverse countries as France
and India and hence there is a need to take account of the
significant variation in the education and skill of employees.
Average earnings will be the most appropriate proxy measure
of labour quality. However, we do not wish to convert between
currencies but require, if possible, some physical measure of
labour quality. A summary measure of the quality of the labour
input, LQ, is constructed by dividing the average hourly
earnings of production workers by the unit price of the output.
Measuring an hour's labour in terms of tons of cement or of
flour has the advantage of showing little variation for factories within a country and substantial differences between
countries.

The labour usage variable, LU, is constructed as the average
number of hours worked by production workers, divided by 2920,
the number of hours that would be worked in total on an eight-
hour shift over a whole year. The labour input, L, is simply
total employment, and this is included in order to isolate
plant economies of scale. Finally, it is assumed that labour
productivity is an exponential function of the average age of
capital, V, with older capital being less efficient than
newer capital.

The results of five regression equations for cement are
reported in the first half of Table 8.6. These equations have
been estimated using data for 15 establishments in six countries. Variations in output per worker appear to be determined
by three factors: the capital intensity of production, the
level of capital usage and the quality of the labour input.
Neither the labour usage nor the scale variable has a

TABLE 8.6 *Least-squares regression explanation for variation in logarithm of output per worker in cement and grain milling*

Explanatory variables	Cement					Grain milling				
Log capital per worker	0.799 (0.128)[a]	0.795 (0.134)	0.806 (0.130)	0.800 (0.133)	0.801 (0.139)	0.611 (0.127)	0.571 (0.123)	0.583 (0.147)	0.603 (0.140)	0.585 (0.143)
Log capital usage	0.574 (0.178)	0.593 (0.190)	0.651 (0.201)	0.526 (0.208)	0.482 (0.257)	0.918 (0.118)	0.886 (0.114)	0.901 (0.129)	0.918 (0.123)	0.901 (0.126)
Log labour quality	0.372 (0.084)	0.371 (0.087)	0.302 (0.117)	0.376 (0.087)	0.422 (0.165)	0.213 (0.107)	0.295 (0.115)	0.206 (0.112)	0.205 (0.120)	0.174 (0.127)
Log labour usage		-0.195 (0.471)					0.877 (0.580)			
Log number employed			-0.103 (0.119)					-0.039 (0.090)		
Average age capital				0.006 (0.012)	0.016 (0.034)				0.004 (0.022)	-0.005 (0.024)
(Dummy) (Average age capital)					-0.010 (0.032)					0.016 (0.018)
Constant	-2.223 (0.463)	-2.229 (0.482)	-1.633 (0.827)	-2.304 (0.508)	-2.336 (0.541)	-1.618 (0.294)	-1.332 (0.337)	-1.411 (0.570)	-1.637 (0.325)	-1.651 (0.329)
R^2	0.954	0.955	0.957	0.955	0.956	0.932	0.944	0.934	0.933	0.937

[a] Figures in brackets are estimated standard errors.

significant impact on labour productivity. Their inclusion,
in the second and third equations for the cement industry,
results in insignificant coefficients and no improvement in
explanatory power. They are not closely correlated with the
other explanatory variables and their inclusion or exclusion
does not greatly affect the size or significance of the first
three coefficients. We conclude that there is no benefit to
be gained at the plant level by raising the level of labour
usage or by increasing the scale of the plant in this industry.
In the fourth and fifth equations for cement, it can be seen
that the age of capital also plays no significant role in the
explanation of labour productivity. The fifth equation allows
the *ex ante* function to differ between the developed and less
developed countries. Thus, average age is allowed to have a
different impact on labour productivity in the eight observations for France, Israel and 'Middle Europe' than in the remaining, less developed, countries. There were insufficient
observations to allow for the existence of a different *ex ante*
function in each country. In neither of the cases reported,
however, did the variable show any signs of making a significant contribution. It was not multi-collinear with any of
the other variables and did not greatly alter the sizes and
significance of the other estimated coefficients, although
the fifth equation showed more signs of change than did the
fourth equation. The coefficients indicate that the average
age of capital does not have a significant impact on labour
productivity in the cement industry.

Table 8.6 also reports the results of the same regression
equations for grain milling. These have been estimated using
data for 16 establishments in seven countries. There are substantial differences between the sizes of equivalent coefficients in the two industries. In grain milling, as in the
cement industry, capital intensity, capital usage and labour
quality play the most important roles in the explanation of
labour productivity. However, the labour quality variable is
not quite significant, at the 5 per cent level, for grain
milling. The scale and vintage variables again make insignificant contributions. The dummy variable for grain milling
has the value unity in the nine observations for Israel,
Japan and 'Middle Europe'.

5 CONCLUSIONS

Our main conclusion is almost identical to that drawn by
Gregory and James.[10] If age can be assumed to be an adequate
reflection of the vintage of capital then, if vintage effects
are present, their impact on labour productivity varies

substantially across industries in each of the countries for
which observations are available. There is also no real evidence from our sample that, for technical reasons, vintage
effects characterise particular industries, because industries
which appear to comply with the vintage hypothesis in one
country fail to do so in others. The detailed analysis of the
cement and grain milling industries reveals that the key
variables in the explanation of variations in labour productivity are the amount of capital per worker, the level of
capital usage and the quality of the labour force.

Our finding that capital per worker is a crucial factor
influencing labour productivity is relevant to the study of
Polish manufacturing industries reported by Gomulka (1976).
Output per worker (Y/L) in new factories was 2.13 times
greater than the average for all industry. As the capital/
output ratio (K/Y) in new factories was only 1.17 times
greater than the industry average, Gomulka (1976, p. 861)
interpreted the large gain in labour productivity as 'pre-
dominantly a vintage effect'. However, it follows directly from
these two statistics that the level of capital per worker (K/L)
in new factories was 2.49 times greater than the average,[11]
and this cannot be ignored when considering the increase in
labour productivity. If we take the elasticity of labour
productivity with respect to capital intensity as being 0.6
(see values in Table 8.6), then the increase in capital per
worker in new Polish factories might be expected to cause a
73 per cent rise in output per worker.[12] We might also expect
workers in the new factories to be better qualified than the
average and there to be incentives to achieve higher rates of
utilisation in the more capital intensive plants. Both these
factors can be expected to give rise to higher levels of labour
productivity. Thus, the large productivity jump recorded for
new factories in Poland may be explained by factors other than
the vintage effect of new capital.

The accumulating evidence suggests that the vintage theory
has reached an important crossroads on its evolutionary path.
It would, even now, be premature to conclude that the vintage
hypothesis is clearly refuted. Despite the lack of favourable
evidence, embodied technical change and the associated vintage
hypothesis remain intuitively plausible. At this stage, it
would be more sensible not to dismiss the concept out of hand,
but to recognise that the fitting of the simplest of vintage
functions to plant level (or more aggregate) data is unlikely
to result in unequivocal support for the vintage hypothesis.
There are, for example, important deficiencies in most of the
studies. Detailed analysis of the role played by trends in
relative factor prices, for example, has, so far, not been
undertaken in the literature. If the price of capital

persistently increased relative to that of labour, even the
simplest of vintage models, with an *ex ante* function exhibi-
ting substitution possibilities, may indicate a labour-using
bias in the choice of new technology. Real world trends in
relative factor prices may differ between industries in a
given country, and between countries for a given industry.
In addition, certain elements of the vintage theory still
wait to be properly developed. A particularly weak link appears
to be the *ex ante* function which is at the interface of R & D
and production. Except for passing reference,[13] there has been
no formal integration of imperfect knowledge and risk into the
ex ante decisions of vintage theory. Rosenberg (1976), for
example, makes a number of comments relevant to this study
and to the work of Gregory and James (1973) and Gomulka (1976).
In particular, he has pointed to teething problems as a reason
why new technology may have relatively higher costs and, in
consequence, firms may choose to buy new capital but of an
older vintage.

APPENDIX

The ISIC numbers shown in Tables 8.1-8.5 refer to the following industry groups: 202 - dairy products; 203 - food canning;
205 - grain milling; 207 - sugar refineries; 231 - textiles;
232 - knitting mills; 251 - wood products; 271 - paper and
pulp; 291 - leather products; 300 - rubber products; 311 -
chemicals; 312 - vegetable and animal oils; 313 - paints;
319 - other chemical products; 331 - building materials;
334 - cement; 339 - concrete and asbestos products; 341 -
ferrous metals; 342 - non-ferrous metals; 350 - metal products;
360 - non-electrical machinery; 370 - electrical machinery;
383 - motor vehicles; 385 - bicycles.

NOTES

1. For a brief review, see Gregory and James, 1973, p. 1133.
2. Haig (1975) and Bosworth (1976, pp. 30-3) provide a number
   of detailed comments, but see also Gregory and James (1975).
3. Gregory and James (1973, p. 1138) dismiss the problem as
   unimportant.
4. *Profiles of Manufacturing Establishments*, vol. 1 (1967)
   UNIDO, Industrial Planning and Programming Series, no. 4,
   United Nations, New York; *Profiles*, vol. 2 (1968) UNIDO,
   Industrial Planning and Programming Series, no. 5, United
   Nations, New York; *Profiles*, vol. 3 (1971) UNIDO, Industrial
   Planning and Programming Series, no. 6, United Nations,

New York.

5. *Profiles* (1967, p. 5) provides a detailed description of the types of establishments that are included in the sample.

6. *Profiles* (1967, p. 3).

7. *Profiles* (1967, p. 9).

8. These results are not reported. However, they can be obtained by writing to one of the authors.

9. Similar functions have been estimated elsewhere; see Griliches and Ringstad (1971, pp. 66-70) and Bosworth (1976, pp. 110-19).

10. Gregory and James (1973, p. 1153) state: 'If our sample of new factories is at all typical, then the age of factories is not an important explanatory agent of the dispersion of value added per worker within each industry.'

11. $\frac{K}{L} = \frac{Y}{L} \cdot \frac{K}{Y} = (2.13)\ (1.17) = 2.49.$

12. $(2.49)^{0.6} = 1.73.$

13. See Johansen (1972, pp. 6-9) and Bosworth (1976, pp. 44-60).

REFERENCES

Bosworth, D.L. (1976) *Production Functions: A Theoretical and Empirical Study* (Farnborough, Hants: Saxon House).

Gomulka, S. (1976) 'Do New Factories Embody Best Practice Technology? - New Evidence', *Economic Journal*, vol. 86, pp. 859-63.

Gregory, R. G. and D. W. James (1973) 'Do New Factories Embody Best Practice Technology?', *Economic Journal*, vol. 83, pp. 1133-55.

Gregory, R. G. and D. W. James (1975) 'Do New Factories Embody Best Practice Technology? - a Reply', *Economic Journal*, Vol. 85, pp. 378-82.

Griliches, Z. and V. Ringstad (1971) *Economies of Scale and the Form of the Production Function: An Econometric Study of Norwegian Manufacturing Establishment Data* (Amsterdam: North Holland).

Haig, B. D. (1975) 'Do New Factories Embody Best Practice Technology? - a Comment', *Economic Journal*, vol. 85, pp. 383-8.

Johansen, L. (1972) *Production Functions: An Integration of Micro and Macro, Short Run and Long Run Aspects* (Amsterdam: North Holland).

Rosenberg, N. (1976) 'On Technological Expectations', *Economic Journal*, vol. 86, pp. 523-35.

9 A Model for Long-run Forecasts of Employment in Industrial Sectors

SÖREN WIBE

1 INTRODUCTION

This chapter presents a simple model for the time path of the demand for labour in a sector in the economy. The model is general in the sense that it can be used for all factors of production, but it has special relevance for labour.

The starting point is the identity

$$v \equiv \frac{v}{q} \cdot q,$$

where v is the amount of the factor in question and q is total production of the good in the sector. The total model, $v = f(t)$, where t is time, is constructed by combining two models, one for the time development of v/q and one for the time development of q. The development of v/q is described by a model of technological progress in the sector and the development of q is described by a model for the time path of total demand.

The central theme of the paper is the introduction of *limits*, both for technological progress and for total demand. Technological progress is pictured as the successive realisation of a 'limited space of possibilities', and the development of total demand as the successive satisfaction of a 'limited space of needs' for the good in question.

The model is tested on three sectors: Swedish Pulp Industry, Swedish Railway Traffic and Swedish Telephone Communication, all for the period 1911-78. These sectors were chosen to achieve dispersion in the categories of goods covered. The total model, $v = f(t)$, is not tested directly, but the two fundamental models (for v/q and q) are tested separately and then combined before comparing these results with real observations (v,t). This procedure is adopted, at this stage, in order to test the empirical explanatory power of the two underlying models before testing the total model directly.

A brief description of the model of technological progress is presented in Section 2. A short presentation of the model for total demand appears in Section 3. The total model is

144   *Employment and Technological Change*

analysed in Section 4, and the empirical results are presented in Section 5. The chapter concludes with a summary in Section 6.

2 THE MODEL OF TECHNOLOGICAL PROGRESS

Let us assume a production function

$$q = f(v_1, \ldots, v_n). \tag{1}$$

When introducing technological progress, we usually introduce a function $A(t)$, and let

$$q(t) = A(t)\, f(v_1, \ldots, v_n) \tag{2}$$

in the case of Hicks neutral progress (generalised to the case of n factors of production). $A(t)$ is a function giving the rate of technological progress, and the usual assumption about the properties of $A(t)$ is

$$\frac{\frac{dA}{dt}}{A} = \left(\frac{\dot{A}}{A}\right) = k, \tag{3}$$

where k is a constant. $A(t)$ then becomes the (well-known) exponential function, and production (with constant amounts of factors) then grows exponentially over time.

The reason for assuming (3) is seldom made explicit, but it seems probable that this form is chosen foremost because of its simplicity. However, it can be fruitful to use other forms for the function $A(t)$, since (3) implies that an arbitrarily great amount of goods can be produced from a given set of inputs. This is not a realistic picture, however; on the contrary, there will generally be a definite maximum that can be produced from a given set of factors, even though we assume that the technological knowledge is developed to its maximum.[1] An alternative assumption is

$$\frac{\dot{A}}{A} = C_1\,(C_2 - A(t)), \tag{4}$$

where the C_i are constants. This gives, for $A(t)$,

$$A(t) = \frac{C_2}{1 + C_3 e^{C_4 t}} \tag{5}$$

where C_3 and C_4 are new constants (C_3 a constant of integration and C_4 determined from equation (4)).

Assumption (4) is an assumption of a 'bounded space' of technological possibilities. It holds that

$$\lim_{t \to \infty} A(t) = C_2 ,$$

(6)

i.e. that there exists an upper limit for $A(t)$.

A short interpretation of assumption (4) can be given if we write (4) as

$$\dot{A} = C_1 \cdot A(t) \cdot (C_2 - A(t)) .$$

(4')

The speed of the technological progress (i.e. $\dot{A}$) is determined by two factors: $A(t)$ and $C_2 - A(t)$. The more $A(t)$ grows, the more the general knowledge of the process in question grows. This knowledge, however, forms a base for future growth, and the possibilities of new discoveries in the field is assumed to be proportional to this base. There exists, however, a finite space of technological possibilities and the more $A(t)$ grows, the more this space is exhausted. The possibilities of new technical discoveries are then also seen as proportional to the 'room of undiscovered possibilities' (i.e. $C_2 - A(t)$). The result of all this is then model (4).

The model presented is 'technical' in the sense that economic variables do not enter as determinants of the path for $A(t)$. This may, however, not be an unrealistic picture. It is well known that many factors influence the rate of technological progress: science; individual inventors; the efforts of individual firms; etc. The total outcome of this whole process may well be a time path that is largely independent of the development of prices, something that appears as just 'given from above' to the individual firm.

In principle, there is nothing preventing us from using model (4) wherever we now use model (3). In fact, it may even be a realistic picture of a whole economy to assume a finite amount of technological possibilities. However, I think that the best application of the model is on separate production processes and specific machines, where the finite technological space can be accurately motivated on technological grounds. This model, or some form of it, is also used in the engineering literature, when picturing the time development of some technical 'figures of merit' (e.g. the degree of efficiency of a machine).

In this chapter the model has also been used on separate
production processes. This allows some rather drastic assumptions to be made about the form of the production function.
I assume here that these are of the Leontief type, i.e. of
the form

$$Q = \min (a_1 v_1, \ldots, a_n v_n), \tag{7}$$

where the a_i are the fixed coefficients of production. In
this production model, technological progress is equal to the
lowering of the input coefficients v_i/q $(=1/a_i)$, and if we
assume the progress model (4), the time path of the input
coefficients takes the form

$$\frac{v_i}{q} = c_1^i + c_2^i \cdot e^{c_3^i t}, \tag{8}$$

where the c_j^i now are new constants, with C_1, $C_2 > 0$ and $C_3 < 0$.

When estimating the input coefficients according to (8), it
is often possible to calculate the value of C_1 theoretically.
C_1 is the lower limit for the coefficient, and this value can
often be determined directly from the physical laws that
govern the process. This is especially true for materials
and energy. The consumption of coke per ton of iron in a blast
furnace is, for instance, at least about 373 kg; the consumption of wood when making pulp is at least 2 m³ per ton; and
so on.

In this respect, the labour factor presents special problems.
It is, as a rule, impossible to calculate a technologically-
determined minimum requirement here. This fact should indicate
that C_1 is given the value 0, but, of course, this would be an
approximation. No process can be fully automated (i.e. the
labour input coefficient must always exceed zero). One way of
estimating the value for C_1 in the case of labour could be to
start with labour requirement per plant, and try to find this
minimum value. The analysis could then proceed to make an
estimation of maximum production per plant. In agriculture,
for example, the space dimension is vital. One farmer cannot
run a farm greater than a certain area. This, together with
the fact that total production per unit of land has an upper
limit, sets the lower limit for the labour coefficient. In
other cases, for instance when we cannot single out individual
production units (e.g. railways, telecommunications), it might
be possible to determine a lower limit required to operate the

whole sector. The lower limit for the input coefficient will
then be determined by the eventually existing upper limit for
total production in the sector.

In the empirical part of this chapter, however, it is assumed that C_1 for labour is approximately 0. It is, I think, a
realistic approximation for all three sectors under consideration.

3 THE MODEL OF TOTAL DEMAND

Concerning the model for total demand, one has to decide
whether to analyse short-run developments (i.e. 10-20 years)
or long-run trends. A suitable model for short-run purposes
is

$$q(t) = \frac{A_1}{1 + A_2 e^{A_3 t}} . \tag{9}$$

This model is frequently used in business economics when
picturing the life cycle of a product. The arguments for its
use might run as follows.

Let us assume that the overall development of an economy
creates a demand for a product. From the point of utility,
there exists an upper limit for its use, and additional output
over this limit will meet no demand. The product can, however,
be used by many persons and firms for a variety of uses. The
more this product is actually used, the more people and firms
receive information about its properties and potential use.
In this manner, new possibilities of using it for special
purposes are discovered. However, the more the product is used,
the more this diminishes the potential possibilities, and demand begins, ultimately, to flatten out towards its equilibrium
value. The most simple model taking account of all this is (9),
a complete analogy to the technical progress model: demand is
stimulated by actual use and hampered by the upper limit of
potential possibilities.

For long-run trend purposes, model (9) can be used, but
$q(t)$ must now be interpreted as demand per capita, and t must
be substituted by income per person, $y(t)$. The reason for
using this model can be found in extensive empirical research.
Many studies have revealed an upper limit for the consumption
per person of certain products, i.e. food, cars, TV etc.
(Prais, 1954; Wold, 1952). Several studies have also revealed
that the Engel curve (i.e. the relationship between income
and demand for a product) has a logistic shape (see, for

example, Aitchinson and Brown, 1954). In all, empirical evidence suggests that model (9), with the alterations made above, is a good statistical description of demand when income per person rises over time.

This paper focuses on long-run trends, and, for the sake of convenience only, model (9) is used directly, without taking into account the rise in population and the rise in income per person. These approximations are not, however, too drastic. The rise in population was only about 0.5 per cent per year in the period studied (which was insignificant when compared to the overall rise in total demand). In addition, if the income per person follows a linear curve over time, it does not matter whether we use t or $y(t)$ in equation (9). As a linear curve actually is a good description for the time period, it is not too drastic to substitute $y(t)$ for t. One must, however, remember that these approximations are made for the sake of convenience only.

4 ANALYSIS OF THE TOTAL MODEL

Combining models (8) and (9) yields the time path for a factor of production,

$$v(t) = (C_1 + C_2 e^{C_3 t}) \left(\frac{A_1}{1 + A_2 e^{A_3 t}} \right). \tag{10}$$

When analysing the properties of the function $v = f(t)$, two cases are considered: (i) $C_1 = 0$; (ii) $C_1 > 0$. These two cases correspond, in general, to labour and 'other factors' respectively. As the analysis is very simple mathematically, just the main results are summarised:

(i) $C_1 = 0$. We have here three cases depending on the relationship between C_3 and A_3.

(a) $A_3 > C_3$. *Properties:* (i) f decreases with time;
(ii) $\lim_{t \to \infty} v(t) = 0$, $\lim_{t \to -\infty} v(t) = \infty$.

(b) $A_3 = C_3$. *Properties:* (i) f decreases with time;
(ii) $\lim_{t \to \infty} v(t) = 0$, $\lim_{t \to -\infty} v(t) = \frac{A_1 C_2}{A_2}$.

(c) $A_3 < C_3$. *Properties:* (i) f has a bell-shaped curve over time;

(ii) $\lim\limits_{t \to \infty} v(t) = \lim\limits_{t \to -\infty} v(t) = 0.$

(ii) $C_1 > 0.$

(a) $A_3 > C_3$. *Properties:* (i) f initially falls with time, reaches its minimum, rises, and approaches $A_1 C_1$ asymptotically from below;

(ii) $\lim\limits_{t \to -\infty} v(t) = \infty,$ $\lim\limits_{t \to \infty} v(t) = A_1 C_1.$

(b) $A_3 = C_3$. *Properties:* (i) f has a logistic curve, rising steadily with time, but with decreasing growth rate;

(ii) $\lim\limits_{t \to -\infty} v(t) = 0,$ $\lim\limits_{t \to \infty} v(t) = A_1 C_1.$

(c) $A_3 < C_3$. *Properties:* (i) f raises towards a maximum point, falls, and approaches $A_1 C_1$ asymptotically from above;

(ii) $\lim\limits_{t \to -\infty} v(t) = 0,$ $\lim\limits_{t \to \infty} v(t) = A_1 C_1.$

5 EMPIRICAL RESULTS

The total model, (10), can be used for a direct statistical estimation by regression. In this chapter, however, the two fundamental models are estimated separately, and then the estimated values (v, t) from these are compared with actual observations.

The factor used is labour. In all three cases, the theoretical minimum value for the input coefficient is assumed to be 0. Data for the labour input coefficient were obtained by dividing total labour input in the sector by total production for each year of observation.

The sectors chosen are: (I) Swedish Pulp Industry (production is here measured as the total production of dry pulp in tons); (II) Swedish Railway Traffic (where production is measured as axle-kilometres per year); and (III) Swedish Telephone Communication (where production is measured in numbers of talking periods during the year - a period is a 3-minute telephone call).

5.1 *Results for Technological Progress*

Table 9.1 gives the results for the technological progress model.

TABLE 9.1   *Results of the least-squares regression with the model $v/q = C_2 e^{C_3 t}$*

Swedish industry	v/q	C_2	C_3	R^2	DW
I Pulp	(h/ton)	56.94	-0.038	0.90	0.37
II Railways	(h/axle-km)	0.106	-0.022	0.89	0.78
III Telephone Communication	(h/period)	0.045	-0.030	0.92	0.36

v/q = labour hours per unit of output. Yearly observations every third year, 1911-78. All estimated C_i significant at the 99% level.

As can be seen from the values of R^2, the estimated curve fits the observations well. The Durbin-Watson values are, however, very low, indicating strong correlation in the error terms. However, considering the long time period involved here, this result is not surprising. Technological progress often follows 'long waves', and was, for instance, considerably slower during the periods between the two world wars than in the period after World War II. However, the result emphasises that we must interpret the curve as a *long-run curve* and not as a curve that can predict what will happen from year to year.

5.2 *Results for Growth of Total Demand and Production*

Table 9.2 gives estimates for the demand model.

TABLE 9.2   *Results of the least-squares regression with the model $q = \dfrac{A_1}{1 + A_2 e^{A_3 t}}$*

Swedish industry	p	A_1	A_2	A_3
I Pulp	(tons x 10^6)	12.5	26.0	-0.0502
II Railways	(axle-km x 10^6)	4704.2	4.5	-0.0485
III Telephone Communication	(periods x 10^6)	53796.0	175.4	-0.0598

q = number of produced units (per year). Data based on yearly observations every third year, 1911-78. All A_i significant at the 99% level.

The objective function cannot be put in linear form, and ordinary regression programs can therefore not be used. The special program used does not give the values of the regression coefficient or Durbin-Watson statistic, so, in order to give the reader some appreciation of the goodness of fit, figures have been drawn showing the estimated curve together with the observations. These curves are shown in Figures 9.1, 9.2 and 9.3. As can be seen from these figures, the curves fit fairly well. Especially for Sectors I and II, one can easily see that the deviations are systematically spread around the curve, indicating a low DW value.

Something must be said regarding the estimation of these logistic curves. The resulting curve is S-shaped. A reliable estimate of the curve requires observations along all its shape, otherwise the estimates of the long-run equilibrium value (i.e. A_1) will be extremely uncertain. Usually, however, observations above the point of inflexion of the curve are very rare. This is because the time period just passed (i.e. the 1950s and 1960s) was a period of rapid growth in almost all industrial sectors. In this special case, the estimations regarding railway traffic can be regarded as fairly accurate. The long-run equilibrium value (4.7 billion axle-kilometres per year) is in accordance with the long-run forecasts of the industry. Turning to telecommunications, however, the estimates are extremely uncertain, due to the rapid growth of production in the last two decades. The result, 54 billion periods, must therefore be viewed with a good deal of scepticism. (Current production is about 20 billion periods.) Regarding pulp, the problems were even greater. Initially, totally unrealistic results were obtained, namely 35 million tons, an amount that would have required raw material amounting to three times the total growth of the forests in Sweden. Instead of adding a production constraint, an additional data point of 10 million tons in the year of 2000 was added. This figure was drawn from the one long-term forecast for the industry. The obtained value of the equilibrium production, 12.5 million tons, is accordingly realistic only if the referred to long-run forecast is also. The method adopted (i.e. combining statistical analysis with information of another kind) does, however, seem reasonable in the type of analysis conducted here.

5.3 *Results for the Total Model*

If the estimates in Sections 5.1 and 5.2 are combined, one
obtains an estimate for the time path of total employment
in the sectors (measured in hours worked). Finally, this
curve is compared with the direct observations. The results
can be found in Figures 9.3, 9.4 and 9.5.

In Figure 9.3, the result for the pulp industry is depicted.
As can be seen, both the estimated curve and the observations
have a bell-shaped form. The maximum for the curve seems to
correspond fairly closely in time to the actual maximum (i.e.
around 1950). However, the curve seems to be displaced downward and somewhat wide compared to actual observations. It
seems that a direct estimation of v against t (with model (10))
should be able to give a better fit.

The result for railway traffic is depicted in Figure 9.4.
As can be seen, the deviations are fairly large, but as a
long-run curve, the estimates seem to be quite reasonable.
The maximum for the curve, however, is around 1940, while the
maximum for the observations seems to be close to 1960.

Finally the result for telephone communications is shown
in Figure 9.6. The observations seem to fit well with the
curve, especially up to 1960. According to observations,
however, it seems that the maximum in employment has already
been reached, as the values for the period 1960–80 are almost
the same. According to the curve, however, a maximum should
occur around 1990 at a value about 15 per cent higher than
the largest observations.

6 CONCLUDING SUMMARY

In this chapter, a model has been presented for the time path
of factors of production, especially labour, in three sectors
of the economy. The model combines a theory of technological
progress with a model of the development of total demand and
production of the product. The model is used for evaluating
a long-run curve for employment in different sectors.

The empirical results point to a good fit for the model of
technological progress. In each case, however, the Durbin-
Watson statistics were relatively low, indicating systematic
errors in the functional form. This result can be explained
by the long-run character of the estimates. A comparison between the actual values of employment and the values predicted
by the curve stressed this point. The deviations were large,
but as a long-run curve, the results were not unrealistic.
The model presented could, therefore, be used as a convenient
statistical tool in analysing the long-run developments for

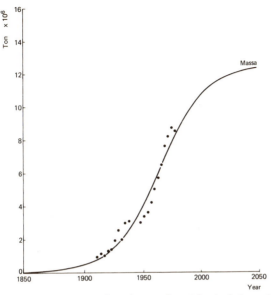

FIGURE 9.1 *Observed production and estimated trend for pulp*

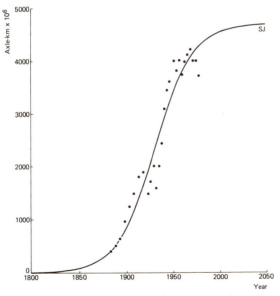

FIGURE 9.2 *Observed production and estimated trend*
for railway traffic

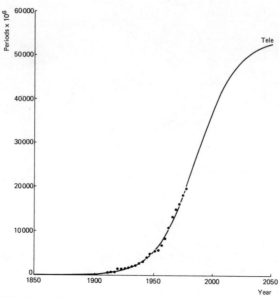

FIGURE 9.3   *Observed production and estimated trend
for telephone communications*

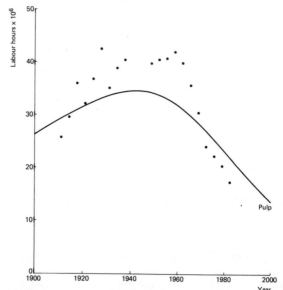

FIGURE 9.4   *Total employment in the pulp industry:
observed values and estimated trend*

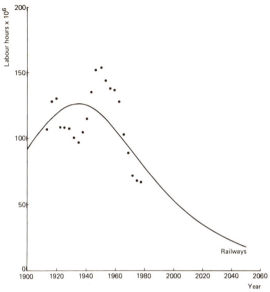

FIGURE 9.5 *Total employment in railway traffic:*
observed values and estimated trend

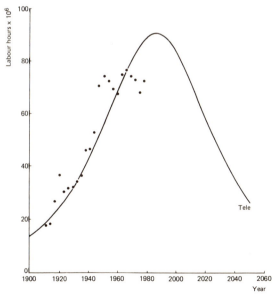

FIGURE 9.6 *Total employment in telephone communications:*
observed values and estimated trend

factors of production in industrial sectors.

NOTE

1. This is the same as saying that factor input per unit of
   output has a lower limit. This is most certainly the case
   for material and energy inputs in most processes.

REFERENCES

Aitchinson, I. and I. A. C. Brown (1954) 'A Synthesis of
   Engel Curve Theory', *Review of Economic Studies*, vol. 22,
   pp. 35–46.
Prais, S. L. (1954) 'Non-linear Estimates of the Engel Curve'
   Review of Economic Studies, vol. 20, pp. 87–104.
Wold, H. (1952) *Demand Analysis* (Stockholm: Almqvist and
   Wiksell).

10 Consequences of Technological Change: the Case of the Shipbuilding Industry

RICHARD HARRISON

1 INTRODUCTION

Despite an awakening of interest in the last decade, it remains true that the shipbuilding industry has attracted less attention from economists and economic historians than its importance to the economy over the last century has deserved. One important reason for this has been the very close link between the shipbuilding and shipping industries, reflected in the existence of close financial and organisational ties between shipbuilders and shipowners and shipping companies throughout the late nineteenth and early twentieth centuries (Robertson, 1974). In the light of Britain's considerable dominance of world trade throughout this period (Hoffmann, 1955, p. 81), economic historians have concentrated on the study of the shipping industry rather than the capital goods industry which supplied it (Jones, 1957, pp. 7-8).

This neglect is surprising, however, given the increasing interest in the process of technological change, all forms of which have a tendency towards spatially, temporally and sectorally localised patterns of evolution (Siebert, 1969). In particular, the development of the shipbuilding industry, both in Britain and the rest of the world, 'offers most valuable lessons for the study of the influence of fundamental technical changes after 1860 on the organisation of the firm, on the accumulation of capital, the growth of the market and the organisation of masters and men for bargaining' (Pollard, 1951, p. iii), and provides specific opportunity for the examination of the employment consequences of technological change.

Technology and technological change are, of course, complex constellations of concepts which defy concise definition. However, in the broadest sense, technology can be understood as 'society's pool of knowledge regarding the industrial arts' (Mansfield, 1968, p. 10), comprising the available set of techniques, processes and products in an economy at any given time. Accordingly, 'the rate at which new technology is produced in any period is the rate of technological progress

157

. . . When an enterprise produces a good or service or uses
a method or input that is new to it, it makes a technological
change' (Schmookler, 1966, p. 2). In this chapter, no differ-
entiation will be made between the invention of a new product,
service, process or input and its diffusion and adoption
through an economic system. If it is accepted that an innovation is an idea perceived as new by an individual, 'it really
matters very little, as far as human behaviour is concerned,
whether or not an idea is "objectively" new as measured by
the amount of time elapsed since its first use or discovery.
It is the newness of the idea to the individual that determines
his reaction to it' (Rodgers, 1962, p. 13). Instead, technological change will be treated as a single transformation process
occurring in and affecting an economic system or subsystem.

As technology can neither be assumed to be given, and thus
effectively ignored, nor taken to be a constant over time (see
Johnson, 1975), technological change has been seen as a primary
constraint on the long-run rate of growth of an economy (Solow,
1957). Many studies of economic growth in the developed world
emphasise that the increase in industrial output which occurred in the nineteenth and early twentieth centuries cannot
be accounted for by increases in the inputs of land, labour
and capital alone (see, *inter alia*, Deane, 1967; Hartwell,
1971; Youngson, 1972; Abramovitz, 1956; Maddison, 1964;
Denison, 1967). While often treated as a residual variable,
accounting for that growth in output not explained by input
changes, the rate of technological change has been observed to
vary between countries (Boretsky, 1975), between industries
and sectors (Salter, 1966; Landes, 1969), between firms
(Freeman, 1974), between regions (Pred, 1966) and, of course,
over time (Cameron, 1975).

Investigation of the employment consequences of technological
change has followed one of two not entirely separate directions.
On the one hand, are studies of aggregate structural changes in
national and international economies, either historically (for
example, Walker, 1980) or with reference to contemporary trends
in employment and unemployment (for example, Rothwell and
Zegfeld, 1979). On the other hand, are detailed micro-level
studies of changes in factor combinations and cost structures
affecting the performance and viability of particular industries and sectors of the economy in specific locations (see,
for example, the case studies in Pavitt, 1980, Part II).
Empirical study of the transfer of specific technologies in
particular industries can be carried out on a number of temporal, geographical and industrial scales. In the case of the
shipbuilding industry, four levels of analysis can be identified, at which employment consequences of technological change
can be observed. First, within the firm, product and process

innovations will lead to changes in the occupational structure
of the labour force and hence to a changing relationship with
the local labour market, particularly if, as is frequently the
case, a shipbuilding concern occupies a dominant position in
the labour market. Second, and related to this, changes in
product and process specifications within the shipbuilding
industry will induce corresponding changes in the industry's
inter-sectoral relationships, through the system of backward
inter-industry linkages.

Changes in the inter-regional distribution of shipbuilding
output and employment in response to differential rates of
adoption of new process and product technologies constitute
the third level of analysis, in which concepts of sub-national
comparative advantage and technical leadership become important. Notable among such changes was the dramatic transfer
north of the centre of gravity of the British shipbuilding
industry, from the Thames to the Clyde and the North-east, in
the late nineteenth century, associated with the introduction
of iron and steam technology into the industry (Pollard and
Robertson, 1979, pp. 49-69). Also important, however, and to
date relatively neglected, is the examination of changes in
the inter-regional distribution of output and employment in
the industry and the contribution made to this by technological
change. The fourth, and final, level of analysis, which will
be adopted in the remainder of this chapter, is concerned with
the evolution of the modern-world shipbuilding industry over
the last 150 years. At this scale, given the paucity of reliable information on which an extensive time series analysis
can be based, data on industry output will be used as a sur-
rogate indicator of employment changes associated with the
international reallocation of industry activity.

2   TECHNICAL CHANGE AND ECONOMIC PERFORMANCE

The historical development of the world shipbuilding industry,
and the relationship between technological and employment
change, can be considered as a sequence of five phases of construction activity, each of which is associated with a significant redistribution of productive capacity.

2.1   *The Pre-industrial Shipbuilding Industry, 1800-50*

Before the first Industrial Revolution, shipbuilding was one
of the few industries in Europe to produce a large product,
handle a large volume of raw materials and bring together a
long list of semi-manufactured and manufactured goods for

assembly (Unger, 1975, p. 56). By the end of the seventeenth
century, Dutch shipbuilders had established themselves as the
most technologically advanced in Europe, producing a wide range
of vessels designed to carry out specific tasks. Throughout
the eighteenth century, however, the advantage bestowed by this
specialisation of design was gradually eroded, as organisational inflexibility led to technical stagnation and the erosion of the industry's competitive advantage (Unger, 1975,
p. 68), and by the end of the Napoleonic Wars, with the defeat
of France, Britain's supremacy in world shipbuilding was,
apparently, assured (Pollard, 1951, p. 1).

By 1850, however, the American industry was supreme and
threatened the existence of the British industry. Exhaustion
of native timber supplies and increasing long-distance transport costs and import duties on Baltic timber made it increasingly attractive for British shipowners to take advantage
of the cost savings of construction in the North American
colonies, close to both a cheap timber supply and several
recently opened and rapidly expanding sea routes (Pollard,
1951, p. 6). By 1774, American-built ships amounted to approximately one-third of total British tonnage (Fassett, 1948,
p. 23). Building on these locational advantages, the American
industry took the lead in the development of new types of
sailing vessel, particularly the fast clipper for long-distance
routes, and new forms of shipping organisation, such as the
introduction of regular sailing packets. By 1800, the combined
effect of these locational and technological advantages was to
reduce American building costs to 30 per cent below the level
in Britain, and, as a result, between 1835 and 1860 American
tonnage engaged in foreign trade grew from 1 million to 2.5
million tons (Fassett, 1948, p. 24; Fayle, 1933, p. 238).

This expansion of the American shipbuilding industry and
the threat it posed to the British industry was based on 'a
high level of intelligence and initiative . . . freedom from
the complex of prejudice and tradition which governed the
thoughts and activities of the old world . . . and unbounded
resources.   . . . In fifty years they contributed as much to
the development of the sailing ship as the whole maritime
world had contributed in three hundred' (Thornton, 1939, p. 5).
Until the late 1860s, sail remained dominant on all but the
shortest sea routes, and despite a late resurgence in sailing
ship design in Britain, America's cost advantage, and dominance of a growing market for new ships, remained. The repeal
of the Navigation Acts in 1849 removed an assured home market
for British shipbuilders and appeared to threaten the very
existence of the industry in Britain (Jones, 1957, p. 10).
Instead, the next half-century witnessed an unparalleled
period of expansion and development in which the British

industry attained a position of unchallenged supremacy.

2.2 *Steam Power and Metal Hulls, 1850-90*

A number of circumstances combined to bring about this change.
Although the share of British ships in the British trade declined in the 1850s, it increased rapidly thereafter at the
expense of American vessels (Pollard and Robertson, 1979,
p. 11). In the trade from the United Kingdom to the United
States, British tonnage increased from 946,000 in 1860 to
1,853,000 in 1866, while American tonnage fell from 2,245,000
to 484,000. In percentage terms, the British share of the
American trade rose from 18 per cent in 1855, to 65 per cent
in 1865, to 84 per cent in 1885, as the American share fell
from 79 per cent, to 26 per cent, to 10 per cent (Bates, 1893,
pp. 141-5, 151-6, 160). This sudden decline in the American
industry was initiated by the depression of 1857 and severely
exacerbated by the Civil War, in which 40 per cent of American
sea-going tonnage was lost and many major shipbuilding areas
went out of production altogether (Cormack, 1930, p. 226).
   Simultaneous with this preoccupation in other fields of
economic endeavour and post-war reconstruction, America's
competitive position was further, and in the long run finally,
eroded by the advent of a series of technological innovations
which were to completely change the character and distribution
of the shipbuilding industry by 1900. As Parkinson (1960, p. 3)
has noted: 'it was the building of iron and steel ships pro-
pelled by steam that worked the change and gave the United
Kingdom, for a time, overwhelming advantage'. By the 1850s,
timber in America was still considerably cheaper than in
Britain, but, for the first time in Britain, iron became
cheaper than wood. Subsequently, American attempts to compete
with Britain, with her high output of cheap coal and large,
skilled, body of engineers in steamship development, were
bound to end in failure, and the introduction of the iron hull
further favoured Britain as a shipbuilding centre.
   The re-emergence of the American industry in modern form,
and the development of shipbuilding in other European countries,
particularly Germany, towards the end of the nineteenth century,
occurred too late to offer economic competition with the
British industry, which accounted for at least 60 per cent of
world tonnage launched up to 1914 and, at a peak, reached almost 80 per cent. This ascendancy was not, however, a foregone
conclusion, and was not solely the result of technological
change. Although the iron hull was first introduced in 1836,
the first time the description 'built of iron' appears in the
Lloyd's register of shipping (Naish, 1958, p. 594), the sailing

ship remained dominant on most routes throughout the third quarter of the nineteenth century. Cost reductions were achieved less through technological change (excepting the introduction of the composite wood and iron and iron hulls in sailing ship design) than from the fact that the general growth in world trade offered greater prospects of picking up return cargoes rather than ballast. Steam power, on the other hand, was less advantageous the longer the voyage, and it was not until after 1880 that sail lost its cost advantage on inter-continental routes (Milward and Saul, 1973, pp. 220-1).

Detailed discussion of the progress made in technical inno-vation in the British shipbuilding industry in the latter half of the nineteenth century is beyond the scope of this chapter (see, for example, Robb, 1958; Pollard and Robertson, 1979; Albu, 1980). However, it is possible to attribute to their sources a number of the most significant technical innovations made in the last two centuries. Although several inventions have been made in one country and exploited in another (good examples are the welded hull and double-helical gear which were invented in Britain and exploited in the United States in the twentieth century), it is clear that throughout the nine-teenth century, British technical competitiveness was absolute.

By 1860, many of the early fears over the use of iron, and difficulties in evolving new methods of construction to handle the new material, had been overcome. This was partly a reflec-tion of the publication and acceptance of the first set of rules for iron construction by Lloyd's in 1854, partly because of difficulties in the supply and irregularities in the quality of imported timber, and partly the need to build ships longer than the 300 feet limit imposed by timber construction forced builders into making greater use of iron. Despite this, and despite the advantages iron construction offered at least some classes of shippers, the attitude of shipbuilders themselves contributed to the slowness of the transition from wood and sail to iron and steam: 'private shipbuilders continued to assimilate haphazardly the inventions poured upon them. Mixing empirical virtuosity in one field with appalling ignorance and backwardness in another, they were innocent of mathematics, averse to science, and hostile to theory' (Pollard, 1952, p. 101; Pollard and Robertson, 1979, pp. 130-50).

This was most clearly seen in the unwillingness or inability of the shipbuilders to develop new skills and techniques appro-priate to the new material, a failing which put many yards out of business. It was only with the development of an efficient marine steam engine after 1860 (in particular, the adoption of the triple expansion engine patented in France in 1871 (Milward and Saul, 1973, p. 220; see also Spratt, 1958)) and the intro-duction of steel for hull construction in 1877 following the

production by Siemens of a mild steel, suitable for shipbuilding, in an open-hearth furnace (Burn, 1940, pp. 52-4), that
the character of the British industry could accurately be
described as revolutionised (Pollard, 1951, pp. 22-39, 99-138;
Jones, 1957, pp. 14-22). Favoured by an island position, shel-
tered ports, a large share of world trade, a relative abundance
of capital, economical and extensive supplies of the necessary
raw materials, and technical skills unequalled elsewhere,
Britain could legitimately be described by the end of the
nineteenth century as the workshop of the world shipbuilding
industry (Moss and Hume, 1977).

There is little doubt that Britain's lead in the process of
industrialisation would have ensured this rise to supremacy
in any case, but the transition from the old to the new was
completed only by the end of the nineteenth century (Jones,
1957, p. 25), and the adoption and implementation of the new
technology had been a faltering and stumbling process which
was encouraged, if not necessitated, by three negative factors:
the disappearance of the American threat after the Civil War,
the difficulties experienced in maintaining an adequate supply
of suitable quality timber in the 1860s, and the continuing
expansion of world trade which necessitated more and larger
ships. Technological change and innovation appears less as a
central element in an aggressively competitive industry than
as a response, necessary for survival, to changed supply,
demand and competitive conditions in the industry.

2.3 *Comparative Advantage and British Hegemony, 1890-1914*

Evidence for this lack of dynamism can be found in an examination of the character of the British shipbuilding industry
at the turn of the century, when its comparative success was
at its height. The slight fall in the British share of world
production which occurred towards the end of the 1890s can
be attributed to the first development of a modern industry
elsewhere, particularly in Germany and the United States,
based on the development of steelmaking and engineering capacity and the needs of an expanding navy and mercantile marine
in these countries (Pollard, 1957, p. 427). However, much of
this growth abroad took place in sections of the industry
which were not open to international competition, either for
strategic reasons (naval shipbuilding) or because of a protective barrier of subsidies and legislation (merchant shipbuilding), and the relative position of the British industry
was, at this time, rather stronger than the data indicate.
Accordingly, by 1914 British yards were still without serious
rivals.

The comparative advantage of British shipyards in this period had its origins in 1860-80, when Britain alone had the capacity to develop a major, modern shipbuilding industry, and continued up to 1914 largely because of three factors. On the demand side, Britain had access to a large shipping market, both at home and abroad (Schwarz and von Halle, 1902, II, p. 88), which provided the opportunity for mass production, specialisation, external economies and the full use of fixed capital. On the supply side, British yards benefited from supplies of steel which were generally lower priced than for their major would-be competitors, either directly from the home industry or indirectly through the dumping policies of American steelmakers (Board of Trade, 1918, p. 41). They also benefited from a radical alteration in the organisational structure of the industry. As shipbuilding became more clearly the medium-technology construction and assembly industry which it was to remain until the present, some of its activities were sub-contracted out to smaller specialist firms, with the economic advantages of specialised knowledge, a wider market and more mobile capital for the trade as a whole (Pollard, 1951, pp. 82-3). As ships became more complex, competition among sub-contractors and suppliers helped reduce the price of components and speed up the rate of technological change (Pollard and Robertson, 1979, p. 232). The advantages of this system of an extensive supplier network were only later to accrue to foreign yards, and for a time gave Britain a continued cost advantage. A third factor in the maintenance of British hegemony was the combination of lower labour costs with a tradition of greater skill and experience in the British shipbuilding industry labour force (Pollard and Robertson, 1979, pp. 173-200). By 1900, the productivity of shipyard workers in the United Kingdom, at 12.5 tons output *per capita*, was almost twice that in the United States and three times that in Germany (Pollard, 1957, p. 438).

However, in one crucial respect, the British industry began to lag behind that in the rest of the world. By the turn of the century, there was little doubt that much of the equipment found in British yards was less advanced than in American and German yards (Schwarz and von Halle, 1902, II, pp. 143-53; John, 1914, pp. 293-4). For the most part, this capitalisation had been undertaken to compensate for the absence of a large pool of skilled labour, but it was a poor substitute which could not be fully exploited until all processes had become more mechanised and shipbuilding had become a true mass production industry (Pollard, 1957, p. 437). Indeed, the caution of British shipbuilders in avoiding over-investment and their slowness in adopting new equipment and techniques was one of the short-term strengths of the industry at this time, contributing to Britain's continued dominance by reducing overhead

charges, which were particularly hard to bear during severe,
often extreme, cyclical downturns in output, and allowing the
production of vessels at a lower cost than was possible in
many of the highly-capitalised foreign yards.

In general terms, this may reflect a wider distinction between 'technological rationality' and 'economic rationality'.
It could be argued that the British erred in being too rational
in their decision making, refusing to accept and adopt innovations because the relative inelasticity of home and foreign
markets and the existence of much still-usable equipment made
new investment financially unattractive, at least in the short
term. In Germany and America, on the other hand, interest in
technical efficiency rather than cost minimisation, and innovation for innovation's sake, led to capital investment which
in strictly economic terms was unwise, and to over-anticipation
of present objective opportunities (Sawyer, 1954). This difference reflects not economically irrational behaviour on the
part of German and American entrepreneurs, but the adoption of
a different and more optimistic time horizon than their British
competitors, who appear, in the shipbuilding industry at least,
to have viewed their long-term prospects in very much the same
light as the short-run outlook, and reacted accordingly
(Pollard and Robertson, 1979, p. 5). The difference was one
of calculation not of rationality: 'the German industrialist
and financier had a longer time horizon and included in their
estimates exogenous variables of continuing technological
change that their British competitor held constant' (Landes,
1960, p. 121).

In 1914, Britain was still responsible for 60 per cent of
world shipbuilding output, and the building capacity of
British shipyards still greatly exceeded that of the rest of
the European industry, particularly in the construction of
large vessels. But despite this, the cautious long-term policy
of investing only in innovations whose profitability had been
thoroughly proved, which enabled Britain to withstand the
challenge from foreign competition up to 1914, left the industry in a weak position to compete on equal terms in the
very different market conditions of the post-war era. The
failure of all but a few British shipyards to maintain technical parity with their competitors was soon to contribute
to the decline of the industry which has become endemic over
the last half-century.

2.4 *The Rise of Foreign Competition, 1918-39*

By the 1920s, Germany, Sweden and Japan had emerged as major
competitors to the British industry (Parkinson, 1960, p. 12),
and the view expressed in the Report of the Departmental

Committee on Shipping and Shipbuilding, that 'there were few
important industries where the predominance of British manu-
facture has been more marked than in shipbuilding and marine
engineering' (Board of Trade, 1918, pp. 35-6), was becoming
increasingly outdated. Between 1924 and 1939, the British
share of world tonnage launched fell from 64 per cent to 34
per cent, while the combined tonnages for Germany, Japan and
Sweden rose from 12 per cent to 36 per cent. A similar pattern
emerges from data on total ship production.

Ostensibly, this decline of the British industry in the
inter-war period can be attributed to the failure to maintain
a suitably high rate of technical innovation, thus allowing
the development of a technically more advanced and competitive
industry abroad. Not only did foreign yards install modern
equipment in the first decade of the century, but they also
took the lead in the introduction of oil-fired marine engines,
automatic welding and new forms of shipyard layout, organisation and management (Jones, 1957, pp. 27-31). To this extent,
the British industry paid the penalty for being the pioneer of
the modern shipbuilding industry, clinging more tenaciously
than any other industry to practical experience and tradition
rather than to scientific training (Pollard, 1969, p. 94).
However, the failure until too late to undertake necessary
structural, financial and technical reorganisation did not of
itself fully account for the failure of the British industry
to maintain the advantages of an early start.

By the end of the First World War the demand for new mercantile shipbuilding had been grossly inflated by the need to
replace war losses, and much of this replacement occurred
through the expansion of foreign shipbuilding industries. War
restrictions had prevented Britain from maintaining a supply
of shipping to neutral countries, and replacement building in
the boom of 1918-20 left no excess capacity to supply a foreign
market (Jones, 1957, pp. 91-3). The result was over-expansion
of world shipbuilding capacity, leading to the introduction of
protective subsidies designed to keep newly-developed facili-
ties in production. This affected British builders in two
ways: directly, in that work for foreign owners was no longer
available; and indirectly, in that British shipowners could
not afford regular replacement of their fleets in the face of
subsidised foreign competition. Adding to the difficulties
posed by over-capacity and subsidised competition, currency
instability and exchange controls in Britain further restricted
the competitiveness of the British industry (Jones, 1957,
pp. 73-6). As an assembly industry with up to two-thirds of
the cost of the final product accounted for by bought-in
materials and components, shipbuilding reflected the state
of the economy as a whole, and if shipbuilding was inefficient

and subject to inflation in the 1920s and 1930s, it was because large sectors of the economy were subject to inflation
and inefficiency (Dougan, 1968, p. 189).

These conditions, in combination, undoubtedly constituted
a severe handicap to the British industry, and this was exacerbated by lower material and labour costs abroad. Up to
1931, British delivered steel prices were considerably higher
than on the Continent, and though devaluation in that year
narrowed the differential, the subsequent rise in British home
prices, which was more marked than on the Continent, gave
continental shipbuilders a further advantage. It is rather
more difficult to evaluate differences in labour costs, but
on the basis of wage rates, efficiency and the length of the
working day, the British industry was less competitive, and
this was reinforced by inferior organisation of work, technique and use of mechanical equipment which still characterised
an industry carrying the legacy of the wood shipbuilding era
(Jones, 1957, pp. 77-83). Despite the rationalisation of the
1930s, achieved through the National Shipbuilders Securities
Ltd, by 1939 many British yards were badly out of date. The
equipment installed in these yards was inefficient, production
methods such as welding and prefabrication were either unknown
or regarded with scepticism, and the quality of design had
fallen behind that elsewhere. Before 1930, the design of cargo
ships 'reposed in a state of quiescence yielding to a placid
and unintelligent policy of repetition, devoid of technical
character, lacking in commercial progress when compared with
the pace of scientific progress in other directions and un-
worthy of the two industries responsible for their creation'
(Ayre, 1930, p. 4), and progress in this field after 1930 was
more than matched by developments abroad.

2.5 *Decline and Fall of British Shipbuilders and the Rise of Japan 1950-75*

This erosion of the comparative advantage of the British shipbuilding industry, in response to a complex of exogenous and
endogenous changes which included technological change, was
followed by an acceleration in the rate of relative decline
and by a decline in the European industry as a whole, with
the rise to world dominance of Japan in the mid-1950s. This
change in relative shares occurred alongside an almost exponential rise in total world tonnage launched, in which Britain
failed to share. Indeed, in 1970, Britain was building less
tonnage than in the 1920s and 1930s, and by 1975 its share of
tonnage had fallen to 3.6 per cent. Japan's growth, however,
has been much less marked in terms of the number of ships

launched, reflecting a considerable rise in the average size
of ship launched. By the mid-1960s, Sweden and Japan, and
later, to a lesser extent, Germany, were building larger ships
than were launched in Britain. Among the innovations which
contributed to this shift in the world centre of gravity of
the industry, the development of the very large crude carrier
and bulk ore carrier stands out as most evident. However, the
decline of the relative technical competitiveness of the
British industry was due to a number of other, equally significant but less visible, technical innovations. If a willingness to generate and adopt innovations is a prerequisite for
maintaining a market share in a highly competitive industry,
relative technical backwardness may be at least as important
in explaining the post-war performance of the British industry
as are the traditionally invoked criticisms of poor management,
bad industrial relations and low productivity.

In the early 1950s, the main challenge to the British industry came from the German and Swedish industries, and was
based on, among other things, the development of mass production techniques, standard vessels and components, and a highly
efficient technology (Pollard, 1969, p. 423). However, the
Suez crisis of 1956 led to a massive increase in the demand
for oil tankers, putting the final twist to changes in the
pattern of supply and demand for oil and oil products which
had their origins in the Second World War. Before 1939, most
petroleum shipments were in the form of finished products
transported from the major sources, particularly the United
States and Venezuela, to major markets, such as Western Europe.
The Second World War brought about two changes: a marked increase in the consumption of oil, leading to the development
of the Middle East oilfields; and the construction of large
refinery centres in or near the market areas of Europe and
Japan. Growth in tanker size, reflected in an increase in
average ship size, was 'an economic requirement growing out
of the fact that the merchandise being shipped is a large-
quantity, single-quality material requiring transportation
over extremely long distances' (Shinto, 1968, p. 57).

This radical change in the pattern of demand favoured Japan,
which had a high level of new capital investment in shipbuilding, shipyard organisation based on strong management teams
and the means to develop specialisation in this field (see,
for example, Yamashita, 1967; Al-Timimi, 1975). In particular,
this was achieved by altering the methods used to build ships.
Assembly from the keel up was replaced by a meticulously
planned system of block construction, based on United States
war-time practice, in which each component construction unit
is prefabricated at the dock-side and welded into position
when finished. The consequent cost advantage which the

Japanese enjoyed through the late 1950s and 1960s stemmed
from three sources. First, the optimum block size was engin-
eered to fit a mass-production system, using techniques first
developed in the aircraft industry. Second, construction
proceeded in parallel: while the units of the bottom structure
were being welded together, other assembly blocks were fabri-
cated by the dock-side. Third, the fittings for each block
were pre-installed, reducing outfitting time at the end of
the production cycle (Shinto, 1968, p. 64). While similar
techniques, organisation and structure were being adopted in
Sweden (University of Newcastle, 1968), the British industry
continued in its pre-war path, only beginning to adopt these
innovations in the late 1960s. Failure to take advantage of
the immediate post-war sellers' market to re-equip and modern-
ise yards (Jones, 1957, pp. 203-35) and the collapse in the
early 1960s of the sea-borne passenger transport market, left
all but a few British yards unable to cope with foreign competition, which continued to receive subsidies to improve
competitiveness and establish the industry as an instrument
of national economic development. By 1970 it could still be
said of the British industry that,

> despite very considerable changes which have taken place
> over the years a shipyard can still fairly be described
> as having a 'craft' technology. The two essential features
> of the technology of shipbuilding are that the product is
> not standardised and that mechanisation and rationalisation
> have not proceeded to any great extent. For the most part
> each ship is individually designed, programmed and con-
> structed. . . . Even though a great deal of equipment is
> supplied by outside sub-contractors, the building of a ship
> depends essentially on the manipulation of tools and materi-
> als by men who have acquired craft skills over a period of
> years. (Brown and Brannan, 1970, p. 197)

The rapid rise of Japan in the 1950s, and the recent development of new shipbuilding capacity in nations such as Brazil,
South Korea and Taiwan, has put paid to the British myth that
long apprenticeships and inherited skills were essential for
shipbuilding (Venus, 1972). That the most successful countries
in recent years have been those which have applied scienti-
fically-based innovations to design and production methods is
suggested by relative rates of increase in average output
(measured in gross tons completed) per employee. Despite a
fall in employment of over 16 per cent in the period 1963-75,
average *per capita* output in the British shipbuilding industry
rose only marginally compared with that in its major competitors. Added to this, the development of low-cost competition

in newly-emerging shipbuilding nations further threatens the
survival in world terms of the British industry.

3   CONCLUSION

In 1973, there was a warning that the British shipbuilding
industry was falling behind its competitors in terms of price,
delivery, labour relations, technology, development and capital investment (Booz, Allen and Hamilton, 1973). Of particular
importance in the survival of the industry will be an increasing emphasis on ship types with high added values based on
increased R&D and design innovation. British government policy
towards the industry has been dominated by the succession of
attempts to save failing yards rather than by the support of
risky innovations (Hogwood, 1979). As expected from a product
cycle model of industry evolution, the development of green-
field sited, low-cost shipyards abroad is particularly suited
to the construction of relatively simple, standard ships, the
design and construction of which follows now established
methods and uses capital equipment and techniques which can
be embodied in the construction of the shipyard. However, it
has been suggested that it will be some time before new shipbuilding nations develop the reserves of skill and technical
knowledge needed to compete in the building of sophisticated,
high value added ships (Venus, 1972). Unless the British industry radically changes its orientation to suit the new economic, technical and political environment within which it has
to operate, it seems likely that the endemic decline of the
last fifty years will become terminal.

REFERENCES

Abramovitz, M. (1956) 'Resource and Output Trends in the
   United States since 1870', *American Economic Review*, vol.
   46, pp. 5-23.
Albu, A. (1980) 'Merchant Shipbuilding and Marine Engineering',
   in K. Pavitt (ed.), *Technical Innovation and British
   Economic Performance* (London: Macmillan).
Al-Timimi, W. (1975) 'Innovation Led Expansion: the Shipbuild-
   ing Case', *Research Policy*, vol. 4, pp. 160-71.
Ayre, Sir Wilfred (1930) 'Presidential Address: Institution
   of Engineers and Shipbuilders in Scotland', *Transactions*,
   vol. 84, p. 4.
Bates, W. W. (1893) *American Marine* (Boston and New York:
   Houghton Mifflin).
Board of Trade (1918) *Report of the Departmental Committee on*

Shipping and Shipbuilding (London: HMSO).

Booz, Allen and Hamilton International (1973) *British Ship-building 1972*, Department of Trade and Industry (London: HMSO).

Boretsky, M. (1975) 'Trends in US Technology: a Political Economist's View', *American Scientist*, vol. 63, pp. 70-82.

Brown, R. and P. Brannan (1970) 'Social Relations and Social Perspectives Amongst Shipbuilding Workers - a Preliminary Statement', Part Two, *Sociology*, vol. 4, pp. 197-211.

Burn, D. L. (1940) *The Economic History of Steel Making 1867-1939* (Cambridge University Press).

Cameron, R. (1975) 'The Diffusion of Technology as a Problem in Economic History', *Economic Geography*, vol. 51, pp. 217-30.

Cormack, W. S. (1930) 'An Economic History of Shipbuilding and Marine Engineering', unpublished PhD thesis, University of Glasgow.

Deane, P. (1967) *The First Industrial Revolution* (Cambridge University Press).

Denison, E. F. (1967) *Why Growth Rates Differ* (Washington: Brookings Institute).

Dougan, D. J. (1968) *The History of North East Shipbuilding* (London: Allen & Unwin).

Fassett, F. G. (ed.) (1948) *The Shipbuilding Business in the United States of America*, vol. 1 (New York: Society of Naval Architects and Marine Engineers).

Fayle, C. R. (1933) *A Short History of the World's Shipping Industry* (London: Allen & Unwin).

Freeman, C. (1974) *The Economics of Industrial Innovation* (Harmondsworth: Penguin).

Hartwell, R. M. (1971) *The Industrial Revolution and Economic Growth* (London: Methuen).

Hoffmann, W. (1955) *British Industry 1700-1950* (Oxford University Press).

Hogwood, B. W. (1979) *Government and Shipbuilding: The Politics of Industrial Change* (Farnborough, Hants: Saxon House).

John, T. G. (1914) 'Shipbuilding Practice of the Present and Future', *Transactions, Institute of Naval Architects*, vol. 56, pp. 293-4.

Johnson, P. S. (1975) *The Economics of Invention and Innovation* (London: Martin Robertson).

Jones, L. (1957) *Shipbuilding in Britain* (Cardiff: University of Wales Press).

Landes, D. (1960) 'The Structure of Enterprise in the Nine-teenth Century: the Cases of Britain and Germany', International Congress of Historical Science, Stockholm, *Rapports*, vol. V, pp. 107-28.

Landes, D. (1969) *The Unbound Prometheus* (Cambridge University Press).

Maddison, A. (1964) *Economic Growth in the West: Comparative Experience in Europe and North America* (New York: Twentieth Century Fund).

Mansfield, E. (1968) *The Economics of Technical Change* (London: Longmans).

Milward, A. and S. B. Saul (1973) *The Economic Development of Continental Europe 1780-1870* (London: Allen & Unwin).

Moss, M. S. and J. R. Hume (1977) *Workshop of the British Empire: Engineering and Shipbuilding in the West of Scotland* (London: Heinemann).

Naish, G. (1958) 'Shipbuilding', in C. Singer *et al.* (eds), *A History of Technology*, vol. IV: *The Industrial Revolution* (Oxford: Clarendon Press) pp. 574-95.

Parkinson, J. R. (1960) *The Economics of Shipbuilding in the United Kingdom* (Cambridge University Press).

Pavitt, K. (ed.) (1980) *Technical Innovation and British Economic Performance* (London: Macmillan).

Pollard, S. (1951) 'The Economic History of the British Shipbuilding Industry 1870-1914', unpublished PhD thesis, University of London.

Pollard, S. (1952) 'Laissez Faire and Shipbuilding', *Economic History Review* (2nd series), vol. 5, pp. 98-115.

Pollard, S. (1957) 'British and World Shipbuilding, 1890-1914: a Study in Comparative Costs', *Journal of Economic History*, vol. 17, pp. 426-44.

Pollard, S. (1969) *The Development of the British Economy, 1914-1967*, 2nd edn   (London: Arnold).

Pollard, S. and P. Robertson (1979) *The British Shipbuilding Industry 1870-1914* (Cambridge, Mass. and London: Harvard University Press).

Pred, A. R. (1966) *The Spatial Dynamics of US Urban Industrial Growth, 1800-1914* (Cambridge, Mass.: MIT Press).

Robb, A. M. (1958) 'Shipbuilding', in C. Singer *et al.* (eds), *A History of Technology*, vol. V: *The Late Nineteenth Century* (Oxford: Clarendon Press) pp. 350-90.

Robertson, P. L. (1974) 'Shipping and Shipbuilding: the Case of William Denny and Brothers', *Business History*, vol. 16, pp. 36-47.

Rodgers, E. M. (1962) *Diffusion of Innovations* (New York: Free Press).

Rothwell, R. and W. Zegfeld (1979) *Technical Change and Employment* (London: Francis Pinter).

Salter, W. (1966) *Productivity and Technological Change* (Cambridge University Press).

Sawyer, J. E. (1954) 'Entrepreneurship in Periods of Rapid Growth: the United States in the 19th Century', paper presented to the Conference on Entrepreneurship and Economic Growth, Cambridge, Mass.

Schmookler, J. (1966) *Invention and Economic Growth* (Cambridge, Mass.: Harvard University Press).

Schwarz, T. and E. L. von Halle (1902) *Schiffbauindustrie in Deutschland und im Auslände* (Berlin: E. S. Mittler und Sohn).

Shinto, H. (1968) 'Big Ships', *Science and Technology*, vol. 75, pp. 56-66.

Siebert, H. (1969) *Regional Economic Growth: Theory and Policy* (Scranton, Pa.: International Textbook).

Solow, R. A. (1957) 'Technical Change and the Aggregate Production Function', *Review of Economics and Statistics*, vol. 39, pp. 312-20.

Spratt, H. P. (1958) 'The Marine Steam-Engine', in C. Singer et al. (eds), *A History of Technology*, vol. V: *The Late Nineteenth Century* (Oxford: Clarendon Press) pp. 141-56.

Thornton, R. H. (1939) *British Shipping* (Cambridge University Press).

Unger, R. W. (1975) 'Technology and Industrial Organisation: Dutch Shipbuilding to 1800', *Business History*, vol. 17, pp. 56-72.

University of Newcastle (1968) 'Report on Study Visit to Swedish Shipyards', University of Newcastle upon Tyne, Department of Naval Architecture and Shipbuilding.

Venus, J. (1972) 'The Economics of Shipbuilding', the 6th Blackadder Lecture delivered at the University of Newcastle upon Tyne.

Walker, W. B. (1980) 'Britain's Industrial Performance 1850-1950: a Failure to Adjust', in K. Pavitt (ed.), *Technical Innovation and British Economic Performance* (London: Macmillan) pp. 19-37.

Yamashita, L. (1967) 'Application of Technical Innovations and Automation to Ships Built in Japan', in C. J. Borwick (ed.), *Automation on Shipboard* (New York: Macmillan).

Youngson, A. J. (ed.) (1972) *Economic Development in the Long Run* (London: Allen & Unwin).

11   The Trade Union Response to New Technology

BERNARD JAMES

1   INTRODUCTION

During the last two or three years, trade unions have become
increasingly aware of the need to decide how to respond to
the new microelectronics-based technology. The attitude of
unions is obviously a major factor determining the ability of
British industry to adapt to the new technology - subject to
the willingness of industry to invest in the first place.
From the union point of view, the security and quality of
their members' working lives is at stake, as is their own role
as protectors of their members' interests in their jobs. The
TUC has paid considerable attention to the new technology. A
special consultative conference was held in May 1979 to discuss
the issues involved. An interim report on Employment and Technology was considered at this conference, and a modified version was presented to the annual conference later in the year.[1]
   A number of unions have decided their own policies towards
the introduction of new technology and produced guidelines
and model agreements for their negotiators. Agreements dealing
with aspects of new technology exist in a variety of industries.
This makes it possible to assess the trade union response,
which is complex and raises many issues. These include the
extent of governmental responsibility for full employment and
economic growth; the limitations of collective bargaining; and
the future of industrial democracy.[2] These are broad issues,
on which it is possible only to make some comments at this
point in time. The immediate issue is the control of work,
both at the level of policy making in the firm and at the
level of the task and the work-place.[3]
   Before examining the trade union response in detail, one
general point should be made. This response is not a negative
one. Unions are aware - perhaps more aware than many - of the
dangers to British industry, and consequently to jobs, of a
failure to make full use of new technological developments.
APEX pointed out in 1979 that 'to adopt a policy of resisting
technological change and the improved technology which it makes
possible, would be a recipe for general impoverishment, low
growth and high unemployment. Improving the productive capacity

of industry . . . should be a major priority for all trade
unionists.'⁴ Indeed, many trade unions emphasise that their
members should take the initiative to ensure that employers
are taking advantage of new technology wherever possible in
order to remain competitive in world markets. As the TGWU
pointed out, the important issue is the control of the new
technology, not whether it is good or bad.⁵ To this one might
add the question of who benefits from it, and trade unions
are only doing their job in ensuring that some of the benefits,
at least, go to workers.

The purpose of this chapter is to consider how far trade
union response to the introduction of new technology and the
new agreements being concluded constitutes a major development
in industrial relations. In particular, a central question is
whether major changes in the control of work are taking place,
or likely to take place. At issue, ultimately, is whether
collective bargaining is an adequate means for furthering the
legitimate interests of all those affected by new technology.
If traditional collective bargaining is inadequate, then alternative forms of industrial democracy will have to be considered to legitimise managerial authority and protect workers'
interests.

The chapter is arranged in five sections. The first examines
a number of features of the new technology which give trade
unions cause for concern, including the major problem of unemployment and the TUC approach to it. The second section
outlines the TUC concept of the New Technology Agreement and
evaluates it as a means of handling change through collective
bargaining. Further sections deal with the characteristics of
individual union policies; the types of technology agreement
which have been concluded; and considers the extent to which
union policy has been implemented in these agreements.

2   NEW TECHNOLOGY AND TRADE UNION CONCERN

The reasons for union concern become clear if one considers
what is 'new' about microelectronic technology from the unions'
point of view. While it is true that protection of workers'
jobs in the face of technical change has always been central
to the role of trade unions, the new technology has a number
of distinctive features. As APEX pointed out, the new technology differs from the computer technology introduced in the
1960s: 'Microelectronic technology . . . is flexible, instantaneous and can be rapidly modified often enabling it to do
a wide range of tasks with very little human effort. It is
reliable; it is available from many competing sources; it is
growing at a rapid rate and most important of all it is cheap.'⁶

Four features of contemporary technical innovation are of special significance to the trade union movement:

(a) the pace at which these changes can be and are introduced;
(b) the extent of the likely impact across the economy;
(c) the way in which old jobs and job categories can be eliminated and new ones created;
(d) the way in which it may transform jobs which do survive, and require fundamental change in work organisation.[7]

The pace of change is important because it threatens the ability of work groups and unions to maintain a degree of control over the jobs affected. If change is slow or limited, demarcation rules and other protective labour practices can be adapted to fit the new circumstances. Where change is rapid and continuing, custom and practice will have little opportunity to evolve and become established.[8] New technology may also transform jobs in ways which make them inherently less amenable to worker control, for example, by reducing the range of tasks carried out by the individual, and making his performance much easier to measure.[9] This has adverse implications for job satisfaction and health and safety, as well as leaving the worker more open to pressure from management.[10] Unions must be concerned to minimise this erosion of their members' positions. It is also worth pointing out that if workers experience excessive worsening of their positions as result of change, a likely response will be to resist all change.

Changing the character of jobs also has important implications for trade union membership. This will be especially so where old jobs are eliminated and new ones created.[11] Workers in the new jobs are likely to be less easy to organise. Jobs which are difficult to subject to a degree of worker control do not form a sound basis for work-place and hence wider union organisation. Also, workers in the changed or new jobs will be characteristically less unionisable than many existing jobs.[12] Two areas of employment particularly threatened are semi-skilled work in manufacturing and a range of clerical and administrative jobs in all sectors of the economy.

The first of these areas of employment is one in which fairly high levels of union membership have been established since the Second World War.[13] The second has become an area of considerable membership growth for white collar unions in the last twelve years.[14] The job and market situations of these workers have increasingly encouraged them to join unions. The same does not apply to many of the professional, technical and de-skilled groups associated with the new technology. If

this is correct, a long-term decline in the level of union
membership is a strong possibility. A further effect of technical change on union organisation and structure will be the
weakening or elimination of traditional demarcation lines between unions. As the boundaries between jobs are blurred or
obliterated, the danger of inter-union conflict about which
union should recruit among the new workers will increase.
Closely associated problems will arise from arguments between
already unionised workers about which groups should have the
new jobs allocated to them. As the TUC points out, during a
period of rapid change there is the danger that 'a disproportionate degree of trade union energy could be dissipated
by internal differences'.[15] The TUC calls for more unity and
closer working between unions at the industry, company and
plant levels, and points out that it has an established role
in helping unions to resolve issues that arise between them.[16]
Technical change could be an important factor in increasing
the trend of unions to amalgamate.

Together with the threats to job control and union organisation comes the danger of large-scale and lasting techno-
logically-created unemployment. The extent of the threat to
jobs both within organisations and across the economy as a
whole has caused the greatest concern to the trade union
movement.[17] It is not the purpose of this chapter to attempt
to identify areas of likely unemployment resulting from new
technology, or to estimate the numbers that would lose or
gain jobs. There have been a number of attempts to do this,
which vary between the 'optimistic' view (as far as jobs are
concerned) put forward by the Central Policy Review Staff and
the Department of Employment, and the 'pessimistic' interpretation of APEX and ASTMS.[18] The TUC, in *Employment and
Technology*, is doubtful of the value of forecasting the employment effects of the new technology. The report argues that it
is necessary to distinguish between unemployment brought about
by this means, and unemployment resulting from government
policy. Furthermore, it points out that 'most of the predictions are based on simple forward projections of past trends,
whereas the effect of technological change on the scale that
is expected will be, through radically changing the process of
production and the pattern of output, to make these past trends
an increasingly unreliable guide to the future'.[19] The report
rejects the 'deterministic' view that a particular level of
unemployment will be associated with a particular level of
technological development, and expresses the belief that unemployment will depend on the relationship between productivity growth and output growth.[20]

The TUC position is, therefore, that the problem of unemployment is a problem of demand in the economy as a whole,
and it needs to be tackled at that level. The report calls

on the Government to develop an Industrial Strategy to lead
to a high output, low unit costs and a high employment
economy.[21] To attain this objective, they put forward three
preconditions for success which are government responsibilities.
They are:

(a) a continuing commitment to the work of the Industrial
Strategy, including the monitoring and containment of
import penetration;

(b) the expansion of services - and the Government should
give a clear commitment to the expansion of the public
services as part of its overall commitment to full
employment;

(c) government action on the international level, in concert
with other countries, to promote expansion in world
trade.[22]

In addition, the report lays great stress on the need for
manpower policy. The provision of public education and training
should be increased, and the Manpower Services Commission
should mount a major action programme.[23] Government should
take advantage of the way in which microtechnology can make
industry more mobile, by encouraging work to come to the work-
force, and the minimum standards of the Redundancy Payments
Act should be improved.[24]

The TUC report suggests that trade unions can help to contain the wider effects of the new technology by giving priority
in negotiations to movements towards:

(a) the 35-hour week;
(b) a reduction in systematic overtime;
(c) longer holidays;
(d) better provision for time off for public and trade
union duties;
(e) sabbatical leave;
(f) early retirement for older workers on improved
pensions.[25]

New technology, therefore, challenges union interests at
the levels of job control, union organisation and the protection of employment. With particular regard to the last,
the TUC sees the need for response both from the Government
and in collective bargaining. Other union interests would be
primarily the concern of collective bargaining.

3 NEW TECHNOLOGY AGREEMENTS

The TUC report further suggests that technological change
might be collectively regulated by means of New Technology
Agreements (NTAs). NTAs would guarantee 'full trade union
involvement' in the process of adapting to new technology.[26]
This involvement should be from the earliest stage in the
introduction of change, and agreements should provide for full
consultation before the decision to purchase new technology
is taken. The first objective should be that 'change must be
by agreement . . . no new technology which has major effects
on the workforce should be introduced unilaterally'.[27] In
return for this, negotiators must be prepared to take the
lead in pressing for joint assessment of the opportunities
for 'using new technological processes and introducing new
products on the basis of agreed plans'.[28] By taking this initiative, negotiators might hope to avoid 'belated and inadequate' management decisions which would have more damaging
effects on the work-force.[29]

Another important principle for NTAs is that new technology
should be implemented 'in a context of seeking greater output
through expansion within existing product ranges or through
diversification'.[30] Unions should play a part in seeking alternative products and markets. In the public sector, new
technology should be used to provide improvements in the
quality of services and benefits.[31] By these means, the TUC
would hope to maintain employment levels. However, realisti-
cally, the maintenance of the 'stock' of jobs is not recom-
mended as a condition for an NTA. Instead, the report suggests
that 'wherever possible, an essential condition for the smooth
introduction of new technology is the guarantee of full job
security for the existing workforce'.[32] The areas which should
be covered in NTAs are detailed in a checklist for negotiators,
and include:

(a) guarantees of full trade union involvement based on
    status quo provisions to ensure that change takes place
    with consultation;
(b) assurances that all relevant information will be made
    available to union representatives prior to decisions
    being taken;
(c) agreed plans on employment and output, including the
    guarantee of no redundancy;
(d) agreed provisions for training and retraining;
(e) a linking of the introduction of new technology to
    reductions in working time;
(f) provisions to ensure that the benefits of new technology
    are distributed amongst the work-force;

(g) reassurance that new technology will not be used for the measurement, regulation and control of operatives by management;

(h) provisions to ensure stringent standards on health and safety;

(i) the establishment of joint management-union arrangements to monitor developments and review progress. [33]

It is important to assess these proposals as a possible departure point for new developments in industrial relations. If unions do become involved in questions of output and markets and in taking decisions on investment by way of such agreements, the collective bargaining entailed would amount to a substantial 'democratisation' of industry in itself. At least, agreements based on the NTA 'model' would have important advantages. In concluding NTAs, management and unions would be deciding important issues of principle for the currency of the agreements. Unions would be conceding to managements the right, in principle, to introduce new technology with union cooperation. In return, a number of principles securing the union role and protecting worker interests would be defined and accepted by management. Joint procedures would also be established to handle change on a permanent basis. By these means, the TUC would hope that the scope for conflict over the introduction of specific changes would be greatly reduced. The negotiation of an NTA may not be easy, but once such an agreement were in force, it would allow for the smooth and hence quicker introduction of change.

The NTA concept is, however, only advice from the TUC to member unions. [34] The following sections are based on analysis of the policies and guidelines produced for negotiators by individual unions, and on a selection of agreements dealing with new technology. At this point in time, the number of agreements in the printing and publishing industries outnumber those elsewhere, and only a small number of these have been taken into account in the analysis.

4   THE POLICIES OF INDIVIDUAL UNIONS

The policies of individual unions and the guidelines which they have produced for their negotiators reflect the main lines of the TUC approach. All unions which are becoming involved in the introduction of new technology are concerned that agreements should be adequate in a number of important areas. [35] Agreements should:

(a) establish the principle that new technology is to be

introduced only subject to discussion and agreement
with the union;
(b) provide security for both members' employment and
their incomes;
(c) establish procedures for the collective regulation of
new technology;
(d) ensure that unions retain or acquire a measure of
control over tasks affected by technological change;
(e) take into account questions of inter-union relations
and union organisation;
(f) have full regard to the health and safety implications
of new technology.

It is, therefore, possible to say that unions have important
strands in common in their policies for new technology agreements without following the TUC mechanically.

Beyond the areas of general concern, union policies reflect
the history of job regulation in their industries, types of
membership, wider union policies and other factors. For
example, ASTMS places a heavier emphasis than do some other
unions on clauses covering consultation on the introduction
of new technology, disclosure of information and procedural
matters.[36] The print unions emphasise job control, demarcation
and relations between unions.[37] APEX wants its negotiators to
pay attention to the impact of new technology in detail on
working conditions from the point of view of health and safety
and job satisfaction.[38] The banking union's policy shows an
interest in obtaining greater influence at both the task level
and at the level of policy making in the firm as a condition
for cooperating in the introduction of new technology.[39] The
TGWU also links the introduction of new technology to the
need to move towards greater industrial democracy.[40] The emphasis of individual unions is often reflected in the agreements which they conclude.

The extent to which a union's policy will be implemented
in agreements will be governed by many factors. These include
the attitudes of local negotiators, management policy, the
policies of other unions and local conditions generally.
Agreements therefore vary considerably both in size and
content.

5 TYPES OF TECHNOLOGY AGREEMENT

Only some of the agreements which have been concluded so far
clearly reflect the approach of the TUC in any detail. It is
useful to divide agreements dealing with the introduction of
new technology into four categories, based on the function

the agreement is intended to fulfil in the process of change.
This analysis draws on the traditional distinction made in
industrial relations between substantive and procedural agreements. Substantive matters arise from the substance of employment relationships and include questions of pay, hours
and other terms and conditions of employment. Procedural
issues derive from the existence of trade unions and joint
regulation and include union recognition, negotiating arrangements, disputes procedures and the role and status of work-
place representatives.[41] The categories are outlined below.

(a) Agreements with a heavy substantive emphasis. These
    agreements deal with the introduction of a single or
    small number of related changes, the extent of which
    is closely defined. They specify the technology to be
    introduced, and the workers who are to be affected,
    and detail the provisions for employment and income
    security, trade union matters and health and safety.
    Collective procedural matters are not dealt with,
    except, perhaps, to refer to points at which issues
    should be referred to existing joint negotiating bodies
    or disputes procedures.

(b) Limited procedural agreements. These agreements esta-
    blish procedures for dealing with projected future
    changes, or at least the principles to govern such
    changes. A framework for handling substantive matters
    might be included without going into the detail found
    in the primarily substantive agreements. However, only
    a limited number of possible technical changes would be
    covered by the arrangements in the agreement (for
    example the introduction of VDUs and associated equip-
    ment and linked systems).

(c) 'Open-ended' procedural agreements. These agreements
    establish procedures for dealing with a wide range of,
    or any, technical changes. These agreements are essen-
    tially procedural, and will, at the most, outline
    principles for dealing with substantive issues.

(d) Framework agreements. Unlike procedural agreements as
    such, framework agreements do not provide for detailed
    procedural arrangements. They establish the principles
    for locally agreed procedures. Framework agreements may
    include some substantive principles, and will be nego-
    tiated at the organisational or industry-wide level.[42]

Of these four types, the first differs from the TUC model
in that it does not provide for agreement on the principles
which govern future changes. The principles of whether change
should be introduced, at what rate, and how control shall be

distributed have, in effect, to be re-negotiated each time
a new innovation is proposed. Changes do take place by way
of such agreements, but they imply a heavy burden of negotiating and the repeated danger of conflict over issues of
principle.

In contrast, the essentially procedural agreements are intended to minimise these problems and are more likely to meet
the TUC objectives. They are the agreements which may most
appropriately be termed New Technology Agreements, and have
the potential to assist the smooth introduction of new technology subject to substantial union involvement. Framework
agreements form a part of the negotiating arrangements for
the introduction of change where bargaining takes place at
a number of levels - their value can be assessed only to the
extent that they are complemented by local procedural and
substantive agreements.

The limited procedural agreement is the outcome of the
reluctance of many trade union negotiators to accept the
principle of ongoing technical change at a time of increasing
unemployment. This reluctance is undoubtedly reinforced by
the failure of employers to involve unions sufficiently in
the decision making process. These agreements allow management-
union cooperation in a limited range of technical changes, but
enable matters of principle to be re-examined when change goes
beyond a point at which its consequences can reasonably be
foreseen. In the present economic climate, and lacking an
accord on new technology between government, employers and
unions, this type of compromise agreement could well become
general. At present, however, agreements seem to be fairly
evenly distributed amongst the four categories.

6   UNION POLICY AND TECHNOLOGY AGREEMENTS

How far union policies are implemented in agreements will be
an important influence on the extent and pace of change, its
employment effects and the control of work. This section is
based on an analysis of union policies, model agreements and
guidelines for negotiators, and a comparison of these with
technology agreements which have been concluded.

This analysis showed that fifteen specific objectives can
be identified which unions always (or almost always) want in
technology agreements. The extent to which these objectives
are met is an indicator of the relative influence of management and unions over technical change. The fifteen objectives
can be divided into four groups: those which unions always
or almost always obtain in agreements, and those which they
usually, rarely or never (or practically never) get. Five of

these objectives, unions always get; two, usually; five,
rarely; and three of them never (or almost never).

The objectives unions pursue, and the likelihood of them
being incorporated in the terms of technology agreements,
are as follows.

(a) What unions always want and always (or almost always)
    get:

> a guarantee that there will be no redundancy
> as result of the proposed technical changes;
> a guarantee that there will be no down-grading
> of individuals which will result in lower
> earnings;
> an assurance that information regarding possible
> health and safety effects will be provided;
> an assurance that details of the new technology
> will be provided in time for discussions in
> advance of change;
> a similar assurance with regard to the likely
> manpower effects of change.

(b) What unions always want and usually get:

> the right to take a disagreement arising from
> proposed change through a disputes procedure
> before the change is implemented;
> an assurance that management will seek redeploy-
> ment opportunities for those displaced by the
> new technology.

(c) What unions always want but rarely get:

> agreement on reductions in hours of work;
> an assurance that information on costs and
> transfer pricing will be made available;
> an assurance that there will be no change without
> prior negotiation;
> a declaration that no major change will take
> place without mutual agreement;
> a guarantee that redeployment opportunities will
> be found for workers displaced by change.

(d) What unions always want but never (or practically never)
    get:

> an agreement to disclose full financial information
> prior to negotiating the changes;
> a declaration that major and minor changes require
> mutual agreement;
> a guarantee that there will be no reduction in
> the establishment of jobs.[43]

This analysis does not include earnings objectives beyond
the guarantee that individuals shall not receive lower earnings

as result of their jobs being down-graded through technical
change. The main earnings objective is, generally, that those
accepting changed working conditions shall be rewarded. However, changes in financial rewards subsequent to technical
change are frequently dealt with in the normal run of substantive bargaining. The proportion of a pay increase due to
the acceptance of technical change may not be specified. Only
a few agreements provide for supplements to be paid directly
related to operating new technology.

The overall picture from the implementation of the fifteen
objectives is that a fine line is being drawn along the frontier of control, without any major changes developing in its
position. This conclusion can be modified to the extent that,
in a number of cases, especially where union organisation is
relatively new, unions appear to be using technology agreements to consolidate their positions. However, it suggests
that technology agreements, in general, have so far done
little to extend formal collective bargaining to higher levels
of decision taking in the firm. These agreements have not
proved the means whereby wider concepts of industrial democracy have been furthered.

The objectives which unions always or usually get are minimal
conditions for the conclusion of agreements. The no redundancy,
no down-grading guarantees, and the assurance of management
willingness to seek redeployment opportunities, reflect the
basic responsibility of unions to protect their members' jobs.
The disclosure of categories of job-centred information, and
the right to take disputed changes through procedure before
implementation, are essential preconditions for meaningful
consultations and negotiations. The objectives which unions
rarely or have never attained would represent very substantial
increases in the scope and effectiveness of collective bargaining, if not major developments in industrial democracy.
Where there are guarantees of no changes without prior negotiations or of major changes without agreement, these reflect
realities in industries such as engineering or printing,
rather than breaking new ground.

NOTES

1. TUC, *Employment and Technology* (London: TUC, 1979).
2. For discussion of collective bargaining as a form of industrial democracy see M. Poole, 'Industrial Democracy:
   a Comparative Analysis', *Industrial Relations*, vol. 18,
   no. 3 (1979) pp. 262-72. Also D. Guest, 'A Framework for
   Participation', in D. Guest and K. Knight (eds), *Putting
   Participation into Practice* (Farnborough, Hants: Gower

Press, 1979).

3. For an analysis of the issues involved in arguments about the control of work see E. Rose, 'Work Control in Industrial Society', *Industrial Relations Journal*, vol. 7, no. 3 (1976) pp. 20-30.

4. APEX, *Office Technology: The Trade Union Response* (London: APEX, 1979) p. 13.

5. TGWU, *Micro-electronics: New Technology: Old Problems: New Opportunities* (London: TGWU, 1978) p. 3.

6. APEX, *Automation and the Office Worker* (London: APEX, 1980) p. 3.

7. The impact of new technology on products and processes, and hence on jobs, has been discussed in a number of places, including the two APEX publications. One of the most detailed analyses is contained in the report of the Department of Employment Manpower Study Group: J. Sleigh, B. Boatwright, P. Irwin and R. Stanyon, *The Manpower Implications of Micro-electronic Technology* (London: HMSO, 1979).

8. An explanation of the evolution of custom and practice in the work-place is given by William Brown in *Piecework Bargaining* (London: Heinemann, 1973).

9. *Automation and the Office Worker*, p. 32.

10. Ibid., p. 38.

11. For a discussion of the effects on job content and the types of job likely to increase or decrease in numbers, see *Office Technology: The Trade Union Response*, pp. 32-4.

12. For a classic examination of the characteristics of work and market situations which affect the willingness of workers to join unions, see D. Lockwood, *The Blackcoated Worker* (London: Allen & Unwin, 1958). See also G. Bain, D. Coates and V. Ellis, *Social Stratification and Trade Unionism* (London: Heinemann, 1973).

13. R. Hyman, *The Workers' Union* (Oxford: Clarendon Press, 1971) includes an interesting account of the factors which encouraged the establishment of union organisation among the semi-skilled in manufacturing, especially pp. 38-45.

14. R. Price and G. S. Bain, 'Union Growth Re-visited: 1948-1974 in perspective', *British Journal of Industrial Relations*, vol. XIV (1976) pp. 345-7.

15. *Employment and Technology*, p. 35.

16. Ibid., p. 35.

17. *Employment and Technology*, pp. 25-32; *Office Technology: The Trade Union Response*, pp. 11-24; and ASTMS, *Technological Change and Collective Bargaining*, ASTMS Discussion Document (London, 1979) pp. 2-4.

18. Central Policy Review Staff, 'Social and Employment

Implications of Microelectronics', mimeo (London: CPRS, 1978); *APEX response to CPRS Report 'The Social and Employment Implications of Microelectronics'*, mimeo (London: APEX, 1979); *Technological Change and Collective Bargaining*, pp. 4-5. The 'pessimistic' view is treated in depth in C. Jenkins and B. Sherman, *The Collapse of Work* (London: Eyre-Methuen, 1979).

19. Ibid., p. 28.
20. Ibid., p. 29.
21. Ibid., p. 56.
22. Ibid., p. 56.
23. Ibid., pp. 60-1.
24. Ibid., pp. 61-2.
25. Ibid., p. 38.
26. Ibid., p. 34.
27. Ibid., p. 36.
28. Ibid., p. 36.
29. Ibid., p. 36.
30. Ibid., p. 37.
31. Ibid., p. 37.
32. Ibid., p. 37.
33. Ibid., pp. 64-71.
34. The TUC recognise that unions face a variety of situations, and will produce solutions which will, in many cases, differ substantially from the TUC 'model'.
35. The ensuing discussion is based on the following statements of union objectives, policies and guidelines for negotiators.

APEX, *Automation and The Office Worker* (London: APEX, 1980).
ASTMS, 'Technology Agreements', mimeo (London: ASTMS, 1979).
Banking and Insurance Finance Union, *Report of the Microelectronics Committee*, for the 1980 Annual Conference (Esher, Surrey, 1980).
Electrical, Electronic, Telecommunication and Plumbing Union, *New Technology Guidelines* (London, 1980).
National Union of General and Municipal Workers (GMWU), *New Technology Report to Congress* (London, 1980).
NUJ, *Journalists and New Technology* (London: NUJ, 1980).
TGWU, *Microelectronics: New Technology; Old Problems; New Opportunities* (London: TGWU, 1978).

Most of the above include draft model technology agreements. Further references to these sources will be by way of the union's abbreviated name and page numbers. Some union policy statements are summarised in *Industrial*

Relations Review and Report, no. 198 (1979) pp. 2-10.

36. ASTMS, pp. 1-2.
37. NUJ, pp. 22, 37-8.
38. APEX, pp. 61-2, 37-49.
39. BIFU, pp. 22-4.
40. TGWU, p. 14.
41. The 'Rules Approach' to industrial relations, in which this distinction is of fundamental importance to the methodology, is discussed in J. F. B. Goodman *et al.*, *Rule-Making and Industrial Peace* (London: Croom Helm, 1977) pp. 12-19.
42. Reviews of agreements dealing with new technology may be found in *Industrial Relations Review and Report*, no. 227 (1980) pp. 2-6; and in the Incomes Data Study no. 220, *Changing Technology* (1980) pp. 18-20. The TUC has also produced a mimeographed paper on New Technology Agreements accompanied by summaries of 22 actual agreements.
43. How far this last group of objectives represents purely nominal negotiating positions is open to argument; they are included here to delimit the 'high union power' end of the spectrum, and because these objectives are usually included in union documents. For example, in 1979 the APEX Annual Conference passed a resolution of support for 'any group of members who seek to ensure that the introduction of these technologies is matched by a corresponding decrease in working hours to ensure the maintenance of job numbers' (APEX, p. 36).

12 Responses to the Employment Consequences of Technological Change

LINDA HESSELMAN and RUTH SPELLMAN

1 INTRODUCTION

It is difficult not to be aware of the various new technologies and applications which are becoming available. Microelectronics is expected to form a dominant technology in the coming decades because of the trend to falling costs and increased capability plus the range of potential applications. Numerous applications of lasers and fibre optics are coming on-stream, for example in the areas of precision measurement, weaponry, communications, and metal-working. Commercially viable applications of biotechnology are also on the horizon, particularly in the areas of food ingredients, agriculture, energy and chemicals. Unfortunately, cataloguing the range of existing and possible technological developments and end-uses is easier than forecasting their overall effects on employment.

There is no standard way to allow for discontinuities in innovation within econometric models, which usually treat technological change as an exogenous constant or represent it by a time trend. It is agreed that the net effect on employment will depend on the balance between the demand creation and job displacement effects of technological change, but their relative magnitudes and timing are disputed. Because of the lack of a general theoretical or empirical framework in which to analyse the effects of technological change, considerable use is made of case studies, though forecasters differ on which cases are the best pointers to the future. Considering the effects of microelectronics, for example, Barron and Curnow (1979) estimate that the labour displacement effects will affect about 16 per cent of the labour force, and if the UK experiences slow growth and balance of payments problems, they 'contemplate levels of unemployment of 10-15 per cent of the workforce or more'. Beenstock (1979), on the other hand, argues that the job displacement effect of microelectronics is modified by the job creation effects after two years, resulting eventually (after sixteen years) in employment levels 0.5 per cent higher than they would have been otherwise. So, depending on the forecast chosen and the time horizon, the

employment effects of microelectronics will be either cata-
strophic or minimal. To support their position, the minimalists
can refer to the 1950s automation scare in the US which never
materialised, and the redeployment of displaced UK agricultural
workers over the past twenty years. Predictions of widespread
future unemployment appear to be based on three different
approaches.

(a) The sectoral approach. By disaggregating the economy
    and looking at potential job losses, sector by sector,
    some alarming totals can be reached on the future scale
    of unemployment. The dynamic effects of new technology
    and the possible interaction between sectors which
    could stimulate demand are often ignored with this
    approach.
(b) The states of technology approach. This is essentially
    a comparative static approach predicting changes in only
    one variable, technology, and calculating the likely
    effects on labour demand. With this approach, it is
    often assumed that technological possibilities are
    economically viable and that there are no constraints
    on labour supply.
(c) The historical/technological approach. This is a mixture
    of extrapolation of past trends (e.g. trends from em-
    ployment in the primary and manufacturing sectors to-
    wards the service sector employment) and assumptions
    about the absorption of new technology.

None of these approaches pay sufficient attention to the details of labour supply, for example the changing skill mix
required, the crucial relationship between job displacement
and creation, or the interaction between industries. An equi-
librating mechanism that evens out the rate of adoption across
industries and over time is almost always assumed. Discontinuities, however, are often the focus of concern at the industry level.

Whatever the incremental effect of new technology on employment, it must be superimposed on a fairly gloomy economic outlook. Looking beyond the current cyclical downturn, there is
little hard evidence for optimism about Britain's medium- to
longer-term prospects. The Cambridge Economic Policy Group's
latest base forecast of 4.4 million unemployed by 1985 is,
admittedly, one of the most pessimistic projections, but none
of them is optimistic. The UK is not alone in its gloomy
prospects, as most advanced industrial countries are now
facing more uncertainty than in the post-war period. Some
explain the current malaise in terms of the down-swing of a
Kondratieff wave. In the early stages of new technologies,

employment is generated by the increase in investment accompanied by the creation of new industries producing new products with new processes. As industries mature, innovation switches to standardisation and cost-cutting. Regardless of the explanation, it is unlikely to be a congenial macroeconomic environment in which to adopt the striking changes in product and process technology which are expected to become available in the next decades.

The next section of this chapter considers why it is rational, given the constraints they face, for various groups to oppose or moderate the pace of adjustment. Ideally, society would wish to adjust in such a way as to maximise potential social benefits, while minimising disruption, dislocation and hardship. To do this involves coordinating both the adjustment to technological change itself (in, for example, patterns of output, employment, skills, location), and the responses of various interest groups with influence on the pace of adjustment. There are two main processes by which this coordination might be achieved, the market mechanism or explicit socio-political coordination resulting from discussion and negotiation between the major interest groups.

The third section considers the role and characteristics of market coordination. It examines the way in which the market enforces adjustment and the significance for the form and pace of adjustment of the various ways in which the actual system deviates from the competitive model. An alternative process, involving explicit discussion and negotiation between major interest groups, is reviewed in the fourth section. Examples of this type of response include: Department of Employment studies, examples of European adjustment policies, proposals by the TUC and individual trade unions, CBI and various Sector Working Parties (SWPs). A summary follows, which also examines the factors which will influence the interaction between market and explicit socio-political coordination.

2 THE PACE OF ADJUSTMENT

The UK is faced with a situation in which there are important technological improvements which seem likely to be adopted by competitors but which may also exacerbate already high levels of unemployment. It is generally accepted that the UK must adopt the new technologies or face further erosion of international competitiveness. There may be short-run adjustment costs, but, if the UK fails to adjust, these would be outweighed by the longer-run costs of lost markets. However, it is also agreed that the UK economy adjusts too slowly.

It is important to distinguish this criticism - that the UK adjusts too slowly because institutions are inflexible, unresponsive to the environment and organised in a way that hinders transformation - from another common criticism, that the UK level of productivity is too low. In fact, the two objectives, the highest possible level of productivity and the ability to adjust, may be antithetical. Measures taken to maximise productivity (large scale, standardisation, formal organisational structures, bureaucratic division of labour, etc.) may introduce rigidities which lock the organisation into a particular system. Such systems, though they may maximise productivity in the short run, may also inhibit flexibility and raise the cost of subsequent adjustment and innovation. This type of contradiction is well documented in the case of the US car industry by Abernathy (1978).

It is the pace of adjustment that is of concern here, and various factors are thought to influence it. To the extent that a new technology is embodied in capital goods, clearly the rate and type of investment is important in determining the pace of technological change. Case studies identify constraints on change in the UK such as management awareness and attitudes, shop floor resistance, the lack of government support and the high cost of new product development. However, the identification of constraints sheds little light on how to relax them. For this, it is necessary to examine the pressures and incentives facing individuals and groups that lead them to oppose technological change or try to control the pace of adjustment, i.e. where individual rationality can lead to socially damaging outcomes. To start, we need to ask: (a) what groups will be affected by the change; (b) what power do those groups have to modify the pace of change; and (c) is it possible to rearrange the incentives the groups face to encourage them to accept a position in which all benefit (e.g. where losers are compensated)?

The problem resembles the prisoner's dilemma. Consider a highly simplified example of a situation that might face workers and the firm that employs them. The workers have to choose whether to accept or reject a new labour-saving technology; the firm chooses whether or not to undertake a strategy of expansion. The hypothetical pay-offs perceived to result from the possible choices are shown in Figure 12.1 below. The numbers in the boxes show the change in employment (W) and profits (F) that result from the various choices. If the workers accept the new technology and the firm chooses the expansion strategy, employment increases by say, 50, and the expected value of profits increases by, say, 100. Alternatively, if the workers accept and the firm does not expand, employment falls by 50 and the expected value of profits

| | | Firm | |
		Expand	Stagnate
	Accept	$W = +50$; $F = +100$.	$W = -50$; $F = +150$.
Workers			
	Reject	$W = +100$; $F = -100$.	$W = 0$; $F = 0$.

FIGURE 12.1 *Hypothetical pay-off matrix*

increases by 150.[1] If the workers reject the new technology
and the firm expands production, employment increases by 100
but the firm makes losses. If workers reject and the firm
does not expand, employment and profits are unchanged. What
should the workers and the firm choose to do? If the firm
expands, it could make a loss of 100, while if it does not
expand, the worst outcome is no change in profits. From the
workers' point of view, if they accept the new technology,
employment could fall by 50, whereas if they reject, the worst
outcome is no change in employment. Risks for both groups are
minimised if the workers reject the new technology and the
firm keeps production static - the bottom right-hand entry.
The Pareto Optimal position, where neither group can be better
off without the other being worse off, in this example, is
the upper left-hand value, accept and expand. Rational risk
averse behaviour by the individual groups in this example
produces a sub-optimal position.

The example has been cast in terms of worker acceptance or
rejection of innovation, and the worker that tends to spring
to mind is a blue collar trade union member. In fact, the
workers concerned are equally likely to be supervisors and
managers. The nature of the tasks required of these people,
and the technical content of their work, are likely to change
dramatically with the adoption of new technology. Since the
present incumbents of these positions may well be unqualified
to handle the environment, they may have strong incentives to
hinder adoption.

There are several ways the reject and stagnate choice may
be avoided or resolved, including the following.

(a) If each group had confidence in the other, the reject
    and stagnate option would not be chosen, but why should
    they have confidence in the other following an irrational
    strategy? In the absence of trust and the presence of
    uncertainty, the firm, quite sensibly, adopts the posi-
    tion that it cannot expand because the chances of suc-
    cessful implementation of the new technology are low.
    Equally sensibly, the workers say they have no confi-
    dence in the firm's willingness or ability to expand

production. If they trusted each other, they could both
benefit, but trusting is risky, though there may be
institutional arrangements which help to establish
common interests, for example profit-sharing, workers
cooperatives, or guaranteed lifetime employment systems.
(b) The Government could try and force both groups to
accept the Pareto Optimal solution through, for example,
enforceable planning agreements. The question is then
whether or not the Government has the necessary knowledge or power to coerce the groups in this way.
(c) The Government could establish an insurance scheme to
provide compensation; for example, if the workers
accept and the firm does not expand production, the
Government would provide 51 jobs so the final change
in employment would be +1; and if the firm expands and
the workers reject, it would give a 101 subsidy to the
firm so the final change in profits would be +1. Notice
that if the groups are rational, compensation under the
insurance scheme need never be paid, since the accept
and expand strategy becomes the rational choice.
(d) Market forces may resolve the problem. The firm which
chooses the reject and stagnate solution may be driven
out of business in the long run by competitors who,
facing a different set of constraints, accepted and
expanded. How long reject and stagnate solutions can
persist, i.e. how quickly and strongly market pressure
comes to bear, are matters of dispute. UK history might
suggest, however, that unsatisfactory solutions can
persist for long periods.

This example is only an illustration. Actual decisions
about the introduction of new technology are not so clear-cut,
and may be contingent on the decisions of other agents, introducing interdependence. Pay-offs are uncertain and may not be
measured only in terms of employment and profits, but also in
conditions of work, control over the production process,
organisational survival, and a host of other variables subject
to dispute. But the issues and conflicts raised by this
example are real, and it illustrates the situation where
worker resistance and unadventurous management may be a
rational strategy in the face of technological change. However,
if this situation is a general one, why should it be more
severe in the UK than elsewhere? A range of answers have
been suggested, including the following.

(a) The situation is aggravated by the existence of groups
with the power to resist change. The UK may have more
powerful groups.

(b) The Government does not intervene, with either the
carrot (compensation) or the stick (coercion), as
much as other governments (e.g. MITI in Japan) or
institutions (e.g. German banks).
(c) Market forces do not work fast enough in the UK,
perhaps because of too much government intervention,
or too much market concentration.
(d) There is less trust and common interest among the
various groups in the UK.

Having examined the problem above, the next sections consider two ways in which it may be resolved. First, the market
mechanism is discussed. Then the political mechanisms to
effect change are considered: either government action or
direct negotiation between the interested groups.

3 MARKET MECHANISM

The market mechanism transmits a variety of signals about
consumer preferences and relative efficiencies through a
large and complex economy. This 'invisible hand' is also free
of administrative costs to the government and political inter-
ference or pressure. Under certain assumptions, a competitive
market will produce a Pareto Optimal allocation of resources
- no-one can be made better off without someone being made
worse off. The present government has argued strongly for the
benefits of the market mechanism, in improving allocation,
incentives, innovation, enterprise and effort; and it has
attributed much of the failure of the UK economy to inter-
ference with its operation. For example, in a recent speech,
the Financial Secretary to the Treasury, Nigel Lawson (1980),
argued that 'prices are still the most efficient signals we
have for transmitting the minimum necessary information about
consumer wants and investment opportunities'. Furthermore,
'while markets are undoubtedly imperfect so is the State . . .
there are very real reasons why the imperfections of state
intervention in the economic field are likely to be not merely
equal to, but greater than the imperfections of the market'.
It is difficult to assess the relative imperfections of the
market versus state intervention, but it may be unwise to
leave the implementation of significant technological trans-
formations to the market mechanism alone, for a variety of
reasons. Even if the outcome is Pareto Optimal, it may be
socially unacceptable; there is no guarantee that the market-
generated distribution of income and hardship would be desirable or acceptable. It may also be that the assumptions
under which the market allocation is efficient are not met in

practice. Price signals may be distorted by taxes and subsidies; while monopolies and oligopolies may be able to insulate themselves from market pressure. Uncertainty, indivisi-
bilities, time lags and the need for large social investments
in infrastructure and training, may impair market responses
to technological change. In addition, if the innovative firm
expects to lose much of the benefit to imitating competitors,
the profit-maximising level of R & D will be socially sub-
optimal. These characteristics and distortions influence the
response to and pace of adjustment.

   There is some evidence on the influence of market pressures
and characteristics on the pace of technological change.
Davies (1979) studied the diffusion of twenty-two process
innovations in various industries in the UK and found that
the speed of diffusion is faster: the more profitable the
innovation; the fewer firms in the industry; the smaller the
size inequality between firms; the greater the labour intensity of the adopting firms; and (weakly) the faster the rate
of growth of the adopting industry. Whether or not the market
mechanism is viewed as the appropriate way to implement technological change in the UK, market forces (amongst others)
create the environment in which the adjustment to technological change will take place. If socio-political coordination
is adopted, it must operate within, and take account of, an
environment in which market forces such as international
competition are dominant. To insulate the UK entirely from
market forces would require the establishment of a command
economy with state control over trade and the allocation of
resources. Short of this, any form of indicative planning or
socio-political coordination has to operate within the constraints imposed by world markets and attempt to adjust to
them. It is to the current socio-political responses as to
direction and coordination that we now turn.

4   SOCIO-POLITICAL RESPONSE

The discussion so far has centred mainly on the more general
effects and responses to technological change; we now turn to
the actual responses from organised groups. Since the changes
discussed do not affect all industries evenly, they require
numerous separate, though not necessarily independent, decisions and actions within sectors, industries, individual
companies and trade unions. An examination of the current
socio-political response requires not only a review of broad
principles, as outlined by the TUC and CBI for example, but
also the response to specific industrial situations by Sector
Working Parties (SWPs) and Economic Development Committees

(EDCs), individual companies and trade unions. At the industry
level, the response to technological change is as diffuse and
varied as the adjustments required. However, the examples reviewed below, some of which are well known, do point to
general concerns and constraints within industries, and these
will be highlighted in the concluding section.

4.1 *National Economic Development Council (NEDC)*

Concern about the difficulty of transition to industries
based on new technology, and about the slow pace of adjustment in the UK relative to its competitors, were motives for
a discussion about adjustment policies at the June 1980
meeting of the NEDC. The paper contributed by NEDO reviewed
the policy measures that have been taken to encourage capital
and manpower to move more quickly and less painfully to growth
sectors in an economy, citing many examples from Europe.

The underlying justification for adjustment policies is
that the market mechanism, particularly in the labour market,
does not work painlessly or without friction. The need for
adjustment policies has increased because of the pace of
technological change, increased international specialisation
and the need to develop new (high technology) products, not
in competition with NICs. Adjustment policies may involve:
assisting companies with research and development; easing
other adjustment costs, for example the state bearing part
of the cost of redundancy pay and training provision; increasing the information flow (e.g. on new technology); or
directing resources to products in which the country has a
continuing comparative advantage.

There are also a number of negative adjustment policies
designed to cushion the effects of market changes on old
staple industries (usually major employers of labour in
particular areas). The focus of policy has, however, tended
to move from subsidising losers, first to backing winners,
and then to a cross-sectoral approach aimed at minimising
supply constraints and easing the process of structural change
in the economy. As far as manpower is concerned there has been
a definite shift away from negative, or at best neutral, job
retention policies, towards an attempt to stimulate job
creation. In Luxemburg, steel industry adjustment is being
achieved by early retirement and re-training, and by finding
new employment for many employees through a special 'anti-
crisis' division set up by the industry. The unions and employers' federations in Norway have agreed upon a framework
for local technology agreements on the introduction of computer-based systems. Training schemes are provided in Sweden

for those who are unemployed or threatened by unemployment, to facilitate moves into areas of skill shortage. A scheme in Germany enables the Government to relate the number of training places provided for young people by industry to the numbers of school leavers each year. A levy is raised to meet the costs of providing additional training places if necessary. On a much smaller scale in Britain, Job Creation Limited, originally an offshoot of BSC, has now set up on a commercial basis to assist new companies in high unemployment areas and to provide expert advice and help in areas such as sources of finance.

4.2 *The National Economic Development Office (NEDO), EDCs and SWPs*

At NEDO, and by means of the SWPs/EDCs responsible for particular sectors, a great deal of work has been done on identifying labour shortfalls and surpluses, the future skill requirements of particular industries, and the role of government and institutions in facilitating the introduction of new technology at company/plant level. Many SWPs/EDCs have produced employment estimates, but these in themselves are less important than the process of identifying the particular constraints and opportunities for sectors, industries and companies where new technology has been, is being or will be introduced.

A good example of an SWP which has seriously examined the effects of the labour market on adaptation to new technology is the Computer SWP. NEDO, through the Computer SWP, commissioned a study from the Institute of Manpower Studies (IMS), *Computer Manpower in the 1980s: The supply and demand for computer related manpower to 1985*. A number of conclusions were reached in this study, with implications not only for computer manufacturers and current computer users but also for all those sectors requiring some type of computer-skilled manpower (i.e. where computer uses can be developed on the production line, in stock control, in product development, etc.). The report concluded that shortages of CSM (Computer Skilled Manpower) could be seriously aggravated by shortages of engineering skills. Technological changes in the production of software will reduce some skill requirements, but in the meantime, the most critical constraint on the application of mini-computers to a whole range of new tasks, is likely to be manpower.

The IMS estimate that the national stock of people with computer related skills is currently at least 275,000 and their conservative estimate is that the immediate overall

shortfall is approximately 25,000 people. There is a national
shortfall of more than 16,000 in the programming/analysis
occupations. In addition, the computer supply sector suffers
shortages of about 6 per cent of key engineers both at the
professional and technical level. They conclude that these
key skill shortfalls, by increasing mobility (20 per cent
between jobs) and thus high training costs, are inhibiting
employers from recruiting and training sufficient new entrants,
and are discouraging new applications. Manpower shortages are
the most important constraint on the rate of current and
medium-term diffusion of technology. As a result, old jobs
are being lost without new ones being created, so that the
social constraint on the adoption of new technology will become increasingly prominent.

The IMS predictions are based on the assumption that the
supply of CSM staff is produced by the educational/training
system rather than from companies' existing staff. Given
this assumption, it is estimated that the incremental requirement of programming/analysis skills will be approximately
500 per month. Even if companies do more in-house training,
there are likely to be serious shortages in the labour market,
regardless of attitudes or other institutional barriers to
technological change.

The successful adoption of technological change in an industry not only requires the appropriate mix of skilled labour,
but often also requires adjustment in production processes.
Several SWPs and EDCs have identified production constraints:
for example, the Electronic Components SWP has reported that
British companies do not make components to the right quality,
price and volume. The Radio, Radar and Navigational Aids SWP
has revealed that only 18 per cent of firms achieved satisfactory delivery performance and that productive resources
are under-utilised. The main constraint in this case is slow
adoption of modern computer-based management techniques. The
Machine Tools EDC is tackling machine makers who have concentrated production on 'pre-microprocessor designs', to
encourage them to expand and accelerate output of advanced
technology production. Applications of computer-based control
systems which will lead to higher productivity have been
identified by other SWPs, including Printing Machinery,
Footwear, Clothing, Cotton and Allied Textiles, and Wool
Textiles. Critical constraints on the introduction of new
technology in the clothing and textiles sector, like elsewhere, are likely to be attitudes to change and possible
employment displacement effects, given contracting markets
and fierce competition from overseas.

4.3 *Government*

There has been a steady and increasing recognition of the
role microelectronics could play in the revitalisation of
industry. The government has responded through organisations
like the National Enterprise Board as well as the programmes
and initiatives undertaken by the Department of Industry and
the Department of Employment.

4.3.1 *Department of Industry (DoI)*: The DoI has been
responsible for two major programmes designed to assist the
introduction of microtechnology into UK industries. These are
MISP (The Microelectronics Industry Support Programme) and
MAP (The Microprocessor Applications Project).

MISP was set up in 1978 as a five-year selective support
programme for the UK microelectronics components industry.
Its purpose was to further research and development, investment in plant and buildings, and to launch products or extend
marketing capacity. The assistance entails the provision of
research or development grants of up to 25 per cent of total
qualifying project costs. In certain cases, the DoI can enter
into a cost-shared contract of up to 50 per cent of total
qualifying project costs (recoverable by a levy on subsequent
sales). In addition, MISP makes assistance available for investment in capital equipment, plant, machinery and buildings.
Currently, the amount allocated under this scheme (against
approved projects) is in the region of £27 million.

The Microprocessor Applications Project (MAP) was also
introduced in 1978 to enable UK-based companies and training
organisations to obtain government grants to develop courses
for engineers in the use of microelectronics. Under MAP,
approved open courses qualify for a grant of 50 per cent of
costs, and in-house courses 25 per cent. The training support
is primarily intended to increase the availability and quality
of microelectronics courses for design and production engineers working in industry. MAP complements the National
Computing Centre's Threshold scheme, started in November
1976. This scheme consists of an integrated course of training
lasting a maximum of forty weeks and is funded by the MSC
under its special training measures programme. It has two
major objectives: to train more computer programmers and
operators (to meet the needs of new technology); and to offer
additional training opportunities for unemployed young people.

4.3.2 *Department of Employment (DE)*: The DE set up a Manpower
Study Group on microelectronics in July 1978 to examine the
manpower implications of microelectronic technology up to 1990.
The study group report (known as the Sleigh Report) was

published in December 1979 (DE, 1979). Sleigh, like others, emphasises that it is failure to exploit new technology, rather than the consequences of applying that technology, which would have the most damaging employment effects.

The study group found that the pace of adaptation to micro-electronics in Britain has been dangerously slow, and there is a real risk of British industry falling behind its overseas competitors. To avoid this eventuality, Sleigh stresses the importance of an adaptable labour force, the provision of appropriate training, and the creation of the right climate for the introduction of technological change. The Sleigh Report starts with a series of premises.

(a) The absolute decline in employment in manufacturing in Britain in recent years was not inevitable nor need it be irreversible. The growth of employment in services is not necessarily associated in the long run with a loss of jobs in manufacturing.

(b) The debate about microelectronics and employment has tended to confuse de-industrialisation with the post-industrial society. Technological change has some job displacement and some job creation effects (which depend on the increase in productivity, and the results as far as the business community is concerned). The overall effect is impossible to gauge, but history suggests a positive relationship between output, employment and new technology.

(c) 'Models' produced in relation to microtechnology tend to ignore the inter-relationships between sectors and the indirect macro-economic effects. Speed of diffusion is also an important factor in measuring or assessing the employment effects of new technology.

The authors of the Sleigh Report visited over sixty companies in Britain, together with a number in America and Japan, and drew several conclusions. Those British companies with formal (or informal) no redundancy agreements are those which experience fewer industrial relations problems over the introduction of new technology. In addition, it was found that the successful management of innovation in British companies was accompanied by effective communications and consultation with trade unions, and a flexible attitude by trade unions to technology agreements. The authors also concluded that although relatively low awareness of the new technology in Britain has meant that key skill shortages have not seriously affected innovation, many companies will experience difficulties unless they are prepared to do their own training and re-training. Massive public expenditures (on training,

for example), even if feasible, are not the answer. However,
continuing attention will need to be paid to the most cost-
effective public training programmes.

The Sleigh Report concluded that the effects of microtechnology on employment in manufacturing would be patchy and
swamped by the effect of the growth of demand for manufactured
goods. Speedy adaptation could help some industries regain
their competitive position (hence securing jobs), and in others
processes will be simplified and streamlined (thus reducing
employment levels). In any company, both effects could be
present at any one time. Those industries which are already
automated or semi-automated will benefit from better control
systems. Concerning services, Sleigh predicts that the effects
of technological change will be to reduce clerical and sub-
clerical jobs over the next five to ten years and to create
new skill needs. The overall impact on jobs will depend upon
the economic and adaptation costs of the new technology (related to the benefits). In areas such as the railways and the
postal service, overall numbers are expected to decline in
line with past trends, with little or no acceleration as a
result of microelectronics; post office telecommunications
employment levels, which have often been regarded as at risk,
are forecast to remain stable.

4.4 *Management*

It is difficult to generalise about the management response
to technological change. However, there is some anecdotal
evidence (e.g. from SWPs and EDCs) which suggests that there
is much more awareness of the potential impact of microelectronic technology in those industries which are already
highly capital intensive (e.g. computers) than in those which
are more labour intensive (e.g. footwear).

4.4.1 *Confederation of British Industry (CBI)*: Earlier in
1980, the CBI issued a document, *Jobs: Facing the Future*
(CBI, 1980), which concluded that the only permanent solution
to unemployment is to create viable new jobs in new and expanding industries. Our prosperity, the CBI argues, depends
upon our ability to incorporate new technologies, increase
productivity, and hence remain competitive in world markets.
However, there are a number of uncertainties regarding employment prospects.

  (a) The level of employment depends on the level of demand
      in the economy, which is influenced by, for example,
      anti-inflation policies.

(b) The impact of microelectronics on employment is likely to be uneven. Some sectors and occupational groups are likely to grow at the expense of others. It is easier to see where jobs may be lost than where they will be found.

(c) Britain's labour force is expected to grow by about two million by 1991. It is difficult to see how this 'extra' labour will be absorbed into employment.

(d) Competition from newly-industrialising countries is penetrating even the less labour-intensive industries and will affect employment in some sectors.

In this report, the CBI stresses the key role of competitiveness and the need for control over labour costs. They conclude that 'the new jobs that are created may be different in location and will almost certainly require new skills from those they replace'. Because of these requirements, the role of an efficient labour market in smoothing out the adjustment problems caused by new technology is emphasised. Skill imbalances need to be corrected by training and re-training, and the MSC can play a useful back-up role, given appropriate action by companies. In addition, flexible apprenticeship schemes are required. The CBI suggests that the 'time served' criterion should be abolished, and trade unions should accept government skill-centre trainees. *Jobs: Facing the Future* sets out a programme of action for government, employers and trade unions, including:

(a) agreement on the potential unemployment problem and the manning implications of new technology;

(b) agreement on the need to stimulate productivity, requiring changes in attitudes by employers and employees;

(c) agreement on the need to improve labour market efficiency, easing skill mismatches and improving mobility;

(d) examination of the costs and employment implications of early or flexible retirement;

(e) examination of the role of education, training and re-training;

(f) examination of the costs and benefits of shortening the working week.

The CBI places the responsibility on employers to: take the initiative on productivity (by better communications and consultation); develop manpower strategies on recruitment, training and resettlement; develop better remuneration packages, including flexible working hours and single staff status; respond to social pressures, such as youth unemployment; and look for job expansion opportunities.

4.5 *Trade Unions*

A BBC2 *Horizon* programme highlighted trade union awareness
of microelectronics, and many trade unions have formed modernisation and technical committees to, for example, discuss the
possible impact of the micro-chip, and launch seminars. In
addition, a number of trade unions have produced their own
guidelines on technology agreements. However, there is, in
general, much less awareness on the shop floor. In addition,
most trade unions appear to believe the gloomier unemployment
projections of the academic experts.

  Trade unions have attempted to quantify the impact of new
technologies on occupational groups, though the calculations
are usually expressed as broad percentage bands with little
pretence of precision. Union working groups have concentrated
on the potential impact of technology on offices, and particularly upon information-handling occupations. For example,
the ASTMS *Discussion Document: Technological Change and
Collective Bargaining* (ASTMS, 1979) warned that almost two
out of three employees were in occupations at risk, with
clerical and related workers particularly vulnerable to displacement. ASTMS estimates the effect will be likely to vary
within a 10 to 30 per cent range of severity. Other studies
concentrating on specific sectors have indicated the following
pattern. In banking, a potential reduction in clerical staff
of between 40 and 70 per cent is forecast. Career structures
and work content are also likely to be affected. In distributive trades, a decline in the demand for labour is anticipated, and it will gather momentum in the mid-1980s. New
technology will particularly affect cash register operators
and those engaged in warehousing/stock control. In engineering,
a net reduction of up to 50 per cent in the demand for
draughtsmen is anticipated, caused largely by computer-aided
design, although there may be an increase in the demand for
service/maintenance craftsmen. In word-processing, on conservative estimates it is thought that 100 to 150 thousand
jobs will be lost each year. In the public services, new
technology has been and will be introduced to bring about
labour shedding. This is particularly worrying for trade
unionists, because, in the past, public sector employment has
grown while manufacturing employment has declined. None of
these projections can be said to have much statistical validity, but they do indicate the concern in trade union circles
about the potential job displacement effects of new technology.
Unfortunately, it is much more difficult to forecast the

possibilities for job creation.

4.5.1 *Trade Union Congress (TUC):* A booklet entitled
Employment and Technology (TUC, 1979) was produced by a
special working group with membership including representatives of a dozen major unions affiliated to the TUC. The
report summarises the development and potential applications
of the new technology, and draws some general conclusions
about the impact on jobs. It argues that there is both a
challenge and an opportunity, and that the task is to ensure
maximisation of benefits (and equitable distribution of them)
whilst minimising costs. It recognises that the trade union
movement will need to 'develop its structures, policies and
capacities to meet these changing demands', and as a result
set out various guidelines for affiliated unions (emphasising
local joint machinery, new technology agreements, etc.).

The Employment and Technology working group of the TUC aims
to coordinate education programmes, gather and disseminate
information, develop expertise in work restructuring, health
and safety aspects of technology, etc. Members of the TUC
Economic Committee visited the USA, and tabled a full report
at the NEDC in January 1980. The visit was intended to create
a sense of urgency about developing microelectronic applications. Recently, the TUC and CBI have begun a series of talks
on a joint approach to new technology which could be implemented through local bargaining mechanisms. The outcome of
these talks is not yet clear, but that they are taking place
at all reveals a growing concern about the effects of new
technology on employment, investment, etc. At the beginning
of September 1980, a joint TUC-CBI statement on technological
change was issued. The statement is currently the subject of
consultation within the CBI.

5 CONCLUSIONS

However socially and economically necessary proponents think
it to be, technological change will be opposed unless mechanisms are established to guarantee an equitable outcome.
Furthermore, it may be impossible to separate issues of
technological change and the process of adjustment from
questions of control and distribution. Those who may bear the
cost of adjustment are unlikely to accept vague promises of
good times after a difficult transition. At the same time, it
is unlikely that those who stand to lose will be able to prevent implementation, given the strength of technological and
competitive pressures, but they can slow it down, and sluggish
adjustment may prove to be the worst of all worlds. It is

failure to exploit new technology, rather than new technology itself, that may produce the most severe economic and employment effects.

The strength of socio-political coordination lies in the explicit attempt to determine a socially acceptable solution, should one exist, which is in the interest of all groups. The NEDO SWP/EDC mechanism attempts to accomplish this by improving information, awareness and trust between management, trade unions and government. However, a positive response by organised groups does not, in itself, guarantee acceptance further down the line, for example at plant level. At a general level, most agree that technological change presents a challenge and an opportunity. But since actual decisions about the introduction of new technology are not clear-cut, and there is uncertainty about pay-offs, there remain substantial differences on specific issues. These differences are aggravated by the hostile macro-economic environment, the structural failure of the UK economy, and traditional antagonisms.

Within industry, there is concern about the unevenness of the transition: the balance between job displacement and demand creation; the changing structure of skills required; and the increasing interdependence across industries. There are important supply constraints in the labour market which will inhibit rapid adoption of new technology and applications. It is on just these details that forecasters resort to gesticulation. As to the Government, there is concern that the State is the only institution capable of managing the transition, yet State intervention is often viewed as distorting and inhibiting change. However these issues are resolved, it will be in a context of a competitive international market environment which is changing rapidly in directions which are difficult to predict.

NOTES

The authors are grateful for the help and advice from colleagues at NEDO, but the paper should be taken as their personal view.
1. If the firm expands production, it is possible that they may not be able to sell the additional output, resulting in over-capacity. Consequently, the expected value of the change in profits is lower with the expanded production choice, in this example. Of course, in reality, the actual pay-offs depend on a variety of factors, known only uncertainly.

REFERENCES

Abernathy, W. J. (1978) *The Productivity Dilemma: Roadblock to Innovation in the Automobile Industry* (Baltimore, Md: John Hopkins University Press).
ASTMS (1979) *Discussion Document: Technological Change and Collective Bargaining* (London: ASTMS).
Barron, I. and R. Curnow (1979) *The Future with Micro-electronics* (London: Francis Pinter).
Beenstock, M. (1979) 'Do Labour Markets Work?', *LBS Economic Outlook*, vol. 3, nos 9 and 10 (June/July) pp. 21-31.
CBI (1980) *Jobs: Facing the Future* (London: CBI).
Davies, S. (1979) *The Diffusion of Process Innovations* (Cambridge University Press).
Department of Employment (1979) *The Manpower Implications of Micro-electronic Technology* (London: HMSO).
Department of Industry (1978) *Microelectronics Industry Support Programme* (London: HMSO).
Department of Industry (1978) *Microprocessor Applications Project* (London: HMSO).
IMS (1980) *Computer Manpower in the 1980s: The Supply and Demand for Computer Related Manpower to 1985* (London: NEDO).
Lawson, N. (1980) *The New Conservatism* (London: Centre for Policy Studies).
NEDO (1980) *Adjustment Policies in Europe* (London: NEDO) p. 33.
TUC (1979) *Employment and Technology* (London: TUC).

13 Innovations in Work Organisation as a Response to the Employment Implications of Technological Change

DEREK L. BOSWORTH and PETER DAWKINS

1 INTRODUCTION

Many of the more fundamental changes occurring around us can
be traced to some underlying technological change. Around
these fundamental changes, new technologies also weave a network of more minor modifications, nuances in the fabric of
society itself. The subject of this Conference has been the
implications of technological change for employment (and unemployment). We should not lose sight of the fact that employment is just one aspect of the overall picture. Indeed, it can
be argued, with some conviction, that it is difficult to build
up a comprehensive picture of the consequences for employment
without considering these wider issues. In particular, we would
want to stress that the literature on induced invention, innovation and diffusion clearly indicates that technological
change is, itself, influenced by underlying economic, social
and legal forces. In addition, it is often very difficult to
separate the parts played by technological changes and the
organisational changes that often accompany them. This chapter
therefore examines some of the broader consequences of technological change for employment, outlines some government responses that will help counteract the more adverse effects and,
in particular, shows how many of these remedial actions lie in
the area of innovations in work organisation.

 ## 2 SKILL LEVELS

A job is comprised of a set of tasks, each with its own mental
and physical actions and degrees of dexterity. Technological
change may not make a particular job redundant, but it may
alter the set of tasks involved and the level of skill required
to carry out any given task. A substantial amount of detailed

case study evidence of this type is being built up (for example, Bell, 1972, and Senker and Huggett, 1973).

Movement down the skill ladder may be physically accommodated quite easily. That is to say, workers with the ability to carry out more complicated and sophisticated tasks are capable of completing simpler tasks. On the other hand, there may be psychological problems with such a change. First, a skilled worker may find it difficult to accept having to work at a lower skill level. Second, a de-skilling change may result in more repetitive work, with consequent health hazards (i.e. stress, particularly where a rapid pace of work is imposed) and impact on the quality of working life. It has been argued by other authors that modern technologies associated with mass production have almost always involved the 'simplification of jobs' and these methods have 'undoubtedly degraded work for many individuals' (Cox *et al.*, 1979, p. 1234). At this stage it is not so clear that this will continue to be the trend as the new technologies, such as microprocessors and industrial robots, are diffused through the manufacturing sector. Nevertheless, it has been argued that while the new technologies may compete with some of the existing repetitive work practices, this will lead to 'an intensification of job rationalisation and simplification' (Cox *et al.*, 1979, p. 1234).

In so far as de-skilling affects the utility/disutility associated with the job, it will affect the position of the supply curve. If it reduces the utility (increases the disutility), it will result in an inward shift of the supply curve amongst existing workers. The effect of a shift in the supply curve is to raise the wage and lower equilibrium employment: a higher wage and lower employment position than would have been the case under the new technology if it had not been de-skilling. If this were the end of the matter, the firm might now face a considerable incentive to search for some form of job enrichment that would effectively shift the supply curve outwards. It would invest in job enrichment up to the point where the rate of return to the investment at the margin was equal to the going rate of interest.

This is by no means the end of the matter, however, as the higher wage and lower training requirement may make it profitable for additional workers to train. This will have the effect of shifting the supply curve outwards in the longer term. There is no knowing, *a priori*, where it will finish up. However, job enrichment may be possible (and even profitable for the firm), no matter how far to the right the new supply curve moves after de-skilling takes place.

Clearly, considerably more research is required in this area. In certain countries, research (and even innovation) in

the area of the 'humanisation of work' is subsidised by the
government (SSRC, 1978, pp. 10-15). Action research in Sweden
was supported by various funds to the tune of £2.5 million
in 1977-8. The 'Humanisation of Work Programme' in West Germany
is funded through the Ministry of Labour and the Ministry of
Research and Technology. This programme links research, investment and technological change; it involved expenditure
of some £30 million between 1974 and 1977. It is worth adding
that all the European partners contribute towards the activities of the European Foundation for the Improvement of Living
and Working Conditions. The Swedish and West German efforts,
however, were of a different order of magnitude than Britain's
commitment through the European Foundation and Work Research
Unit.

Japan is a country that we tend to associate with rapid
technological change. Until recently, however, there has been
little evidence that Japan's technological change was linked
with any major innovations in work organisation. It is becoming
clear, however, that such links do exist: while Japan has been
involved in a large number and a wide range of work organisation innovations, information about them has been slow to
spread because of language difficulties (Cooper, 1978, p. 28).
Examples of the success of such Japanese programmes are described by Takezawa (1974), Kobayashi (1970), Yoshida (1973)
and Kondo (1973). The results of the experiments point to the
potential for a higher quality of working life.

The Japanese experiments also showed some other, quite
remarkable results. The new forms of work organisation substantially reduced absenteeism and improved productivity
levels. It is probably fair to say that innovations in work
organisation were often associated with some changes in technology, and, while it is difficult to disentangle one cause
from another, changes in work organisation appear to have as
radical an effect on productivity (and, thereby, factor demands) as technological change. The final point to make regarding the Japanese experience is that the changes in work
organisation were often tied up with changes in the structure
of management, the nature of the power relationships within the
firm, and the degree of worker autonomy and participation.

Movement up the skill ladder may result in other, new tasks
(e.g. the need to programme an n.c. machine tool, rather than
just set it). Here the psychological barriers present in de-
skilling are replaced by fears of attaining the necessary
skill levels (see Mishan, 1971). As the change now involves
some degree of training, the effects on supply are likely to
be different. The satisfaction associated with the job may be
rising (disutility falling), while the rate of return associated with the necessary training for the job declines as the

amount of extra training increases (assuming some element of
the training to be of a 'general' kind), unless the wage rate
offered is commensurately larger. Clearly, under such conditions, questions of job enrichment are likely to be much less
important, and questions about training and retraining are of
much greater importance.

A large number of question marks arise concerning the impact of technological change in this area. First, to what
extent are such changes de-skilling? Second, what is the
relationship between skill level and workers' health (i.e.
because of stress problems)? Third, to what extent do workers
accurately take these effects into account when making their
supply decisions? Fourth, what is the relationship between
job enrichment and skill requirements? Fifth, to what extent
do firms have information about the effects of de-skilling
and job enrichment on labour supply? Finally, to what degree
do firms undertake some form of optimal investment programme
in job enrichment? Here we may find grounds for government
intervention, whether because of imperfect information,
externalities or because of meeting minimum socially acceptable criteria.

3   WORK PATTERNS

Evidence is accumulating that indicates that technological
change is a major determinant of employees' work patterns
(i.e. shiftwork/overtime combinations). Our attention focuses,
in particular, on the impact of technological change through
increases in capital intensity and the more rapid obsolescence
of existing technologies.

3.1 *Capital Intensity*

Labour-saving changes (whether because of biased technological
change or through the substitution of capital for labour
around an isoquant formed from existing alternative techniques) have been important in the post-war British manufacturing industry. Indeed, because of the existence and
growth in the incidence of shift-working, capital per man
on the main shift is at a higher level and growing at a
faster rate than the traditional measures of capital per
employee would indicate (Bosworth and Dawkins, 1981a, Chapter
13); see also Wabe and Camara (1979) and Wabe and Bosworth
(Chapter 8 above). Capital intensity is a major determinant
of the mix of work patterns adopted within manufacturing
(see Bosworth and Dawkins, 1981a and 1981b; and Bosworth

et al., 1981a and 1981b). In addition, the growth in capital
intensity has been a key influence on the post-war growth in
overtime and shift-working. Finally, differences in capital
intensity are a major determinant of variations in capital
utilisation and shift-working across industries.

3.2 *Obsolescence*

The second major dimension of technological change concerns
the rate of obsolescence. The evidence relating to obsolescence is less clear-cut. On the one hand, economic theory
is unequivocally able to demonstrate the central role played
by obsolescence in determining the marginal capital savings
that accrue from shift-working and, thereby, its importance
as an influence on the optimal degree of capital utilisation
and shift-working (Marris, 1964 and 1970; and Bosworth and
Dawkins, 1981a, Chapter 13, and 1981b). On the other hand,
deficiencies in the available data have made it almost impossible to test this theory.

3.3 *Work Patterns and Employment*

Technological change is, therefore, an important factor
underlying the choice of work patterns and, as work patterns
are an important dimension of employment, this link automatically lies within the remit of this chapter and the
Conference overall. However, the choice of work patterns is
even more relevant than might at first be imagined. In particular, because the human body has its own biological time
rhythms, for example 'circadian rhythms' (Luce, 1973), it has
been argued that certain patterns of work interrupt the
body's natural functions and activities (Colquhoun, 1978,
pp. 682-5). This alone would probably be sufficient to give
rise to the fear of adverse effects on health (and safety).
In addition, it has been argued that these effects are likely
to be compounded by the adverse social and psychological
implications of 'abnormal' work patterns. While the medical
evidence is ambiguous (Harrington, 1978), and it may well be
that the premia paid for work during 'abnormal' hours of the
day (or week) compensate employees for the additional disutility of the experience (Bosworth and Dawkins, 1980),
nevertheless, the European Commission and International
Labour Organisation both have plans for protective legislation in this area (Bosworth and Dawkins, 1978 and 1981a).
There is, however, still a large amount of work to be carried
out before a proper cost benefit analysis can be undertaken

in this area.

Not only do work patterns have potential health effects, they also have very close ties with the numbers of jobs made available. While the precise degree of substitution between men and hours is to be determined, the longer the average hours per employee per period, the smaller the number of workers demanded. We return to the question of manipulating hours of work in order to create jobs and share work in Section 6 below.

4 HEALTH AND SAFETY

We have already touched upon certain aspects of health, in so far as repetitive work may give rise to problems of stress, and 'abnormal' or 'unusual' times of work may interrupt normal body rhythms and cause social and psychological problems. Here, we turn to the broader questions of health and safety. It is a moot point whether health and safety have been improving at work. Conditions may well have been radically altered in traditional occupations and activities by the Factories Acts (Bosworth and Dawkins, 1981a, Chapters 3 and 4) and, to a lesser extent, by international rules and guidelines laid down by such bodies as the EC and ILO (Bosworth and Dawkins, 1981a, Chapter 12). There are, however, serious grounds for believing that a great deal remains to be done to improve health and safety at work (Department of Employment, 1980, p. 459). The continuing division of workers into departments and set groups in modern industry, which is in part linked with the pervasive moves towards specialisation and the division of labour (see Section 2 above), has given rise to the question of the influence of human factors on health and safety, for example, caused by the reliance of each worker on the performance of at least one other member of a group (CIS, p. 41).

One can imagine conditions under which health and safety problems might be minimised. Apart from the need for firms to have some incentive to introduce health and safety precautions, these conditions might involve: unchanged industrial techniques; zero structural change; zero economic growth; low rates of labour turnover; and rapid learning of tasks. It is quite clear, therefore, that (in so far as technological change results in innovations in industrial techniques, substantial structural change, and rapid economic growth) technological change may be a potential cause of health and safety problems. However, we should not get the role of technology out of perspective in respect of its descriptive influence on employment. For example, it has been argued that the potential for replacing workers by capital embodying the

latest technologies is perhaps more limited than we had
thought and, also, that its most significant impact is likely
to be to improve the working environment in the area of health
and safety matters (Department of Employment, 1980, p. 461).

Again, we have touched upon an area where a great deal more
research (with an important economic content) remains to be
undertaken. The Government already plays a substantial role
here, through the network of protective legislation it has
evolved and, thereby, through the Health and Safety Inspec-
torate. Nevertheless, there remains the important question
of whether its involvement is optimal. If individual workers
and firms take into account the perceived private costs and
benefits of the health and safety aspects, there must be some
other reason for government intervention. Imperfect knowledge
on the part of one or both sides of industry may imply a
certain role, perhaps in the form of provision of information
(e.g. along the lines of health warnings on cigarettes). A
potentially more important role for government may arise
because of the externalities involved in the labour supply
decision, where the impacts on the family and the wider community are not properly taken into account in the private
decisions.

5   ROLE OF WOMEN IN EMPLOYMENT

There is a considerable amount of historical evidence that
technological change has affected the types of jobs that
women can do. Mechanisation, in particular, removed many of
the physical constraints on the employment of women and the
rapid introduction of relatively inexpensive female and child
labour created, or at least threatened to create, considerable
problems of unemployment. In many ways, we have observed
analogous trends in female employment over the post-war period
(Elias, 1980, p. 180), and many of the associated fears for
unemployment. Technological change has played a dual role:
reducing the grounds for objective discrimination against
women in employment and, thereby, raising job prospects *vis-
à-vis* men; freeing women from domestic constraints in the
home and allowing a greater participation in the labour
market.

5.1 *Technological Change and the Demand for Women Workers*

A great deal of segmentation still occurs in the labour
market (Hakim, 1978). While there is a central pool of jobs
that can be filled by either men or women, other groups of

tasks have tended to polarise into jobs that 'only men can
do' and jobs that 'only women can do'. While we feel a little
dubious about accepting the results at face value, recent
survey work for the EOC has thrown some light on the reasons
for the existence of these extreme categories (IFF, 1979).
For a more detailed review see Bosworth and Dawkins (1981c).

Each establishment was asked whether there were certain
jobs that one sex or the other could not do, given the present
level of training and present technology. The survey records
the percentage of establishments in that industry reporting
jobs that women could not do without extra training or some
technical modification. The responses ranged from as low as
8 per cent of establishments in professional services, up
to 88 per cent in textiles. Comparable figures for the percentage of establishments reporting one or more jobs that men
cannot do without any change again indicated a considerable
variation across industries, ranging from zero in transport
and communications and utilities, up to 39 per cent in clothing
and footwear. Comparison of the results for men and for women
immediately shows a considerably higher percentage of establishments reporting jobs that women cannot do than jobs that
men cannot do, with the exception of professional services
and finance. In all but two industries (professional services
and finance), the ratio of establishments reporting jobs
women cannot do to those reporting jobs that men cannot do
exceeds unity. Clearly, more detailed information is required
about the types of jobs that the respondents had in mind,
and their importance within the production process of each
establishment.

The responses indicated that, in many of the establishments,
this constraint on entry into particular jobs could be removed
by additional training. The survey indicates the equivalent
percentages of firms that would report a barrier to entry into
certain jobs even after training. In certain instances, such
as electrical engineering, the reduction in barriers that
would be caused by extra training was substantial for females
(i.e. from 46 per cent of establishments down to 11 per cent).
In the main, however, the improvement for women was much more
modest than for men. Thus the ratios of establishments reporting jobs that women could not do to establishments reporting jobs that men could not do after training generally
exceed the equivalent ratios without training, the only
exception being electrical engineering.

The results also indicated that a further reduction in entry
barriers could be achieved by technical modification to the
job. In the main, this improvement appears to help break down
barriers of entry for women more than for men, with the exception of other engineering and miscellaneous services

(where it is fair to add that the percentages of establishments reporting barriers for males were already quite small).
As a result, the ratios of establishments reporting jobs
women could not do to those reporting jobs men could not do
decline after technical modification to the job. Nevertheless,
although technical modification of the job in general improves
the position of women *vis-à-vis* men, the improvement is a
relatively minor one.

Earlier, we pointed out that it would have been useful to
have information about the numbers of jobs involved and their
relative importance in each establishment. This is clearly
again true when considering the reduction in entry barriers
caused by additional training and technical changes. Were the
establishments indicating the reduction in barriers important
either in the range of jobs where barriers existed or in the
relative importance of their jobs? In addition, it would also
have been useful to have had some idea about the relative costs
of each option and how the reduction in barriers might have
varied with increased expenditure on training or technical
change. Information of this type might have led to a cost-
benefit analysis of the policy options.

5.2 *Technological Change and the Supply of Women Workers*

Technological change has almost certainly also affected the
supply of female workers on the market. Higher standards of
living have brought the purchase of durable goods within the
range of a much larger proportion of families. Such goods
have increased productivity in the home, thus freeing the
constraints (caused by the timing of certain chores) that
were a particularly large barrier to women supplying themselves into paid employment. While it is easy to speculate
about the impact of technological change on labour supply,
particularly of female workers, there is insufficient data
to undertake more rigorous economic work (Elias, 1980, pp.
194-7). If we are correct, however, and technological change
has been a positive stimulus to the supply of female workers
at each wage rate, then the effect has been to shift the
supply curve outwards. With a given demand curve, the effect
is to reduce the real wage on the market or, in the face of
downward rigidity of wages, produce unemployment (although
some proportion of this may remain hidden if it is formed
from women who fail to register as unemployed).

6 UNEMPLOYMENT: THE POTENTIAL ROLES OF JOB CREATION AND WORK SHARING

In a world of homogeneous labour and a single labour market, unemployment can be considered as the difference between the number of workers supplied and the number demanded at the given wage rate. In addition, however, unemployment can clearly occur when the number supplied is equal to the number demanded, but where there are occupational or geographical imbalances which, overall, off-set one another. The Government has a plethora of alternative instruments by which it could resolve such an imbalance (Burton, 1979). Historically, the majority of these have involved some form of price mechanism that has effectively made labour less expensive than capital or which has produced some overall change in the level of activity. Our attention turns to a limited number of innovations in the area of work organisation which, although they cannot be considered new, have been resurrected and revitalised. These measures relate to the manipulation of work patterns (i.e. shift-work and overtime) in order to create jobs or share work. Thus, we define job creation and work sharing: job creation is associated with a net increase in employment opportunities by the creation of extra jobs, the hours of work of existing workers held constant; work sharing is associated with a net increase in new jobs freed by the reduction in the hours of work of the existing work-force.

6.1 *The Potential Employment Creating Effects of Shift-working*

Trade unions have traditionally been opposed to shift-work, both on the Continent and in the UK. The trade union movement, in parallel with the ILO and the EC, have been in favour of restricting the amount of shift-working on health and social grounds. Such actions have proved extremely difficult to introduce during the present recession (Taylor, 1977), and nothing has been done to implement the provisions of the EC draft directive on shiftworking (EC, 1977). Indeed, certain unions and associated researchers have advocated a growth in shift-work in order to cut the length of dole queues (Taylor, 1977).

The most comprehensive statement of the potential employment benefits of encouraging shift-work in the UK is to be found in Hughes (1977). In particular, he argues that shift-working: (i) can offer an 'early and sizeable' increase in employment, given the existing capital stock, as demand for UK goods and services develops; (ii) promises significant gains in capital productivity with lower capital costs per unit of output (sufficient to outweigh the higher costs of recruitment, training and shift pay), 'depending on demand conditions'.

If firms have been doing their private calculus correctly, they should already have reached their optimal position in terms of the real private costs and benefits that they face. In this case, further increases in shift-working may well cause a reduction in profitability as output expands, product prices fall and labour and other costs (e.g. maintenance costs) rise. The Government must, therefore, weigh the social benefits that can be reaped against the extra private and social costs.

In all this, we must always bear in mind that increasing the incidence of shift-working is a necessary, but not sufficient condition for job creation. If two men are employed one after the other, rather than side by side, no extra jobs have been created. With this in mind, it might be argued that the increased use of shift-working would not seem to be a viable short-term strategy, in so far as any stimulus to employment will result in higher output. This, in turn, will, other things being equal, produce lower prices, lower profits and a smaller increase in employment than would have been hoped for. Such effects are reinforced by a reduction in the demand for capital goods (and, thereby, employment in the capital goods sector) as shift-working increases, at any given level of output.

A more realistic strategy would be for the Government to change the relative costs of shift-work and overtime in favour of the former, *as the economy moves out of recession*. The marginal cost of expansion would then be changed in favour of more employees rather than more hours. A rapid response of domestic industry to increased domestic demand by this route may cut back the threat of being swamped by imports. This is particularly useful in so far as the expansion is unlikely to be stifled by such rapid increases in labour costs at the margin. If this strategy were to result in high absolute profit levels (and, therefore, because of the nature of the expansion, higher profit per unit of capital), the result should be a greater inducement to investment, an activity of which the UK has been starved.

6.2 *Normal Hours, Overtime Working and Employment*

The principle of shorter working hours to achieve higher levels of employment has been advocated from time to time over an extremely long period, in many countries, including the USA and UK. In the USA in 1887, for example, Gompers argued that 'so long as there is one man who seeks employment and cannot obtain it, the hours of labour are too long' and, later, that 'we must find employment for our wretched Brothers and Sisters by reducing the hours of labour or we will be overwhelmed and destroyed' (Levitan and Belous, 1977; and Dankert, 1965, pp. 161-3). While an economist might argue that this seems a rather peculiar way of looking at the problem, nevertheless, it does focus our attention on an anomalous and potentially unacceptable situation, in that, by the end of the 1970s, over 30 per cent of all operatives were working an average of over 8 hours of overtime in an economy with over 6 per cent of its economically active population unemployed.

The reason for this is clear from Section 3 above. The trends towards higher levels of capital intensity and interest rates, and the reduction in the length of the normal working week, have led firms to rely increasingly on overtime working in order to maintain their desired lengths of operating hours. Those in employment, on the other hand, may have been reluctant to risk the goodwill they hold with employers and may have experienced a positive inducement from the increased standards of living that overtime working can offer. At the same time, trade unions may make conciliatory gestures towards their unemployed membership; nevertheless, the election and re-election of officials is much more likely to depend on the votes of the larger body of workers who remain in employment and who would probably look favourably on overtime working.

Hughes (1977), writing about the UK position, argued that 'even if shift-working accelerated economic growth rates and dented the unemployment figures, it would need an altogether bolder approach to mop up the larger part of existing unemployment. The reduction in the working week *could* - if certain conditions were fulfilled - overcome much of the structural unemployment of the British Economy'. Levitan and Belous (1977, p. vii) argued that we might be 'overlooking a potent weapon in our arsenal that could reduce forced idleness and minimise inflationary pressures. . . . Reduced worktime, flexible hours, and alternative work patterns have been almost ignored by government policy makers as a possible tool in fighting unemployment levels that are far higher than any experienced since the end of the Great Depression.' This is very much closer to main-line union thinking. Tyler (1978) states that 'in Britain, along with countries like Belgium, the most popular union answer is to fight for the shorter working week, simply because - more than job subsidies, early retirement, longer holidays, or even cutting overtime - it could channel large numbers of people into jobs'. The TUC, in their *Economic Review* (TUC, 1978, pp. 12-13), argue that the level of employment can be increased (and unemployment decreased) by a reduction in normal working hours or overtime working.

A considerable debate has grown up concerning the employment-creating effects of a reduction in normal hours, a debate that is far from fully resolved. There are clearly a number of difficulties associated with transforming hours freed in this way into jobs. First, there is the question of whether the unemployed workers have the 'correct' skills to fill the jobs made available. Second, are the unemployed workers in the same geographical areas as the jobs that are made available? Third, the job creation effect will be considerably muted if the existing workers start moonlighting as they move on to a shorter working week in their main job. Fourth, as we have already emphasised, some of the new jobs will never appear if existing workers fill the hours gap through extra overtime. Fifth, the extra workers will either require new capital or will move on to a shift system, both of which will probably raise the per unit cost and lower the employment-creating effect. It is clear that a reduction in normal hours must be augmented by other policy measures (particularly concerned with the mobility of labour) if substantial improvements in employment prospects are to be obtained.

In the UK, the TUC seem more hopeful that a reduction in overtime might provide a stronger impetus to employment. While changing the level of overtime does not avoid the majority of the points made above, it may at least avoid the most immediate reason why the policy may prove stillborn. It would be mis-leading, however, to argue that overtime could be translated directly into extra jobs, for a number of reasons (TUC, 1978, p. 13). First, overtime is supplied to fulfil the function of a pool of labour services which can quickly be called into use and removed from use as the cycle demands (TUC, 1978, p. 13). It might prove more difficult to hire and fire workers to allow labour services to vary in the same way that overtime working allows. Nevertheless, it is worth noting that overtime working has, at least in aggregate, become a permanent feature of the employment scene, as Whybrew (1968) has shown. Second, workers already in the job are in the right geographical area and have the pre-requisite skills, while the unemployed may need moving, training or re-training. Third, relating to both the previous points, there is an economically optimal length of working day (from both the employees' and the employers' points of view). The employer, for example, has in some sense found it more profitable to increase hours of work above normal hours (and pay an overtime premium) than to expand the number of workers. Finally, long overtime hours may become the 'norm' for certain groups of workers, in an attempt to attain an acceptable wage (TUC, 1978, p. 13).

It seems clear that the Government could induce a higher

level of employment (and a smaller level of unemployment) by offering financial inducements/penalties to firms that effectively discourage overtime, or by introducing legislation limiting the maximum working week. As the latter is already a feature of legislation protecting women and young persons, this could also be justified on grounds of equality between the sexes. It is also clear that restrictions placed on overtime would make reductions in normal hours a much more effective means of stimulating employment. It seems essential that overtime be limited in some way that is not harmful to the firm or to the individual. One strategy that might be followed is to introduce legislation (allowing some time for compliance) that effectively bans overtime, but which allows for exemption (along the lines of the current Health and Safety Executive exemptions for women and young people). We would shy away from such a course, however, in so far as it seems likely to effectively increase industry's costs without providing a real alternative mechanism by which the firm can adjust to longer-term changes in the demand for its product. An alternative strategy would seem to be to attempt to change the relative prices of men and hours. It seems likely that the pay-roll taxes and other non-wage labour costs are not neutral in their impact on the choice between men and hours. Work sharing might be increased by lowering those costs that vary *per man* and raising those related to the *number of hours worked*. This might be achieved through a more sophisticated National Insurance contribution scheme.

REFERENCES

Bell, R. M. (1972) *Changing Technology and Manpower Requirements in the Engineering Industry* (Sussex University Press, in association with EITB) Z338.4762.

Bosworth, D. L. and P. J. Dawkins (1978) 'Proposed Changes in the Extent and Nature of Shiftworking: Some Important Policy Issues', *Personnel Review*, vol. 1, no. 4, pp. 2–5.

Bosworth, D. L. and P. J. Dawkins (1980) 'Compensation for Worker Disutility: Time of Day, Length of Shift and Other Features of Work Patterns', *Scottish Journal of Political Economy*, vol. 27, no. 1 (February) pp. 80–96.

Bosworth, D. L. and P. J. Dawkins (1981a) *Work Patterns: An Economic Analysis* (Farnborough, Hants: Gower Press).

Bosworth, D. L. and P. J. Dawkins (1981b) 'Optimal Capital Utilisation in British Manufacturing Industry', in *Proceedings of the Symposium on Natural Resources and Production, Karlsruhe, 1980* (Wurzburg-Wien: Physic Verlag).

Bosworth, D. L. and P. J. Dawkins (1981c) 'Barriers to the
  Employment of Women', *Equal Opportunities International*,
  vol. 1, pp. 25-31.
Bosworth, D. L., P. J. Dawkins and A. J. Westaway (1981a)
  'Explaining the Incidence of Shiftworking', *Economic Journal*,
  vol. 91 (March) pp. 145-57.
Bosworth, D. L., P. J. Dawkins and A. J. Westaway (1981b)
  'The Causes of Shift Working in Great Britain', D. Currie,
  D. Peel and N. Peters (eds), *Microeconomic Analysis*
  (London: Croom Helm).
Burton, J. (1979) *The Job Support Machine: A Critique of the
  Subsidy Morass* (London: Centre for Policy Studies) 338.942.
CIS, *Human Factors and Safety*, CIS Information Sheet 15.
Colquhoun, P. (1978) 'Working Efficiency, Personality and
  Body Rhythms', *Department of Employment Gazette* (London:
  HMSO, June) pp. 682-5.
Cooper, C. L. (1978) 'Work Humanisation in Japan', *Department
  of Employment Gazette* (January) pp. 28-30.
Cox, T. *et al.* (1979) 'Job Stress: the Effects of Repetitive
  Work', *Department of Employment Gazette* (December) pp.
  1234-7.
Dankert, C. E. (1965) 'Automation, Unemployment and Shorter
  Hours', in C. E. Dankert, F. C. Mann and H. R. Northrup
  (eds), *Hours of Work* (New York: Harper and Row).
Department of Employment (1980) 'Employment Policy', *Department
  of Employment Gazette* (May) p. 459.
Elias, P. (1980) 'Labour Supply and Employment Opportunities
  for Women', in R. M. Lindley (ed.), *Economic Change and
  Employment Policy* (London: Macmillan) pp. 180-239.
European Commission (1977) 'Memorandum on Shiftwork', Euro-
  pean Commission Discussion Paper V/1135/77-EN.
Hakim, C. (1978) 'Sexual Divisions within the Labour Force:
  Occupational Segregation', *Department of Employment Gazette*
  (November) pp. 1264-8.
Harrington, J. M. (1978) *Shiftwork and Health: A Critical
  Review of the Literature*, the Centenary Institute of Occu-
  pational Health, London School of Hygiene and Tropical
  Medicine (University of London).
Hughes, J. (1977) 'Shiftwork and the Shorter Working Week',
  Personnel Management, vol. 9, no. 5 (May) pp. 18-20.
IFF (1979) *Women and Work*, survey for the EOC/SSRC Joint
  Panel.
Kobayashi, S. (1970) 'The Creative Organisation: a Japanese
  Experiment', *Personnel* (November/December).
Kondo, T. (1973) 'How Much Progress in the Quality of Working
  Life', *Management Today* (November).
Levitan, S. A. and R. S. Belous (1977) *Shorter Hours, Shorter
  Weeks: Spreading the Work to Reduce Unemployment* (Baltimore,

Md: Johns Hopkins University Press; London: Reed).

Luce, G. Gaer (1973) *Body Time: The Natural Rhythms of the Body* (St Albans: Paladin).

Marris, R. (assisted by I. MacLean and S. Berman) (1964) *The Economics of Capital Utilisation: A Report on Multiple Shiftwork* (Cambridge University Press).

Marris, R. L. (1970) *Multiple Shiftwork*, NEDO (London: HMSO).

Mishan, E. J. (1971) *Twenty One Popular Economic Fallacies* (Harmondsworth: Pelican).

Senker, P. and C. Huggett (1973) *Technology and Manpower in the UK Engineering Industry*, Occasional Paper no. 3 (Watford: EITB).

SSRC (1978) *Research Needs in Work Organisation* (London: SSRC).

Takezawa, S. (1974) 'The Quality of Working Life: Trends in Japan', unpublished paper, Rikkyo University.

Taylor, R. (1977) 'Start Shifting the Jobless', *Business Observer*.

TUC (1978) *Economic Review, 1978* (London: Trades Union Congress).

Tyler, C. (1978) 'Unions Crusade for the Shorter Working Week', *Financial Times*, 2 June.

Wabe, J. S. and J. G. Camara (1979) 'Capital Utilisation, Capital Intensity and Efficiency: a Comparison of Factories in Developing and Industrialised Countries', Discussion Paper, Centre for European Industrial Studies, University of Bath.

Whybrew, E. G. (1968) *Overtime Working in Britain*, Royal Commission on Trade Unions and Employers Associations, Research Paper no. 9 (London: HMSO).

Yoshida, K. (1973) 'Work Restructuring in Tokyo Gas Company', unpublished paper.

Name Index

Name Index

Subject Index

foreign countries *and*
United Kingdom
London Chamber of Commerce
and Industry, 98, 99, 107
Luddites, 9, 27

manufacturing industries, 4,
40, 43, 97, 111, 112-25,
127, 140, 159, 176, 190,
201, 202, 204, 209, 211
aircraft industry, 169
cement, 127, 128, 136-9
chemicals, 135, 189; bio-
technology, 189
clothing and footwear, 199,
202, 215
electrical engineering, 215
electronics, 199; computers
(and computing), 34,
47, 117, 175, 197, 198-
9, 200, 202, 204, 210;
fibre optics, 189;
lasers, 189; micro-
electronics, 4, 5, 6,
21, 27, 34, 47, 52, 57,
62, 97-109, 119, 174,
175, 178, 189, 190,
200, 201, 202, 203,
204, 205, 209; silicon
chips, 58, 97-109;
visual display units,
182; word processors,
104, 204; radio radar
and navigation, 199
engineering, 163, 185, 204,
215; instrument engin-
eering, 102; machinery
(non-electrical), 135;
machine tools (and n.
c. machine tools) 199,
210; metal products,
135, 189; printing
machinery, 199; textile
machinery, 18;
robotics, 209
foods, 129, 189
grain milling, 127, 128,
136-41

iron and steel, 3, 146,
159, 161-73, 197, 198;
see also British Steel
motor vehicles, 46, 119,
124, 192
printing and publishing,
180, 185
shipbuilding, 3, 5, 157-73;
metal hulls - *see* iron
and steel
sugar refining, 135
textiles, 135, 215
wood products, 135
market structure (including
monopoly), 10, 36, 39,
69, 196
microprocessors, *see also*
manufacturing industries
- microelectronics
Microprocessors Applications
Project, 200
Microelectronics Industry
Support Programme, 200
multiplier, 29, 30, 33, 37,
38, 40, 43, 44, 82, 112,
117
employment multiplier, 16,
17, 18, 19

non-manufacturing industries,
111, 190
agriculture, 40, 146, 189,
190
electric power, 119, 124
energy inputs, 144, 146,
156, 189; oil (and
North Sea Oil), 97,
168; energy research,
47; steam power, 46,
58, 119, 124, 159, 161-
3
materials, 144, 146, 156,
159, 162, 163, 166, 167
wood pulp, 143, 146, 149-52

occupations, 21, 22, 159,
199, 203, 204, 213, 217;
see also skills